Words and Meaning in Metasemantics

Words and Meaning in Metasemantics

Grounds for an Interactive Theory

Juan J. Colomina-Almiñana

LEXINGTON BOOKS
Lanham • Boulder • New York • London

Published by Lexington Books
An imprint of The Rowman & Littlefield Publishing Group, Inc.
4501 Forbes Boulevard, Suite 200, Lanham, Maryland 20706
www.rowman.com

86-90 Paul Street, London EC2A 4NE

Copyright © 2022 by The Rowman & Littlefield Publishing Group, Inc.

Juan J. Colomina and David Perez-Chico, "A Solution Based in Ordinary Language to the Psychological Objection." Linguistic and Philosophical Investigations 12: 11-33 (2013), Addelton Academic Publishers-New York ©

All rights reserved. No part of this book may be reproduced in any form or by any electronic or mechanical means, including information storage and retrieval systems, without written permission from the publisher, except by a reviewer who may quote passages in a review.

British Library Cataloguing in Publication Information Available

Library of Congress Cataloging-in-Publication Data

Names: Colomina Almiñana, Juan José, author.
 Title: Words and meaning in metasemantics : grounds for an interactive theory / Juan José Colomina-Almiñana.
 Description: Lanham : Lexington Books, [2022] | Includes bibliographical references and index. | Summary: "In Words and Meaning in Metasemantics, Juan José Colomina-Almiñana argues that language meaning determination requires close attention to the constant interaction between speech communities, speaker's intentions, and the audience's uptakes"-- Provided by publisher.
 Identifiers: LCCN 2022025947 (print) | LCCN 2022025948 (ebook) | ISBN 9781793609465 (cloth) | ISBN 9781793609489 (paper) | ISBN 9781793609472 (epub)
 Subjects: LCSH: Semantics--Psychological aspects. | Meaning (Psychology)
 Classification: LCC P325.5.P78 C65 2022 (print) | LCC P325.5.P78 (ebook) | DDC 401/.43--dc23/eng/20220628
 LC record available at https://lccn.loc.gov/2022025947
 LC ebook record available at https://lccn.loc.gov/2022025948

Per a Nicole i Ausiàs,
without whom everything is meaningless

Contents

Preface	ix
Introduction	1
Chapter 1: The Traditional View	9
Chapter 2: The Psychological Relevance of Propositional Content	23
Chapter 3: The Conventionality of Propositional Content	37
Chapter 4: The Interactive Theory	53
Chapter 5: Expanding the Interactive Theory	81
Chapter 6: Application 1: Tensed Sentences	107
Chapter 7: Application 2: Disagreements	119
Chapter 8: Application 3: Presupposition Projection	139
Conclusion	155
Bibliography	159
Index	175
About the Author	183

Preface

My primary research interest has always been to better understand the relationship between language and thought. When I permanently moved to the United States in 2010, my research evolved theoretically and methodologically, expanding to more pragmatic realms. An essential part of my work now focuses on analyzing how and what external elements influence how people talk and, in general, society's role in such an equation. Without forgetting the importance of analytic and formal approaches, I began investigating the impact and constraint of factors such as speaker intentions, attitudes and ideologies, implicatures, presuppositions, age, gender, and many other social constituents of ordinary speech. My research then moved toward the influence and magnitude that both semantic and pragmatic processes, in unison, have on our daily language's meaning and usage. I employ interdisciplinary views that include methodologies borrowed from the analytical philosophy of language, semantics, pragmatics, and even sociolinguistics and linguistic anthropology. The main reason for this multidisciplinary approach, which I have intentionally adopted, is that it provides a better explanation of empirical data than abstract models (reductions and reconstructions). It allows me to think more freely about the relationship between language and reality, accounting for the type of knowledge speakers possess when saying that they know a language and the mechanisms that explicate its acquisition and production. Therefore, my uncompartmentalized approach more accurately answers questions regarding the nature and understanding of language, its origin and structure, and, more importantly, how our ordinary natural languages work.

I am not alone in this endeavor. I have witnessed several scholars working hard to break through the classical hermetical ways of understanding language and meaning in both the philosophy of language and linguistics. Against the traditional monistic view, these academics argue for pluralism regarding content. It is assumed that, given any sentence, one and only one proposition needs to be associated with it, a proposition accessible to both the speaker and audience of any natural language in which such a sentence can be uttered. The new approach posits that this tradition underdetermines meaning since there are many scenarios where sentence content is, at best, ambiguous. The reasons are numerous, from an embedded misunderstanding of sentences as bearers of truth (and, hence, proposition carriers) to a defective approach about the proper function of language and the role that speaker and audience have in meaning production. Therefore, I am happy to say that I belong (or, at least, so I like to believe) to this new generation of thinkers, as I hope this book makes clear.

This new framework is where the new theory this book introduces and explains is located. The ontological reasons for endorsing pluralism regarding linguistic content have been mapped in prior work, primarily delving into the notion of metaphysical points of view (cf. especially Colomina-Almiñana 2018). A point of view is like a window, a place to contemplate reality. It is the basis for any scientific model, and it is a priori neutral regarding the content of its bearer. Points of view then are primitive metaphysical entities, real possibilities for cognition and language. They formally express how the available features of the world are relative to the perspective adopted and metaphysically grounded within primary relations such as determinable-determinate, whole-parts, etc. These perspectives always offer limited access to knowledge, which may indicate the presence of bias in scientific explanation and other types of discourses (cf. Colomina-Almiñana 2021). Therefore, this new perspectivism develops an original methodology employed for remolding the traditional ways our language describes the world. It approaches and explains thin-border objects, such as clouds or shadows, and social categories, such as race, culture, and ethnicity. Besides the previous more evident and direct applications, points of view offer an explanatory background to re-evaluate classical ontological approaches and revitalize how social categories are constructed. It is, therefore, easy to see why many are reticent to accept this view as a viable alternative. The approach I just depicted has encountered strong opposition by some gatekeepers that still believe in the rigid compartmentalization of the disciplines involved in the analysis of Language and languages. *Words and Meaning*, therefore, offers arguments in favor of semantic pluralism regarding linguistic content and meaning more generally, often taking a detour to entertain the metaphysical foundations and implications of my arguments without repeating any of the points made in previous work on the matter at hand.

A few materials included in this book are adapted from previous publications. Portions of chapter 2 are a substantially revised version of my contribution to the article "A Solution Based on Ordinary Language to the Psychological Objection" (coauthored with David Pérez Chico), which appeared in 2013 in *Linguistic and Philosophical Investigations* (12, 25–48).

An early version of chapter 6 was published in 2015 as "Disagreement and the Speaker's Point of View" in *Language and Dialogue* (5[2], 224–246). Chapter 7 is a revision of my 2018 article "Relativism, Contextualism, and Temporal Perspective," which appeared in *Daimon* (75, 131–143). I thank my coauthor, the journals, and the publishers for granting permission to employ these previously published materials.

This book has been in the making for a long time. I do not lie when I say that it has been cooking in my head since Nati García Navarro introduced me to the ordinary language philosophy and Francesc Bodí Beneyto explained to me Nietzsche's perspectivism during my high school years. My interest in the philosophy of language and the metaphysics of propositions has, of course, expanded greatly since and fed from many hours of strenuous reading and intense study during my college years and numerous conversations with fellow academics during my professional years after that. Nevertheless, at least in its current form, the book has immensely benefited from the input and feedback provided by many individuals and audiences during the past five years or so. My teaching has helped me immensely refine some of the arguments employed in *Words and Meaning*, especially the most basic and crucial ideas. I am in debt to many cohorts of students for pushing me to clarify assumed concepts in the philosophy of language and linguistics whose significance I had sometimes taken for granted. Specifically, I appreciate the patience and encouragement provided by the students in my courses on the history of analytic philosophy, radical translation and mistranslation, cross-cultural communication, sociolinguistics, semantics, pragmatics, applied linguistics, and language acquisition offered during these last years.

Many thanks to the audiences at Boise State University, Emory University, Harvard University, Kansas State University, Louisiana State University, Ohio State University, Swarthmore College, Texas A&M University, Towson University, Universidad Autónoma de Querétaro, Universidad de La Laguna, and the University of Puget Sound for questioning some of the caveats of the theory this book introduces, which allow me to fortify its presentation. I must also thank the participants and respondents to my talks during the 1st Workshop on Cognitive Science (Universidad de Zaragoza); the 114th American Philosophical Association Eastern Division annual meeting; the 114th, 115th, and 116th American Philosophical Association Central Division annual meetings; the 133rd Annual Meeting of the Modern Language Association; the 2015 International Society for Language Studies annual meeting; the 2017 Linguistic Society of America annual meeting; the 42nd, 43rd, 44th, 45th, and 46th Linguistic Association of the Southwest annual meetings; the 81st Southeastern Conference on Linguistics; and the 88th, 92nd, and 94th American Philosophical Association Pacific Division annual meetings for the comments and suggestions to early portions of this manuscript.

I am grateful for the conversations and comments generously offered by Luvell Anderson, Louise Antony, Hans Boas, Ray Buchanan, James Cox, María de Ponte, Cory Juhl, Christopher Hom, Manolo Martínez, Jacob Mey, Domino R. Perez, Kathryn Carpenter Rech, Katherine Ritchie, Vicente Raga Rosaleny, Cristian Saborido, Sandro Sessarego, Pablo Stinga, Michael Wilson, Dan Zeman, and the members of the LEMA research group (particularly Antti Hautamäki, Manolo Liz, and David Pérez Chico). This book benefitted from their research project RTI2018–098254-BI00: "Personal Perspectives. Concepts and Applications," Programa Estatal de I+D+i orientada a los retos de la sociedad, Ministerio de Ciencia, Innovación y Universidades, Gobierno de España. The final manuscript was composed and revised thanks to a leave granted by my current institution and funded by the Bill and Carol Fox Center for Humanistic Inquiry at Emory University. My most sincere gratitude goes to the center's administration and the fellows during 2021–2022.

Thank you to Holly Buchanan, Jana Hudges-Kluck, Alexandra Rallo, and Sydney Wedbush, my editors at Lexington Books (Rowman & Littlefield), for the encouragement and support while writing this book and for the extension granted when I most needed it. I will forever be indebted to the myriad reviewers that commented and provided the most needed and valuable feedback during the many different stages the manuscript endured. Once more, it is proven that when well performed, academic peer-review processes are helpful and necessary for the progress of scholarly endeavors and the safeguard of research excellence.

I dedicate this book to Nicole M. Guidotti-Hernández and Ausiàs March Colomina-Guidotti. You both have been with me during this challenging period of my life and have taught me (and still keep doing so) that viewpoints are genuine and, frequently, indispensable. Your help, constant support, and unconditional love kept me afloat, even though sometimes I might not have deserved it. Without you, everything is meaningless.

Introduction

The majority of us, in our ordinary lives, simply talk. We usually do not pay much attention to how we do so. We want to get our message across, making sure that our audience, the hearers of our utterances, entertain what we want to say by what is said. In the same fashion, we do not usually put any particular effort into grasping the mechanisms employed by others to display what they say. It simply happens that we are inclined to engage with what their message says because we entertain their communicative intentions. In a nutshell, this is the Gricean program. It is named after Paul Grice, who recognized the relevance of speaker intentions and other nonlinguistic elements in determining the meaning of our natural language as part of a broader and complex rational behavior.

The above-mentioned theory is usually understood as contraposed to the semanticist view of meaning. Instead of prioritizing speaker intentions, the defenders of the semanticist position believe everything one can say is already encoded in the sentences of our natural language because they can be reduced to their components and relations, what they call the logical form. They present a conception of language as a set of invariant representational models under the notion of *proposition*, which states that words have truth conditions that must match the facts of the world they represent in language to acquire some truth value and, therefore, become meaningful. In a few words, the meaning of a sentence is what it *literally* says, as contraposed to what a speaker means as Grice defends.

This classical conception of language started with the works of Gottlob Frege and Bertrand Russell. It assumes that our natural language deserves a homogeneous semantic theory in which every sentence would be associated with precisely one propositional content. Therefore, it assumes that the structure of our natural language is entirely compositional, and our language mirrors reality at face value. They not only assume that their metaphysics backs up our theory of meaning. They are also convinced that we are obligated to construct a logical theory of meaning capable of explaining all linguistic phenomena and the nature and structure of language itself.

Furthermore, suppose one has any aspirations to contribute to the study of language and meaning. In that case, one must do this without appealing to the speaker's intentions, the audience's interpretations of one's words, or any other psychological state, pragmatic process, or anthropological construct. Therefore, the semanticist view relies on the fact that fundamental metaphysical features of the world determine all linguistic facts, which are the grounds for constructing this semantic model.

Words and Meaning presents and develops an alternate theory regarding semantics and metasemantics, which I dub the *Interactive Theory*. As mentioned, the classical approach to semantics analyzes meaning from a logical standpoint, reducing the meaning of words and sentences to their logical aspects, such as reference, sense, implication, logical form, etc. One determines the meaning of a name, word, or sentence by appealing to their references and truth conditions. These are the facts of the world that determine truth value, literally the objects and state of affairs that would make a sentence true or false, or its truthmaker. This ontological requirement is usually called metasemantics since it establishes the foundations for any theory of meaning or, in other words, marks the basics for how any linguistic expression acquires its meaning. Therefore, metasemantics study and analyze the criteria that grant reference and meaning to any word and sentence. In this sense, the semanticist view considers that meaning is the literal, invariant content of words and sentences (the reference and truth value each word and sentence uniquely carry as determined by their truth conditions), which is established by the principle of compositionality (traditional metasemantics). To summarize, the semanticist view argues that all meaning depends on the meaning of their parts and their correspondence with reality (truth conditions).

Because it addresses the reference and meaning of words and sentences, *Words and Meaning* provides a critical overview of prior approaches to its logical, lexical, and representational aspects. The reason why is because this reductive image of meaning is hard to digest. Even Frege and Russell (the fathers of the conception of language depicted above) recognized that our natural language does not always operate in such a fashion. Our language is full of names lacking reference (such as "Pegasus" and "Sherlock Holmes"), expressions that seem to lack truth value (like instances of the so-called future contingents), and a good amount of other words where content is not so clearly identifiable after all (such as expletives and several ambiguous words). For the followers of the semanticist approach, though, meaning still depends upon the content determination of such words and sentences. Meaning depends upon the logical form (often simply hidden and that proper analysis must unveil) that structures our language and individuates the adequate reference and truth values. Therefore, a semantic theory accomplishes the disambiguation of the propositional content that any linguistic item carries by purely appealing to linguistic mechanisms overtly or covertly present in the language.

The Interactive Theory in *Words and Meaning* defends that a reductive approach to language undermines semantics' scope and leaves many of its foundational aspirations unexplained. The meaning of our words and sentences is not, and cannot be, only dependent on any content words possess by themselves but needs to be grounded in their societal usage, their utterance in a given context, and the intention that the speaker has when uttering such words and sentences and all possible interpretations by their audience. After all, as the motto says, not words but speakers using them mean things with words. If this is the case, as this book demonstrates, we must abandon the illusory endeavor of finding a unitary theory of language and focus our attention on the analysis of ordinary speech that highlights the different pieces involved in meaning-fixing, from societal conventions to pragmatic processes, from lexical elements to audience's potential uptakes.

Words and Meaning puts forward a new way for understanding the foundations of the linguistic and philosophical study of language. The proposed Interactive Theory says that any linguistic item's meaning is its cognitive content and not only its representational content. Nonetheless, the cognitive content of words and sentences depends upon three different but interconnected elements. On the one hand, the speaker's intentions when making a statement are complemented by the audience's potential uptakes. On the other hand, the linguistic conventions established by the proper speech community allow both above-mentioned phenomena to occur, which establish a complex compound of dynamic and constantly evolving norms whose scope must be understood operating locally in specific circumstances. On the surface, this theory does not seem different from others that take the context of use in the analysis of language seriously. Nevertheless, the Interactive Theory is different in a number of aspects.

First, it is the only theory to my knowledge that successfully combines the speaker's intentions, audience's possible uptakes, and conventions to explain the meaning of our natural language altogether. Second, the meaning that a given audience would entertain is always different and determined by the particular conditions established by the salient speech community in any determined circumstance. Any speaker can utter a sentence in any of the over seven thousand natural languages (and their dialects) spoken on Earth and will always be sanctioned differently by the speech community to which the speaker belongs (or the linguist exchange occurs). Therefore, each speech community constrains what is said and how one can say it differently because each establishes different norms regarding how to accomplish it. Third, given that the speaker always wants something concrete out of their utterance, determining the content of such an utterance obligates us to pay attention to what that might be. We need to include also the speaker's intentions when choosing what is said in our analysis of language and meaning. Therefore, the Interactive Theory explains why and how each language sentence gets associated with cognitive content and, as a corollary, why and how truth value shifting can occur. As a secondary goal, it argues in favor of pluralism regarding propositions from the view that different speech communities impose different conditions to determine their languages' content and meaning. *Words and Meaning*, therefore, proposes a hybrid theory that accounts for our intuitive view about what content our audience entertains and a pluralistic approach to the criteria that individuate linguistic content. More specifically, it proposes a more accurate and realistic account of how meaning is produced, considering the proper way our natural languages work.

The structure of this book is as follows. As an alternative to contemporary semanticist and pragmatic approaches to linguistic content, my account criticizes the classical Fregean-Russellian approach, what in chapter 1 I call "The Traditional View." That chapter overviews different attempts to amend the classic semanticist theory by appealing to several disambiguation mechanisms. In my view, such a strategy fails in offering a proper explanation of language because it neglects to account for a crucial element: the fact that language is a human instrument and, as such, must serve the speaker to convey the meaning that she intends to communicate. In other words, language evolved to serve humans and, therefore, needs to reflect its psychological importance without necessarily being restricted to the speakers' mental lives.

Chapter 2, "The Psychological Relevance of Propositional Content," critically engages with improved semanticist theories, particularly a new version of literalism: the so-called minimalism. Contemporary accounts of linguistic content usually do not take account of the relevance that speaker intentions (as well as other related psychological states) have in determining the content of the sentences uttered in our ordinary life. This carries, as a consequence, a psychological unrealism about natural languages. Chapter 2 analyzes the contemporary debate between some defenders of these accounts and some unsuccessful pragmatic alternatives to propose a more realistic view of linguistic meaning. First, the chapter delves into how minimalism and contextualism understand the psychological nature of language and how their opposed positions confront criticism. Second, the chapter demonstrates how minimalist and contextualist positions fail to account for the psychological realism required to understand the nature and structure of the linguistic content of our natural language. Third, the chapter proposes an alternative solution based on a new interpretation of ordinary language theory, incorporating it into the Interactive Theory.

If the previous chapter critically engages traditional theories for not taking the importance of psychological aspects in the determination of meaning seriously, chapter 3, "The Conventionality of Propositional Content," does it for not taking the role of the speech communities construction of meaning seriously. This chapter critically delves into the current debate between semanticist and pragmatist approaches regarding the context of utterances' role in meaning-determination. After presenting a broad introduction to the topic, the chapter analyzes the minimalist proposal that only a few context-sensitive terms inhabit our natural language. Therefore, the context plays no role in fixing the truth conditions of our sentences. This position is hard to digest, as I demonstrate through a critical analysis of the most attractive alternative account in the market, at least in my view: Elizabeth Camp's semantic perspectivism. I agree with Camp that a speaker must make clear what she means to determine what is said. Nevertheless, the audience must entertain the perspective from where the speaker says it. The problem in Camp's view resides in the fact that she gives too much credit to the speaker in the process. While minimalism is psychologically irrelevant, Camp's perspectivism seems to fall in a speaker's solipsism.

Based on the insights developed in previous chapters, chapter 4, "The Interactive Theory," offers an alternative approach to meaning fixing. The Interactive Theory argues that the proper determination of the meaning of occasion sentences requires to account for the knowledge speakers acquire with the learning of a language (observation sentences) and the ordinary information speaker and audience share (available in the common ground), the pragmatic presuppositions that occur in regular communication, and any unarticulated constituent present in the context of utterance. The Interactive Theory argues in favor of epistemically relevant elements in the context of utterance that speaker and audience share without necessarily being conscious about them and that complete a sentence's truth conditions when taken as part of the maximally local context of utterance. This is, of course, part of the background that speakers and interlocutors share. Both learned it from the speech communities to which they belong and, as such, must be distinguished from the set of norms that normatively rule them. To reiterate, the Interactive Theory defends that what one needs to determine the context-sensitivity of the meaning of our natural language's sentences is to pay attention to the conventions established by each relevant speech community, the speaker's intentions, and the audience's possible uptakes. This cannot simply be reduced to semantic elements, not even to scattered pragmatic processes. Therefore, the Interactive Theory appeals to rational frameworks to which speakers and audience refer to ensure that their communicative intentions are adequately understood. This is to determine what they meant by saying what they said by matching what they intend to say to the expectations the audience might have as part of a concrete speech community taken in maximally local scenarios.

Chapter 5, "Expanding the Interactive Theory," delves into the required empirical data to ground the Interactive Theory. The chapter's main caveat is that linguistic acts require constant interaction between speaker and audience and that a speech act is not itself established by the speaker or the audience in isolation but in constant interaction with the speech community to which they belong. The speech community determines the speech act that the speaker performs with her utterance. It also constrains how the audience must interpret it, or at least grounds its different potential uptakes. The norms ruling the act performance and the audience's interpretation are confronted to conventions, which determine what the speaker must say, how, when, to whom, etc., to display certain specific content. The proposition in question is this. It is a somehow "institutionalized" behavior.

Moreover, the speaker must decide what of the possible behaviors the relevant speech community makes available would select to accomplish her intentions, make communication successful, turn her action felicitous, etc. To summarize, chapter 5 argues that the speaker's intentional decision of displaying specific content when uttering a concrete sentence and the proper institutionalized act performed by uttering such sentence altogether with the audience that adequately recognizes and interprets the speaker's intentions determine the proposition within an utterance. Therefore, the dynamic and evolving interaction between a speech community's conventions, the speaker's intentions, and the audience's potential uptakes constitute the propositions of our natural language.

As chapters 4 and 5 demonstrate, the Interactive Theory provides the required tools to assess several concrete case studies. Chapter 6, "Application 1: Tensed Sentences," proposes a new analysis of temporal sentences. It claims that strictly speaking, there is no such thing as temporal truth value shifting sentences under the traditional semanticist view. Therefore, sentences that include temporal indeterminacy elude all analysis. Furthermore, any amending of such theory with the inclusion of temporal operators (disambiguation) is also condemned to failure.

Nevertheless, I firmly believe that temporal sentences are still significant, even though are semantically incomplete. Chapter 6 introduces an analysis based on what the Interactive Theory defines as *the speaker's point of view*. The idea behind this claim is twofold. First, the statements through the use of sentences, not sentences themselves, can be either true or false. Second, a statement's truth value cannot change because it is strictly determined by its truth conditions, which are determined by the time intended by the speaker when uttering such a sentence.

In contrast with contextualist and relativist solutions, the Interactive Theory considers how only under a particular interactive perspective (the relevant point of view from the adequate speech community under question) can one approach the truth of any statement speakers make. Such a perspective always includes objective temporal coordinates even though they still depend upon the relevant point of view. Temporal coordinates are, therefore, beyond speaker and audience. They are embedded in the common communicational ground. They are part of the reality we live in as competent speech community members. Therefore, chapter 6 argues that to account for the truth of any temporal statement properly, one must figure out which perspective the sentence belongs to and then apply the proper temporal coordinates to the sentence in question. Sometimes Truth is not the adequate dimension of evaluation. Suppose this was the case, as the Interactive Theory demonstrates. In that case, we need to account for the objective temporal features delimiting the relevant point of view, which depend upon some interactive conditions that indicate whether such a sentence is or not successful or felicitous within such a point of view as belonging to a specific speech community since these conditions have to do with the proper employment of the sentence under the appropriate circumstances for such a community.

Similarly, chapter 7, "Application 2: Disagreements," argues that the Interactive Theory can reframe the discussion about epistemic and linguistic disagreements. By combining modality with a perspectival notion of meaning, the Interactive Theory demonstrates how a speaker's utterance is a speech act necessarily related to the interlocutor's interpretation. This interpretation is another speech act since integrating the communicative function into a dialogic interaction helps determine the meaning of utterances. In other words, if our linguistic analysis restricts itself to logical truth conditions, the speaker and the addressee become irrelevant and are not necessary for expressing the meaning of their utterances, which turn contradictory any disagreement scenario. By adequately attending to the speaker's point of view, a claim emphasized by the appeal to pragmatic presupposition and common ground in the determination of meaning as defined by the Interactive Theory, one can determine the adequate circumstances of evaluation under which to evaluate any utterance, making room for these disagreements to be faultless and complementary.

Chapter 8, "Application 3: Presupposition Projection," offers an alternative satisfactory response to the projection problem for presuppositions from the Interactive Theory at the same time that confronts classic semantic and pragmatic accounts to presupposed content in complex sentences.

Chapter 1

The Traditional View

This book introduces and argues for a new theory regarding the grounds of meaning, a novel theory in metasemantics that I dub the Interactive Theory. It claims that to determine meaning, we must pay attention to three different but interconnected items: the conventions that speech communities build, the intentions that speakers have when making statements, and the audience's different possible uptakes of such statements. Before presenting the new approach, this chapter critically overviews what I call the Traditional View about meaning. This classical approach started at the turn of the nineteenth to the twentieth century with the works of Gottlob Frege and Bertrand Russell. Against the idealism of their time, the Frege-Russell position understands meaning as content independent of any subjective perception that linguistic terms carry, almost in an essential way. The differences between their approaches are various and profound and, at some point, incompatible. However, both agreed that, no matter what, every word and sentence in our natural language must have an independent arbitrarily attached meaning, which all competent speakers of the language can grasp. This content is nothing other than the conditions any linguistic item must meet to be true—their truth conditions. These truth conditions are the world's circumstances, the facts and state of affairs that the item represents in language. Therefore, for any item to have meaning, it must carry the appropriate content to make what the item says true or false. That content is called *proposition* and is the abstract object whose properties are represented in language. These abstract objects are the concept somehow associated with all linguistic items. Once the content is determined, it simply does not change. It cannot change.

This approach presents problems, given the abundance of vagueness and ambiguities in our everyday modes of talking. What does exactly the sentence "this ball is red" mean? What does "this" mean? What does "red" mean? What does "red" mean when it is a part of a compound name, such as "the color red"? The founders of the Traditional View were well aware of these facts and amended their theories to accommodate the above-mentioned difficulties.

Nevertheless, with further developments, new insights about these problems were offered. Peter Strawson's criticism of Russell's denotational theory emphasized that meaning is not what a linguistic item has but its use in context. Keith Donnellan's distinction between the attributive and referential uses of descriptive definitions improved the problem's solution by fixing their proper reference in context. Moreover, Saul Kripke's notion of rigid designator further empowers an alternate theory about referentiality.

Therefore, this chapter describes the Traditional View and its dominant foundational semantics to highlight flaws and explain why we need the Interactive Theory. The Traditional View presents meaning as content associated with words and sentences for once and for all in one of the two following ways. On the one hand, as sections 1.1 and 1.2 demonstrate, the Frege-Russell position explains reference and meaning determination in terms of descriptive states when associating concepts to linguistic terms. On the other hand, as section 1.3 proves, reference-fixing and meaning can be explained in terms of facts about speech communities. Section 1.4 claims that these two approaches are flawed if considered separately. Any account to meaning that purports to be successful must combine them to explain how the constitutive conditions of our speech communities and the speakers' psychologies contribute to reference determination of the words and meaning-fixing of the sentences in our natural languages.

1.1 FREGE ON SENSE AND REFERENCE

At the end of the nineteenth century, mathematician Gottlob Frege introduced a revolutionary and promising reductive program that would affect the subsequent common understanding of natural languages. Following a methodology he developed and hoping to reproduce his success in logic and mathematics, Frege suggested that natural languages, like mathematics, can also be reduced to the logical analysis of their components and relations.[1] By this, Frege means that, in the same way mathematical concepts do, our ordinary language operates under a complex but concrete structure produced by a closed set of rules. These rules indicate that each natural language item can be employed to determine the embedded meaning of any sentence one can build. Therefore, an artificial language that reproduces this logic can be constructed with totally independent meaning arbitrarily assigned to every term.

This reductionist view was started by Leibniz's logical works, among others, who presumed all sentences of our language could be reduced to a basic algebra that eliminates any ambiguity in natural language. It was commonly thought that ambiguity was created by way of inference. Therefore, to eradicate flawed inferential thinking, the construction of an artificial language with specific rules to clarify what concepts are associated with which linguistic items was seen as necessary. Since then, many logicians and mathematicians followed that lead and built models containing any possible term and relation without ambiguity. Frege expresses this intention in a letter to Peano dated September 29, 1896:

> A conditional definition of the sign for a concept decides only for some cases, not for all, whether an object falls under the concept or not, it does not therefore delimit the concept completely and sharply. But logic can only recognize sharply delimited concepts. Only under this presupposition can it set up precise laws. The fallacy known by the name of "Acervus" rests on this, that words like "heap" are treated as if they designated a sharply delimited concept whereas this is not the case. Just as it would be impossible for geometry to set up precise laws if it tried to recognize threads as lines and knots in threads as points, so logic must demand sharp limits of what it will recognize as a concept unless it wants to renounce all precision and certainty. Thus, a sign for a concept whose content does not satisfy this requirement is to be regarded as meaningless from the logical point of view. It can be objected that such words are used thousands of times in the language of life. Yes, but our vernacular languages are also not made for conducting proofs. And it is precisely the defects that spring from this that have been my main reason for setting up a conceptual notation. The task of our vernacular languages is essentially fulfilled if people engaged in communication with one another connect the same thought, or approximately the same thought, with the same proposition. For this it is not at all necessary that the individual words should have a sense and meaning of their own, provided only that the whole proposition has a sense. Where inferences are to be drawn, the case is different: for this it is essential that the same expression should occur in two propositions, and should have exactly the same meaning in both cases. It must therefore have a meaning of its own, independent of the other parts of the proposition. (Frege 1980, 114–115)

The purpose of constructing this logical model is, of course, to eliminate all ambiguities ordinary language contains and fix the reference and meaning of every linguistic item in our natural language. As Frege admits, we often employ names lacking reference, complex expressions without truth value, and words whose content is not immediately identifiable. These cases problematize a well-established theory of meaning: John Stuart Mill's approach to meaning as referentiality.

Mill's idea was that certain words' meaning is nothing but its reference and that sentences with these merely referential words are cognitively irrelevant. To be fair to history and Mill's philosophical system, his theory of language is based on his syllogistic, for Mill considers language a fundamental instrument of thought (Mill 1843). Mill acknowledges a distinction in words: they can have a denotation and a connotation. A word denotes the object of the world it represents in language but connotes specific properties of such object. Connotation, therefore, determines denotation in the sense that to know the connotation of a word, speakers must know the necessary and sufficient conditions that determine what object such a word denotes (that is, its truth conditions). Nevertheless, not all words have connotations. Words lacking connotation do not attribute any specific properties to any object but pick up its reference, its denotation. They are a mere marker to refer to concrete individuals. For this reason, Mill calls them singular words.[2] They are equivalent to what we call proper names, words such as "Cicero," "Ulysses," and "Ausiàs" that are employed to refer to specific individuals. So far, so good. The problems arise because Mill insists that these words are not cognitively relevant when used predicatively in sentences with a copula (especially in sentences stipulating identity). After all, they do not offer any information about the world but only about a merely verbal proposition. Think about the sentence "Tully is Cicero." According to Mill, this sentence does not say anything about the world since it simply states an individual's identity with himself, given that Cicero was Tully. Therefore, Mill concludes that this type of proposition only provides information about the conventional ways we employ language to refer to things but not factual information about how the world is. This is the starting point of Frege's famous differentiation between sense and reference.

To account for these cases, Frege (1892) distinguishes two components of meaning for any linguistic item: sense and reference. On the one hand, we have words, which reference is the objects of the world that those words represent in language. Their sense is the specific properties that the speaker associates with such objects. On the other hand, we have sentences. For Frege, sentences express functions applying to arguments. In a sentence such as "Ausiàs is asleep on the couch," we have a sense (an abstract object, a thought) and a reference (its truth value, which right now at the time of writing this is True, since my son Ausiàs is asleep on the couch). In this sentence, the subject (the proper name "Ausiàs") picks up my son, a real object of the world, while the predicate refers to a concept. In sentences, concepts are functions from objects to truth values. Therefore, the above-mentioned sentence can be understood as representing the concept "___ is asleep on the couch" as applied to my son Ausiàs.

The sentence "Tully is Cicero" also has a sense and a reference. The reference is True since it happens that Cicero was Tully. However, even though the prior sentence and the sentence above about my son Ausiàs have the same reference (True), they do not have the same meaning. Therefore, something else must help determine this sentence's meaning. This is its sense. The sense is the thought that the sentence expresses, which in this case is that the individual named "Tully" is the same that the individual named "Cicero." In other words, the sentence represents the concept "___ is Cicero" as applying to Tully. If this is the case, it cannot be true that the sentence is cognitively irrelevant, as Mill said, since it offers crucial information: the fact that the individual named "Tully" also is the individual named "Cicero." According to Mill, this sentence is trivial because it simply informs the convention that two different names refer to the same individual. Frege argues that this is not the case.

Sentences such as "Tully is Cicero" offer information about the world since it could be the case that a speaker did not know that Tully and Cicero are the same person. This is what his famous example, "The morning star is the evening star," is all about. Suppose we accept, with Mill, that such a sentence is trivial because it only states that an object (the reference of the two linguistic items) is identical to itself. In that case, we must equate the prior sentence to some tautological, a priori knowledge, something like "Venus is Venus" (given the fact that Venus is the object that both "the morning star" and "the evening star" stand in language for). However, that is not what the sentence "The morning star is the evening star" says. The sentence is significant and does not state a mere tautology. The sentence states that a discovery has been made, new information is provided, and cognitive gain occurs when someone realizes that the two objects, "the morning star" and "the evening star," have the same reference.

The distinction between sense and reference raises an interesting conundrum. If the reference simply is a mechanism for a word to pick up the object of the world it denotes, to fix a name's reference, what is the sense? Is it some kind of mediation between these objects of the world and what the subject attributes them? Does one simply express their thoughts about the objects of the world? If this were the case, ordinary language would only reflect subjective perspectives about the world, something like the speaker's perceptions of objects as having some properties but not others. However, this is not what Frege says. As his correspondence with Peano pointed out, object properties attribution depends on Thought, but not on any individual's thought. The meaning of any sentence is independent of any subjective thinking. The sense is the concept associated or displayed by any sentence and that any speaker of a given natural language (the "vernacular" Frege talks about) would understand. An intuitive level understands this relation as a direct correspondence between what we say and what we mean. This is, a verbatim correspondence between the content of our mental states (meaning of thoughts) and the content of our words (words meaning) and the external conditions which make both true (truth conditions). This, of course, necessarily binds what we say, what we think, and what we do. Therefore, this correspondence can be understood under a radical realist approach that claims meaning is a part of the world. After all, as Frege says, language and thinking have to do with things and properties, with reality, and not with what we make of them. In a few words, "no psychological investigation can justify the laws of logic" (Frege 1979, 175, sentence 17).

1.2 RUSSELL ON PROPOSITIONAL FUNCTION AND DEFINITE DESCRIPTIONS

Bertrand Russell, like Frege, also believes in building a logically ideal language capable of describing the world free of any accidental and imprecise misleading natural language surface structures. This formal language allows describing states of affairs in virtue of logical terms and connectives and gives an accurate description of what meanings are arbitrarily associated with linguistic items. Russell considers many of our ordinary language statements open to doubt because they refer to entities that may be known only through inference and not actual knowledge of reality. In other words, like Mill, Russell believes that much of our language offers information only about the rules of language (*de dicto*) and not about how the world is (*de re*).[3]

Despite his admiration, Russell (1905) pointed to some flaws in Frege's theory. Under Frege's approach, sentences such as "Pegasus is fast" are meaningless since they lack reference. Remember that, for Frege, the reference of sentences is their truth value, which is established by composition (by combining the references of all terms in the sentence). If a sentence includes a term that lacks reference, such as "Pegasus," it lacks truth value and meaning, even though it offers cognitive information because speakers associate some sense to the sentence. This is problematic for Russell.

He agrees that terms such as "Pegasus" lack reference. Nevertheless, Russell disagrees that the sentence lacks truth value or meaning. Even though they do not stand for a real object, the name and the sentence that includes it still express something. However, what do they express? The easy answer is that they may express a concept, as Frege would say, the sense speakers associate to the words in question. Nevertheless, this is a mistake. This is precisely the problem Russell points out. If we consider that a sentence like "Pegasus is fast" expresses a concept, we must admit that either incomplete, undetermined propositions exist or all denoting items stand for an object. The first position (Frege's) leads us to admit, against our intuition and experience, that some sentences are meaningless because they lack a reference (truth value). The second position (Meinong's) ends with the extreme ontological realist position that a name must necessarily denote either an existent or a nonexistent object.[4]

Russell introduces a distinction between propositions and propositional functions to solve the problem.[5] If a proposition requires a complete logical form, every term provides a reference. However, natural language is undetermined. Therefore, natural language cannot be all about propositional logical forms. It must be some other logical form that saves the intuitive idea that a linguistic item expresses meaning even though it may lack reference. Consider again the sentence "Pegasus is fast." If we believe that this sentence's logical form is propositional, we fail in expressing meaning because "Pegasus" lacks reference. However, Russell says, we can think of it as having a different logical form. We can think of it under the propositional function model. Instead of assuming that the sentence expresses meaning after accumulating the meanings (references) of all its parts, we can remove any specific individual from its propositional content. If we do so, instead of having "Pegasus is fast," we have something like "x is fast" (or "___ is fast"). This second logical form expresses a perfectly valid meaning without necessarily associating it to anybody or anything yet. Even though it has no truth value, it is significant because no individual is represented by the empty slot occupied now by the variable x. Furthermore, it alleviates Frege's problem relying on the speaker-based association of senses to words and sentences. In other words, Russell reshaped Frege's theory and introduced a function from objects to propositions that solved the problem generated by undetermined sentences such as those including empty names in purely logical and quantificational terms.

If we think about Russell's purpose, with his distinction of logical forms, Russell provides an answer to the question regarding the proper individuation of linguistic items' reference so that we can make claims about them within the structure of language itself. Russell's application of propositional functions elegantly answers Frege's problems with sentences including words lacking reference without appealing to the cognitive content offered by senses. However, Russell's caveat expands beyond cases of empty names. Propositional functions also provide solutions to other problematic cases. For instance, propositional functions explain indexical sentences such as "This is big." If we read the sentence under the propositional logical form model, the sentence is incomplete because the term "this" is undetermined and ambiguous. Under the propositional function model, though, the sentence says, of whatever object that could potentially fulfill it, that the unidentified object has the property "to be big." Terms such as "this," "that," and so on, are what Russell calls *logically proper names* since they have necessarily associated referents, even though they are undetermined in language until circumstances make the speaker and audience aware of the object the word picks up in a specific occasion.

In addition to these terms, Russell mentions the difficulties of descriptive phrases, which a priori do not seem to be referential. Russell says that these linguistic items contribute to the meaning of a sentence even though they have no meaning by themselves:

> If "the author of *Waverley*" meant anything other than "Scott," "Scott is the author of *Waverley*" would be false, which it is not. If "the author of *Waverley*" meant "Scott," "Scott is the author of *Waverley*" would be a tautology, which it is not. Therefore, "the author of *Waverley*" means neither "Scott" nor anything else—i.e., "the author of *Waverley*" means nothing, Q.E.D. (Russell 1959, 85)

If this is true, then definite descriptions such as "the author of *Waverly*" have a completely different role in explaining meaning. But why? Recall that Russell looks at these linguistic items as part of significant sentences that make a claim, what for Russell implied saying of something that has some property. In other words, a sentence is significant if and only if it expresses a complete proposition of the subject-predicate form. The logical form determines the type of proposition expressed by a significant sentence. In subject-predicate sentences like the above-mentioned examples, the sentence expresses a proposition constituted by whatever the linguistic item in the subject place refers to and the property predicated of that object by the copulative side of the sentence. Russell calls this a *singular proposition*. The sentence's meaning is the proposition, and the parts of the sentence have as their meanings the contributions they make to such proposition. Therefore, the linguistic item that has a subject's role contributes the object of the world to the sentence that the proposition is about. This object is the meaning of the linguistic item acting as a subject. As said before, any proper name (or even any logically proper name) is the perfect example of this kind of linguistic item since it necessarily links an object to the proposition expressed by the sentence.

Nevertheless, as mentioned before, we cannot consider sentences with an empty name (a word lacking reference) under the subject-predicate type or the propositional logic form. If this were the case, the subject's role fails to be significant. These sentences do not express a complete proposition but a proposition with an empty space where the contribution of the name should be. Russell says that if we find linguistic items that mention objects without necessarily picking them up, these objects must be their meanings. If they have objects as their meanings, Russell concludes, they will be able to fill the subject's role in significant sentences.

These linguistic items are descriptive phrases, such as the definite descriptions "the author of Waverley" and "the king of France." When we consider sentences with descriptive definitions in the subject position, such as "The king of France is wise," Russell says, the sentence is significant because it expresses a complete proposition. The sentence is meaningful because it appears to have a subject-predicate form (propositional logical form) where the property "wise" is predicated on the object that "The king of France" refers to. Nevertheless, this is incorrect because there is no such thing as a king of France. Since the definite description does not refer to any current object of the world, according to Russell, the sentence must either be meaningless or fail to be a subject-predicate sentence. The sentence is significant since any competent speaker of English would understand what the sentence says, even though it must be false (since, in the present, there is no king of France). Therefore, the sentence must have a different structure than the usual subject-predicate sentence, primarily because, as seen before, definite descriptions are not referential terms and, therefore, cannot function as normal subjects. If this is the case, the sentence must be associated with a complete proposition that is not singular (that is, that is not about a specific item). However, if this is true, then the definite description does not contribute an individual item to that proposition and, therefore, it is not a referring expression.

A question, nevertheless, persists. If the sentence has meaning and the expressed proposition is complete, then the proposition must reflect the definite description. Sentences including definite descriptions are uniquely existential sentences, and definite descriptions are quantificational expressions. The definite description then plays two different roles within a sentence. On the one hand, it signals that the sentence containing it expresses an existential proposition, and, on the other hand, it contributes a property to that proposition even though it does not contribute any individual object.

To sum up, Frege and Russell agree that proper names have both a sense and a reference, that proper names without a reference still have a sense (which allows for building significant sentences), and that there is no difference between proper names and definite descriptions. Russell explicitly claims that the meaning of proper names is equivalent to the meaning of the descriptions that speakers associate with them. Frege employs definite descriptions to explain the sense of proper names, the thoughts that speakers associate with them. Russell and Frege had different views about definite descriptions, though. Russell but not Frege thought of them as quantifier phrases. Nevertheless, Frege and Russell agreed that sentences with definite descriptions are significant not because they refer to any concrete individual (after all, they do not contribute their reference to the sentence) but to a propriety (what is predicated) of anything that could satisfy such condition.

1.3 CRITICISM AND EXPANSION

The two prior sections detailed the crucial differences between Frege and Russell regarding the meaning-fixing of the sentences of our natural language. Nevertheless, they also highlighted the common points. Both Frege and Russell agreed upon the need to construct a formal language free of any ambiguities that could establish a well-founded and independent set of rules to determine the conditions under which any linguistic item could be meaningful.

Peter Strawson (1950) criticizes Russell's denotational theory because referring is nothing that words do but something that speakers using words can do. Strawson distinguishes between a sentence, the use of a sentence, and the utterance of a sentence. Sentences *per se* are not true or false since only the statements that speakers make when uttering these sentences can have truth value. He focuses on sentences including definite descriptions such as "The king of France is wise." This sentence is significant but false for Russell since the definite description "The king of France" lacks reference. Strawson also considers that the sentence is significant. However, he believes that the sentence can be neither true nor false (it lacks truth value) since nobody would utter such a sentence if they knew that there is no king of France. Therefore, for Strawson, a sentence such as "The king of France is wise" presupposes that the speaker believes France has a king.

Keith Donnellan (1966) argues that both Russell and Strawson are wrong. Each is partly right because they focus on just one of two different uses of definite descriptions. Moreover, despite their opposition, they share some false assumptions. Donnellan uses Russell's definition of denoting: "a definite description denotes an entity if that entity fits the description uniquely" (Donnellan 1966, 271). However, like Strawson, he refers to a relation between a speaker and what she talks about. Therefore, for Donnellan, linguistic items denote, but people refer. Although a person cannot refer to something without being aware that she is referring to it, she can use an expression that denotes something without knowing that she is denoting it.

Donnellan then distinguishes two different uses of definite descriptions. On the one hand, we have the attributive use: "A speaker who uses a definite description attributively in an assertion states something about whoever or whatever is the so-and-so" (Donnellan 1966, 267). On the other hand, we have the referential use: "A speaker who uses a definite description referentially in an assertion . . . uses the description to enable his audience to pick out whom or what he is talking about and states something about that person or thing" (Donnellan 1966, 267). Think about the following scenario. In a forensic examination, where there is no evidence about Smith's murderer, the coroner says: "Smith's murderer is insane." The coroner uses the sentence attributively because the speaker says this without having any particular person in mind, basing his claim solely on the violent manner in which Smith was killed. Now, think about this other scenario. In the trial where Jones has been charged with Smith's murder and where his behavior is distinctly awkward, the prosecution's attorney says: "Smith's murderer is insane." The attorney uses the sentence referentially because, independently of how Smith was murdered, the speaker is uttering the sentence to refer to Jones specifically.

Donnellan argues that Russell's theory applies at most to the attributive use of descriptions but fails to account for the referential use. Therefore, Russell gets one of the two uses (the attributive) but misses the other. Strawson's theory, instead, accommodates the referential use, but "it goes too far in this direction" (Donnellan 1966, 271) because referential use does not successfully occur even though nothing satisfies the description. Therefore, Strawson gets the referential use only partly correct. Both Russell and Strawson agree that when nothing fits the description, the sentence's truth value is affected. For Russell, the sentence is false. For Strawson, it is neither true nor false. However, this is a mistake. Donnellan believes that both Russell and Strawson are wrong about the referential use.

Donnellan claims that a speaker may referentially use a sentence to say something true even though the description acting as the subject is empty. One may succeed in referring to something by employing a description that does not correctly describe the thing one is referring to. For example, consider again the referential use of "Smith's murderer is insane." It is perfectly possible that, after all, Jones is not guilty of the crime because Smith was not murdered. In this case, the description "Smith's murderer" lacks reference because it does not apply to anyone. Neither Jones nor anyone else would ever fit the description. Nevertheless, Donnellan claims, the attorney used the sentence to say something true. She said of Jones, the man she expressly referred to with the inappropriately employed description "Smith's murderer," that he is insane. If Jones is, after all, insane, the speaker has said something true of Jones, even though the description does not apply to him.

Saul Kripke (1972) further criticizes the Frege-Russell view. For Frege and Russell, the problem was to explain how the words of our natural language get associated with their referents. This is, how we manage to link arbitrary symbols with the things they stand for in language. The descriptivist states that names connect with their referents due to a process of association. The speakers of language associate words with specific properties in a descriptive way, and these words refer to whatever object of the world happens to have those properties. This elegant picture explains how sentences containing seemingly incomplete propositions are, after all, meaningful.

Nevertheless, Kripke says that this is mistaken. He presents three different arguments to prove his point: the so-called modal, semantic, and epistemic arguments. Under the Fregean-Russellian theory of names, most linguist items (mostly definite descriptions) do not fix reference and, hence, have trouble explaining meaning. The core of Kripke's arguments is the notion of *rigid designator*. A rigid designator is any linguistic item that essentially designates the same object (or predicates the same property) in every possible world. The question is, how does a rigid designator fix reference? Kripke offers as an alternative his causal theory of referentiality.[6] This theory says that some original baptism happens (some object gets associated with a specific name, either by ostension or description). From this original baptism, a causal chain of transmission occurs in which the name is passed from one speaker to another to refer to the same object as intended by the original individual.[7] To summarize, Kripke's account of reference is opposed to the descriptivist approach offered by Frege and Russell. The Frege-Russell view explicates the determination of reference and, hence, the meaning of our sentences in terms of facts about the psychological states of individual language users. Kripke, instead, explains reference-fixing and meaning in terms of the constitutive facts of our speech communities.

1.4 WHY IT MATTERS

As we saw in section 1.3, by defending that sentences such as "The king of France is wise" are not false but lack truth value, Strawson defied the rules of classical logic, which constrained natural languages to a framework where every sentence must be either true or false. This is one of the reasons why Russell never accepted this option, since it goes against all basic logical rules and, by extension, threatens the entire Fregean-Russellian program. For Strawson, though, formal logic has little to offer over ordinary language. Logic takes a narrow view since it reduces everything in language to the content words carry (its semantics). Nevertheless, this ignores essential elements that are also present in language, such as the speaker's intentions and a good number of pragmatic processes that help complete the propositions expressed by the sentences of our ordinary language. Any reductive approach to language, therefore, gets semantics wrong. On this basis, chapters 4 and 5 introduce and defend the Interactive Theory of meaning. My theory correctly accounts for the meaning of natural language by rejecting the Traditional View above detailed: the idea that meaning is determined once and for all in terms of either the conventions of speech communities or the speakers' associations among words and senses. A proper account of meaning must explicate the existing interconnection between conventions, the speaker's intentions, and all audiences' possible interpretations. Before that, though, the next chapter critically evaluates contemporary reductive semantic accounts that depart from and expand upon the Traditional View.

NOTES

1. This reductive program is called Logicism. Frege is not alone in this endeavor. Others like Charles Sanders Pierce, Lewis Carroll, and Bertrand Russell endorsed it.

2. They contrast with general words. These are words such as "Roman," "three," or "unicorn." These words have a connotation because they attribute proprieties to the object associated with them. Therefore, they inform the necessary and sufficient conditions for such association, even though not all general words necessarily have a denotation. As Carnap would say, these words have intension but not necessarily an extension.

3. This is implicit in his famous differentiation between knowledge by description and knowledge by acquaintance.

4. Russell, at some point, agrees with Meinong but later drops this strong ontological thesis in favor of his theory of types.

5. This distinction is introduced in Russell (1905) but is substantially expanded in Russell (1911).

6. Even though nobody doubts the prominent role Kripke has in expanding the so-called "new" theory of reference, we must remember that the origin of such causal theory is due to Ruth Barcan during the 1950s, which is materialized in Barcan Marcus (1962). It is time and my moral duty to recognize her long-time-ignored crucial contribution to the history of analytical philosophy. Cf. Humphreys and Fretzer (1998) and LaVine (2020).

7. "Someone, let's say a baby, is born; his parents call him by a certain name. They talk about him to their friends. Other people meet him. Through various sorts of talk the name is spread from link to link as if by a chain. A speaker who is on the far end of this chain, who has heard about, say Richard Feynman in the market place or somewhere, may be referring to Richard Feynman even though he can't remember from whom he first heard of Feynman or from whom he ever heard of Feynman. [. . .] A certain passage of communication reaching ultimately to the man himself does reach the speaker. He then is referring to Feynman even though he can't identify him uniquely. He doesn't know what a Feynman diagram is. . . . Not only that: he'd have trouble distinguishing between Feynman and Gell-Mann. So, he doesn't have to know these things, but, instead, a chain of communication going back to Feynman himself has been established, by virtue of his membership in a community which passed the name on from link to link, not by a ceremony that he makes in private in his study: 'by "Feynman" I shall mean the man who did such and such and such and such'" (Kripke 1972, 91–92).

Chapter 2

The Psychological Relevance of Propositional Content

One controversy in the debate about the determination of sentence content has to do with the boundaries between semantics and pragmatics. As said in the introduction and chapter 1, semantic literalism was the norm during a good part of the twentieth century. According to its defenders, a sentence's meaning is nothing more than "what is said" when uttered. In other words, what the sentence *literally* says (the proposition it carries). Therefore, meaning is reduced to the semantic content of the sentence and its components. Given the difficulties of explaining semantically incomplete sentences, there is a current tacit agreement that contextual elements are required to fix meaning and, hence, some pragmatic process is required. The debate centers around how much of that work falls on each side of the semantics/pragmatics divide. On the one hand, semanticist positions defend that meaning still depends on what a sentence says and that only a minimal part of our language is sensitive to context. On the other hand, contextualist accounts of meaning claim that the content of a sentence mostly depends on all the different utterances speakers may perform and, therefore, contextually sensitive sentences abound in language.[1]

Before moving forward, though, I want to address the distinction between semanticism and contextualism. Following literalism, semanticism claims that sentences represent the world in a certain way and their truth value depends on how the world is. Therefore, semanticism determines the truth conditions of every sentence in a compositional fashion. If this is the case, the speaker has no role in fixing a sentence's truth conditions. In contrast, following Gricean and Strawsonian caveats, contextualism argues that the sentences of our natural language do not have truth conditions *per se* but conventional meanings that inform their employment to say things that are true or false, to make statements. Therefore, what properly has content is the speech act performed by the concrete sentence uttered on a given occasion.

Sections 2.1 and 2.2 focus on minimalism, a new form of semanticism. Minimalism suggests that the content of a sentence incorporates contextual ingredients, but only when the meaning of the sentence requires it. The number of times it is needed, though, is minimal, and only a handful of linguistic indexical terms such as "I," "she," and "now" are context-sensitive. For minimalism, the analysis and determination of meaning occur at the semantic level, negating the contextualist distinction between the content of the speech act and the sentence's content. The question is, then, as Carston (1988, 2002, 2004a, and 2004b) noted, if semantic content is always (either in overt or covert form) operating at the semantic level when determining meaning, why must one appeal (even just minimally) to contextual factors for the completion of specific sentences? Furthermore, if semantics is the only thing required to fix meaning, what is the role of the speaker when uttering a sentence? It is evident that what, according to minimalism, determines what a sentence says bears no relation to the speaker's psychological content, associations, or intentions and, hence, the existence of speakers is irrelevant for the existence of meaning and language whatsoever.

Cappelen and Lepore (2005) respond to this criticism by claiming that, first, semantic content has a psychological role indeed and, second, the semantically uttered content of any sentence is enough to guarantee communication success beyond any possible mistake a speaker might make, avoiding incorrect interpretations by the audience. Therefore, minimalism claims to respond to this psychological difficulty. In fact, as section 2.3 highlights, Cappelen and Lepore insist that the contextualist does not have a proper answer to this psychological requirement. Under the contextualist framework, no participant knows all the relevant factors involved in determining both the meaning and the possible ways the whole audience is involved. Furthermore, there are no reasons to ensure that the sentence's content is represented in an intrapersonal way from the utterance since direct access to the sentence's supposed implicature is not allowed. Consequently, contextualism defends an unrealistic psychological notion of meaning. In the contemporary debate between semanticist and contextualist accounts to meaning, therefore, the following general principle is in place:

(PO) The Psychological Objection: The speakers' mental states are irrelevant in determining the content of the sentences of our language.

If PO is a problem for both semanticism and contextualism, the determination of linguistic content must then transcend the level of semantics and pragmatics, given that it is evident that the speaker's intentions have a role.[2] Section 2.4 introduces the Interactive Theory of meaning, which is further developed in chapters 4 and 5, as an alternative solution to PO. This theory emphasizes not only the truth conditions of utterances and the statements one can make with them but, more importantly, the felicity conditions of speech acts. Furthermore, the Interactive Theory highlights the critical role of a speaker's intentions (and other mental factors) and speech communities in determining linguistic content.

2.1 SEMANTICISM, MINIMALISM, AND THE ROLE OF THE SPEAKER

The Gricean analysis of meaning distinguishes between what a sentence says (sentence meaning, or *what is said*) and what a speaker intends to say with her utterance (occasion meaning, or *what is meant*). This distinction is essential since it differentiates between the content of a sentence semantically implicit in any utterance and the implicatures that such sentence carries. Carston argues that the Gricean "what is said" is cognitively redundant because it requires the presence of a fully aware speaker for the determination of sentence content. From here, she says, if the only thing that Grice can offer is a dichotomy between sentences whose content is implicit in linguistic form and sentences whose content is redundant, then in many cases, the Gricean "what is said" is implausible to play a role in the speaker's mental life (Carston 1988, 156–168). A framework that only offers this sort of "what is said"—one that plays no role at all in the speaker's mental life—should be rejected because it, in her own words, "ignore[s] the nature of communication and of cognition in general in the interest of a formal principle which has no bearing on human psychology" (Carston 1988, 165).

Carston analyzes sentences in which slight shading provides a different reading of what a sentence says. She reformulates the sentences by making the content explicit, reconstructing Gricean implicatures. With this in mind, taking the core of the Gricean "what is said," a sentence such as

(1) The park is some distance from where I live

means

(1′) The park is some distance (whatever this distance is) from where I live.

Since (1), the literal reading, is a trivial sentence regarding some contexts, it is more probable that what the sentence means is something like

(1″) The park is far away from where I live.

Carston defends that sentences such as (1) need to be understood as necessarily pragmatically enriched. They are equivalent to what Grice calls an implicature, which appears when the conversational maxims are applied over what a sentence says. The relation established by Grice between implicatures and other phenomena has traditionally shown weak and forced, she says, and therefore we must understand them as functionally independent. However, even though implicatures could play an outstanding role in the speaker's mental states, this is nothing compared to the role played by explicatures. Therefore, either we keep the Gricean "what is said" or explicatures (what makes cognitively redundant the role of the content). Nevertheless, it is possible to reject both and accept implicatures because there is nothing that semantic content can do that implicatures cannot do. If this is the case, the Gricean "what is said" neither plays a role when fixing a sentence's content nor has any particular function that an implicature also plays. Thought this way, everything an explicature could explain can also be explained by an implicature, which turns irrelevant whatever the Gricean "what is said" enacts. Minimalism, therefore, is redundant.

Grice differentiates between "what is said" and implicatures. He offers a distinction between conventional and conversational implicatures and further differentiates between generalized conversational implicatures (GCI) and particularized conversational implicatures (PCI). According to Grice, GCI are inferences that gather the speaker's intuitions about what she is concerned (what Grice calls a normalized interrelation), which must be interpreted as a kind of standardized utterance that already includes what it is implicated, something that every competent speaker could inferentially understand. On the other hand, PCI are sentences that do not share this normalization. Think about the following example:

(Question): "Do you have a cigarette?"

(Response, as GCI): "I am sorry, but I do not smoke" (to implicate that you do not have any cigarettes, though you have said seemingly something else).

(Question): "Would you like to come to the cinema with me?"

(Response, as PCI): "Bite me!" (as a negative answer to the question, absolutely saying something unexpected that should be interpreted differently from the usual meaning of the mere words).

Grice's analysis of implicatures was not concerned with conversational comprehension but an analysis of the GCI and its normalized interpretations—a differentiation between the semantically established aspects of meaning and those that require a pragmatic enrichment process. According to this view, Grice is concerned with the elements required for specifying linguistic content (cf. Levinson 2000 and Carston 2004b).

According to Carston, then, if the Gricean semantic content is cognitively redundant, it is implausible that it plays a distinctive role in a speaker's mental life (Carston 1988 and 2002). Nevertheless, if the proposition a sentence expresses plays some role that semantic content may also play, then semantic content does not have a distinctive function in the speaker's mental life. Therefore, it cannot play a role in determining the linguistic content of a sentence, as minimalists claim. One must conclude that it is cognitively irrelevant.

In the same way, if the meaning of a sentence plays a role that semantic content could also play, it will be cognitively redundant. It is implausible that semantic content plays a role in the speaker's mental life. Hence, Carston concludes, this renewed semanticist position also "ignore[s] the nature of communication and of cognition in general in the interest of a formal principle which has no bearing on human psychology" (Carston 2002, 40).

In agreement with this criticism, Recanati holds that "there is a central role for rich pragmatic processes to play in determining the correct analysis of the literal meaning of an utterance of a given sentence [. . .] in addition to there being a role for such processes in determining the contextual implicatures of the utterance" (Recanati 2004, 18). According to Recanati, we should focus on pragmatic factors rather than semantic elements to determine the linguistic content of speakers' utterances. As minimalists summarize, the contextualist believes that "the proper focus of theorizing here must be the pragmatically enriched *explicature*" (Borg 2004, 45).

Recanati (2004, chapter 1, section 4) formulates criticism of minimalism's lack of psychological awareness. Consider a sentence like the following:

(2) Mr. Jones has three children.

According to minimalism, what (2) says is what their parts say. Its meaning must be reduced to, and only to, its literal content. Consequently, the proposition expressed by (2) will be "Mr. Jones has at least three children (but he may have more)," given that the verb is unspecific. However, ordinary language philosophy, first, and contextualism, second, have shown that in specific contexts the literal meaning corresponds precisely to what a speaker intends to say ("what is meant"), which is entirely different from the literal meaning of the uttered sentence. Recanati's contextualism is based on what the speaker intends to say as "an expanded version of the sentence's semantic content and is identified by process of *free enrichment*, free because the sentence already expresses a proposition, not the one [the speaker] means but merely a *minimal* proposition" (Bach 2007, 487). According to Recanati, when one asks how many children Mr. Jones has, what the speaker means by (2) is "Mr. Jones has exactly (no more, no less) three children." Nevertheless, this is not the only proposition (2) contains. A sentence like (2) has different meanings, depending on the context of utterance. The number of contextual factors the audience has at hand determines the meaning in each case. Appealing both to the speaker's intention and a process of free enrichment should help the audience recognize what the speaker means by her utterance of the sentence on any concrete occasion.

Recanati also uses a distinction between primary and secondary processes of recognition: "[R]ecognition of what is said is the result of *primary* processes [that operate on an item which is not consciously accessible to the agent and yield an item which is available to consciousness], and implicatures are recognized through *secondary* processes" (Bach 2007, 488). This differentiation allows for an already available item to be taken and yields a further consciously accessible item. The former is mandatory and optional, even though it is reduced to intuition and introspection, which are not ordinarily conscious processes. The latter is inferential and, therefore, conscious.

Indeed, there is just literal meaning for the minimalist, and it is determined by a handful of pragmatic, contextual factors. However, according to Recanati, examples like (2) show that at least two different cases are available. On the one hand, there are cases where a sentence implicates meaning. These are cases where the speakers are aware of both "what is said" and "what is meant" simultaneously, just as minimalism holds. On the other hand, there are cases where the speaker is more conscious of "what is said" than of "what is meant." Therefore, minimalism "respect[s] the intuition that the constituents of 'what is said' correspond to constituents of what the sentence used to say, except that when the sentence is semantically incomplete" (Bach 2007, 489).

If this is the case, minimalism confuses what pragmatics and semantics offer. Furthermore, as Recanati states, all sentences require some availability constraint to have meaning. To be precise, what a sentence says should be "determined by the *intuitive truth condition* of the utterance, even if it departs dramatically from what is predictable from the semantics of the uttered sentence" (Bach 2007, 489). Therefore, "what is said" is always consciously available to the participants in a linguistic exchange, whereas "what is meant" does not belong to a different level but could become unified, making it fully accessible to the speaker's consciousness (Recanati 2001, 79–80). This is possible only because the speaker's conscious intuitions regarding "what is said" really depend on the common knowledge of the conditions that make a sentence true.

For Recanati, this identification is prior to all indirect speech acts that the speaker's intention could explain (Recanati 2004, 25). In opposition to those who consider that the only way of explaining these intuitions about "what is said" consists of some appeal to the speaker's opinion uttered in an indirect style about the corrections performed, such as "He said that . . . " or "What he meant is . . . " (as Cappelen and Lepore 1997 claims), Recanati defends that we have an alternative way to explain the speaker's intuitions regarding truth conditions. This alternative offers different images of specific scenes and requests that helps the speaker to identify the uttered proposition as true or false. This presupposes that every speaker chooses the same evaluative constraint since it depends on a conscious level of linguistic understanding that "what is said" and "what is meant" share. The availability requirement ultimately elucidates utterance meaning.

An Availability Principle is, then, according to Recanati, required. It establishes that "'what is said' should always be intuitively available to the participants of a conversational exchange (unless something does not work adequately and the participants will not be considered as 'normal interpreters')" (Recanati 2004, 31). The reasons to defend this principle are clear. First, minimalists equate meaning and conversational implicatures, as if these would just have the role of contextual ingredients and were not the conventional meaning of the sentence. Since minimalism eliminates them from the intuitive meaning of the utterance, the proposition becomes unavailable to the participants in a communicative exchange. This shows how the contextual characteristics of a sentence utterance become a constitutive element of "what is said." Second, these elements are necessary because if they were optional, as minimalists defend, one should leave aside the context of utterance, and our expectations will be truncated. Therefore, contextual elements of any sentence utterance require fixing linguistic content. Third, pragmatic processes (such as saturation, free enrichment, and so on) are often necessary to determine utterance-meaning because processes of truth value interpretation are pragmatic. Accordingly, abandoning minimalism and accepting the Availability Principle is necessary.

2.2 OBJECTIONS FROM A MINIMALIST STANDPOINT

In order to recover psychological realism in meaning determination, Cappelen and Lepore not only respond to criticism but also see contextualism as being psychologically unrealistic. If only a set of pragmatic processes help determine a sentence's content, the speaker's mental states are irrelevant when fixing meaning because all the relevant elements for this endeavor are a part of the context, and none of them seem to depend on the speaker, at least according to Cappelen and Lepore. Furthermore, Carston's criticism of Gricean semanticism does not affect minimalism at all because, first, she seems to misrepresent minimalism, and second, Carston's account is closer to minimalism than she would like to recognize.

Concerning Carston's erroneous image of minimalism, Cappelen and Lepore attack her neo-Gricean version of the Relevance Theory. For her, semanticism assumes that, in any linguistic exchange, the speaker communicates speech act content, that for them is nothing but what the sentence says. The only thing a speaker communicates is "what is said" through the sentence uttered, asserted, claimed, stated, suggested, asked, and so on. As stated before, Carston believes that a sentence's semantic content can never be understood entirely under the minimalist program because the only meaning expressed is always hidden. For Cappelen and Lepore, this is a mistake because contextualism does not pass Carston's tests for context sensibility. According to them, any contextualism disables communication and is internally inconsistent. This objection applies to all forms of contextualism as well, including Travis (2006) and Bezuidenhout (2006) (Cappelen and Lepore 2005, chapters 7–9).

Think about radical contextualism (Sperber and Wilson's [1986] version of the Relevance Theory). It denies that minimal semantic content is expressed in any well-formed sentence utterance (in English, at least) because every sentence requires some pragmatic enrichment. On the contrary, for minimalism, this content is an indispensable part of correctly realizing all communicative exchange since it plays a role in the speakers' cognitive life. Hence, any theory that does not recognize minimal semantic content is empirically inadequate and internally inconsistent.

According to Cappelen and Lepore, minimalism agrees with Carston's theory about determining sentence content. For them, the contextually implicated elements of any sentence determine what that sentence says. Meaning is determined because contextually shared content is required for implicature recognition. The notion of minimal semantic content is not identical to the Gricean "what is meant" because it does not play the same cognitive role. The semantically expressed content (the proposition), therefore, "is our minimal defense against confusion, misunderstanding, mistakes, and it is that which guarantees communication across contexts of utterance" (Cappelen and Lepore 2005, 185). The proposition semantically expressed in every uttered sentence is the safe conduct that protects the speaker and her audience from possible mistakes or misunderstandings. The content known by speaker and audience is what one communicates by using the appropriate words independently of the utterance context. For minimalism, what a sentence says is what the speaker successfully communicates. Therefore, the notion of semantic content that Carston criticizes in Grice is not the same notion that minimalism accepts. If this is correct, Carston's criticism is, at best, inaccurate.

Cappelen and Lepore (2005) argue that what determines the content of "what is said" (the propositional content of an explicature) in Recanati's theory assumes that speaker and audience information sharing is previous and always available to any communication. According to this view, the speaker's and audience's perceptions and shared context provide all available information. However, the amount of information one individual grasps would depend upon their cognitive capabilities (or their adequate disposition to the communicative exchange or, even, their sincerity). If this is so, as Recanati insists, all communicative exchange participants must always be aware of all the factors fixing what a sentence says, which is too strict.

As Cappelen and Lepore (2005, 187) further state, the great variety of situations in ordinary language does not consistently achieve these requirements. For example, a speaker could make a statement about her own beliefs (for instance, "I believe that he is guilty") even though the conditions that make that someone guilty might be unknown. In other words, opaque scenarios like those involving propositional attitudes are hard to account for since determining truth value has nothing to do with the individual speaker's beliefs. The same would be the case when the Gricean condition of sincerity is not satisfied or, quite simply, the speaker sees the world from a different point of view. In these cases, the speaker would not share any information with the audience, and communication would be in jeopardy.[3]

Cappelen and Lepore (2005), therefore, argue that, since it is not possible to guarantee the awareness of every factor required to determine what a sentence says, contextualism is wrong because no agent could ever have direct access to an explicature. Even worse, the same psychological access requirement can never be satisfied. Appealing to such vital awareness requirements in ordinary language situations is unrealistic because the communicative exchange is possible without the speaker being always conscious or aware of what is communicated.[4] Therefore, Cappelen and Lepore suggest abandoning the Availability Principle.

This directly attacks Recanati's (2004) position. For Recanati, "what is said" is consciously present in the process of understanding an utterance of any sentence because it corresponds to the information intuitively shared by speaker and audience in any linguistic exchange under normal conditions. However, as Cappelen and Lepore (2004, 188) point out, how does this happen? Furthermore, is it indispensable that something normal (in terms of awareness) has to be present in the speaker's mind to understand what an utterance says? Numerous counterexamples exist. There are cases where speech conditions are abnormal, even if the speaker thinks that they are not. There are cases where the speaker may believe that the conditions are not entirely normal, but they are. There are cases in which the speaker believes that she is not normal, and, nonetheless, she is normal after all. Although the conditions of speech are normal, there may be cases in which the speaker could still not be aware of the factors required to make adequate such a linguistic situation. Therefore, if univocally distinguishing what is normal from what is not in any speech situation is required to determine what a sentence says, one cannot entirely do so in every possible case. To conclude, a speaker does not always correctly represent what a sentence says because not all information is always accessible in a communicative exchange, so "Recanati's 'what is said' is not psychologically real" (Cappelen and Lepore 2005, 189).

Both theories critically accuse each other of being psychologically irrelevant. Nonetheless, semanticism and contextualism are unable to properly account for the relevance of the speakers' mental states in meaning determination. From my point of view, this means that neither semantics nor pragmatics by themselves can determine natural language meaning. However, the next section analyzes a minimalist attempt to overcome the psychological objection before addressing this.

2.3 SPEECH ACT PLURALISM

Cappelen and Lepore (2005, chapter 13) present what they dub Speech Act Pluralism (SPAP). SPAP is not a *systematic theory* of speech act content but a collection of instructions to ensure speakers communicate some information when uttering a sentence. SPAP is a *general theory* about the relationship between a sentence's semantic content and the content of the performed act.

The main idea behind SPAP is that what an utterance says, asserts, claims, asks, and so on corresponds to what it semantically expresses. When a speech act is done, the speech act content changes with every new utterance of the sentence, but the sentence's semantic content remains the same. Cappelen and Lepore combine what Nathan Salmon (2004 and 2005) differentiated as two different notions of semantics. On the one hand, he advanced an expression-based notion of semantics according to which intrinsic semantic features of propositions do not depend upon their possible utterances. On the other hand, he advanced a speech act-based notion of semantics where propositions' semantic features are acquired when expressed in a specific speech act. Putting together the two notions of semantics is a mistake. If this is true, minimalism is not so different from contextualism after all (Stainton 2006). Cappelen and Lepore, of course, negate this assessment (Cappelen and Lepore 2006b, 487–491).

SPAP's central thesis (what Cappelen and Lepore call "the Central Observation") is that any uttered proposition expresses a plurality of different contents regarding the different speech acts that their utterances perform. Nevertheless, these are not the content. The content of these speech acts depends upon the logical relation between the proposition's semantic level and the conversational level of utterances and other logical implications that they may compose (as, for instance, the facts of the world or the truth conditions of such proposition). However, it does not depend on context-sensitivity or contextual elements (Cappelen and Lepore 2005, 193 and 199–200; Cappelen and Lepore 2006a).

To recapitulate, SPAP argues that any time someone utters a sentence, the speech act she performs has a different content. Emphasis on all possible interpretations determines the content of each utterance. When uttering a sentence, all possible speech acts speakers can perform share the same semantic content: the content expressed by the uttered proposition.[5] The content is available to any possible participant in the communicative exchange because the truth conditions of the different speech acts are intuitively accessible. This would be so even if the speaker has neither privileged access to the content of the utterance (Cappelen and Lepore 2005, 202) nor a necessary, sincere belief about what she says (Cappelen and Lepore 2005, 203). Therefore, these minimally semantic propositions are psychologically relevant under all possible scenarios.

To me, Cappelen and Lepore's SPAP theory is hard to digest. First, it confuses the truth conditions of propositions with the felicity conditions of speech acts. If we consider propositions, then we have to point out whether a proposition is true or false. Nevertheless, if we have speech acts in mind, it is not enough to appeal to truth conditions. Moreover, even though the uttered proposition performing a concrete speech act could be false, the speech act could still be successful. We must appeal both to the factual truth conditions that tell whether an utterance is true or false and the normative conditions that allow the felicitous performance of specific speech acts. From my point of view, what Cappelen and Lepore defend is highly problematic. If the only way participants in any communicative exchange are aware of a sentence's content is by grasping the sentence's truth conditions that allow performing different speech acts, they fall short for the normative conditions of such speech acts to be set aside. This has a primary and fatal consequence, what I call "the Semantic Fallacy"[6]:

(SF) If the content of a specific expression fulfills certain semantic truth conditions, the semantic truth conditions must also characterize the semantic function of all possible speech acts performed, independently of the speaker's illocutionary purpose and speech act's felicity conditions.

If the sentence's truth conditions are the content of the speech acts performed when we utter such a sentence, these truth conditions never fulfill the normative conditions under which a communicative exchange participant would recognize how certain speech acts can be achieved. Furthermore, the speaker and her audience will not recognize the felicity conditions of any speech act at all. Therefore, if one agrees with such a view, one must accept that a sentence's truth conditions are not psychologically relevant because they do not consider the speakers' mental states or the contextual and pragmatic elements required for establishing all possible speech acts' felicity conditions.

In my view, speakers and their speech communities play a relevant role in the meaning determination of natural language sentences. The previous examples demonstrate that the speaker's intention (and other mental conditions) has a crucial role in meaning-determination. More importantly, the examples demonstrate that neither semantic nor pragmatic accounts alone can adequately explain such a role because a sentence's truth conditions or pragmatic processes are not enough to determine our natural language meaning.

2.4 WHERE TO GO FROM HERE

The question now is, in what sense is an intention (a sincere one), or any other psychological element, required for meaning-determination? My answer to that question is inspired by ordinary language philosophy. We must distinguish between the content of a sentence, the statement one makes with any possible utterance of such a sentence, and the different speech acts that each of those utterances can perform. I argue that linguistic content comes from the speech act in a concrete utterance a sentence performs. A sentence expresses some content from the very moment in which it is uttered. The Austinian theory of speech acts is based upon the assumption that psychological states and conventions coexist as a requirement for linguistic content determination. This is important for at least two different but related reasons. First, the existence of certain mental elements *colors* what the speaker means. It gives any act the same *tonality* expressed by our words. Second, the audience's possible uptakes would determine utterance meaning and what action has been performed. The audience recognizes what the speaker meant when she expresses her states by saying what she said. The Interactive Theory that chapters 4 and 5 develop will use this conception as the starting point. However, first, we must address how speech communities establish conventions and their role in meaning-fixing.

NOTES

1. This distinction between semanticism and contextualism is partial and incomplete. Contextualism can be further divided into different accounts according to the concrete understanding of the determinative role of the pragmatic processes involved in natural language. They range from moderate contextualism (which defends that undetermined, incomplete sentences need to go through a process of free enrichment, as defended by François Recanati [2004]) to radical contextualism (based on the Relevance Theory, which claims that virtually all sentences require some pragmatic refinements, as Robyn Carston [2002] argues). The market offers other contextualist positions such as Barwise and Perry's (1999) situational semantics, Korta and Perry's (2011) role-management contextualism, and a form of contextualism that claims that truth conditions are relative to the speaker's assessment (chapter 7 carves deeper into this last position). Minimalism is just one of the various approaches that explain linguistic meaning in semantic terms. Among these accounts, we must differentiate between, for instance, the truth conditions semanticism defended by King (2007), Collins (2007), Stanley (2007), and Szabó (2006); among others, the expression conditions semanticism advocated by Nathan Salmon; Predelli's (2005) "formal" semanticism; and the "tinge" minimalism held by Manuel García-Carpintero (2007), Manuel García-Carpintero and Pérez Otero (2009), and Emma Borg (2004 and 2012). There are more positions on both sides, but this list does not pretend to be exhaustive but illustrative. Next chapter offers some additional insights.

2. For a further explanation of the different labor that semantics and pragmatics do in fixing meaning, see Bianchi (2004), Szabó (2005), and Ezcurdia and Stainton (2012). I believe semantics and pragmatics have different roles in the process but are not as distinct as many believe. The idea in this book is that a good part of the work of fixing meaning goes beyond this classical differentiation, and attention to the speech community that builds conventions and the speech acts behind those conventions is a requirement.

3. An interesting question is whether one encounters a case of miscommunication when a speaker is not adequately understood or, instead, a case where communication does not occur at all, given that both speaker and audience seem to live worlds apart. (See, for instance, Anderson 2017.)

4. Think about this case, introduced by Austin (1962). Suppose a bridge player raises a bet without noticing that she cannot win. She was unaware of what she was doing, but this does not mean that she did not do what she did because she indeed did it: she raised her bet, even though she did it without noticing that she could not win the hand.

5. Bach (2006, 437–438) points out that, if this is the case, then Cappelen and Lepore fall for propositionalism, how he dubs the core thesis of the Traditional View. They defend the thesis that when a speaker expresses a proposition, she always expresses a thought because it always appeals to some extra element (which is different from the purely semantic elements that compound the sentence itself) to determine the meaning of the uttered proposition. This is because, as they admit, to determine what a sentence says, we need to reconstruct all allowed utterances of such sentence

to determine the expressed thought, and this task can be done in many very different ways (Cappelen and Lepore 2005, 192). In my view, Bach pays attention just to SPAP's first part. Although Cappelen and Lepore radically deny propositionalism, when they state that the semantically expressed content of an utterance is just one of the many possible asserted propositions (Cappelen and Lepore 2005, 200), they accept, as Bach does, that it is not necessary to appeal to any sensible contextual elements to determine the content of the propositions expressed by our utterances (Cappelen and Lepore 2006b, 469–473). In other words, a proposition's semantic content is the content that all possible utterances of the same sentence share, independently of the context of utterance (Bach 2006, 442).

6. The Semantic Fallacy is the correlate of what has been called "the Pragmatic Fallacy": "(PF) If the use of a particular expression fulfills a certain illocutionary purpose of the speaker, then that purpose must also characterize the expression's semantic function with respect to the speaker's context" (Salmon 1991, 306). I accept PF for my primary purpose here, but I think this fallacy is also problematic (at least in its current form).

Chapter 3

The Conventionality of Propositional Content

As the previous chapter makes clear, since at least Morris (1938), it is usual to explicitly distinguish between semantic and pragmatic approaches to language when analyzing how meaning is determined. The distinction is, supposedly, of method and scope. According to the original distinction, semantics only describes the conditions that would determine the truth value of any sentence of any given natural language. At the same time, pragmatics analyzes the contextual elements that help fix what a speaker means besides what is said. Therefore, semantics has to do with truth conditions, and pragmatics engages with the use of a sentence in context.[1] Many insist that an adequate explanation of meaning requires properly addressing the existing relationship between the arbitrary signs that constitute our natural languages and the world's facts these stand for in any particular language. In other words, explaining meaning-determination requires describing what facts will make true or false any unit of language, leaving pragmatics as a mere accessory whose study is not relevant for linguistic and philosophical purposes.

Nevertheless, in contrast with this *descriptive semantics*, there are good reasons to push for the relevance in a proper analysis of language of what has been called *foundational semantics*:

> A descriptive-semantic theory is a theory that says what the semantics for the language is, without saying what it is about the practice of using that language that explains why that semantics is the right one. A descriptive-semantic theory assigns *semantic values* to the expressions of the language and explains how the semantic values of the complex expressions are a function of the semantic values of their parts.
>
> Second, there are questions, which I will call questions of "foundational semantics," about what the facts are that give expressions their semantic values, or more generally, about what makes it the case that the language spoken by

a particular individual or community has a particular descriptive semantics. (Stalnaker 1997, 535)

Stalnaker is digging here into a distinction that David Lewis established between languages and language:

What is the connection between what I have called *languages*, functions from strings of sounds or of marks to sets of possible worlds, semantic systems discussed in complete abstraction from human affairs, and what I have called *language*, a form of rational, convention-governed human social activity? We know what to *call* this connection we are after: we can say that a given language £ is *used by*, or is a (or the) language *of*, a given population P. (Lewis 1975, 165–166)

The same idea is contained in the following passage:

The fact that a word or phrase has a certain meaning clearly belongs to semantics. On the other hand, a claim about the basis for ascribing a certain meaning to a word or phrase does not belong to semantics. "Ohsnay" means snow in Pig-Latin. That's a semantic fact about Pig-Latin. The reason why "ohsnay" means snow is not a semantic fact; it is some kind of historical or sociological fact about Pig-Latin. Perhaps, because it relates to how the language is used, it should be categorized as part of the pragmatics of Pig-Latin (though I am not really comfortable with this nomenclature), or perhaps, because it is a fact about semantics, as part of the Metasemantics of Pig-Latin (or perhaps, for those who prefer working from below to working from above, as part of the Foundations of the semantics of Pig-Latin). (Kaplan 1989, 573–574)

According to the traditional view, what is required to fix meaning is semantics, which determines any linguistic unit's truth value. Metasemantics only answers sociological and historical questions regarding how words get associated with their meaning but cannot explain such meaning because metasemantics has nothing to do with such words' contents.

I disagree. As the previous passages demonstrate, metasemantics is the conjunction of whatever extralinguistic mechanism capable of making sense of why any linguistic unit gets associated with its truth value. It is a primary function of metasemantics to explain why and how such association occurs in the first place, which has usually been neglected when determining meaning. Therefore, a good approach to language must explain how and why a linguistic unit means what it means by clarifying how and why such a linguistic unit has its truth value (cf. García-Carpintero 2012a and 2012b for a summary of a few relevant cases).

The previous chapter delves into why a proper account of meaning requires explaining the role of the speaker's intentions in fixing meaning. It critically engages with semantic and pragmatic theories that do not take it seriously because they fall under what I called "the psychological objection." It concludes that often meaning-determination requires centering the speaker's point of view before addressing the context of an utterance of what is said to entertain what is meant. This chapter overviews why some semantic and pragmatic positions resist the idea that conventions accomplish a role in meaning-determination. In other words, it explains meaning-fixing from below. It explains why an adequate approach to meaning requires considering the conditions a speech community demands from a speaker for her to be able to mean what she says and accomplish certain things with her words. Briefly, why and how an adequate approach to meaning-determination requires to center the speech community viewpoint (conventional meaning) before addressing the question about the speaker's meaning.[2]

3.1 SEMANTICS AND THE CONDITIONS OF MEANING

As seen before, minimalism reduces meaning to semantic content. Therefore, minimalism is a classic example of descriptive semantics that approaches meaning from above. It reduces meaning to truth conditions independent of any speaker and extralinguistic element. Cappelen and Lepore (2005, 53) explicitly reject the "mistaken assumption" of taking semantics to explain the ordinary intuitions regarding a speaker's speech acts when employing language. Semantics for them can only be descriptive since its function is to reduce such intuitions to propositional content. They employ three different tests to prove this point. Nevertheless, how Cappelen and Lepore present them does not straightforwardly explicate contextual linguistic phenomena such as metaphor.

For example, according to Camp (2007), metaphor is precisely sensitive to context as a nonliteral linguistic phenomenon. Nevertheless, this contextual dependency does not imply that metaphors have nothing to do with semantic content or cannot be reduced to propositional content (as, for instance, Stern 2000 demonstrates).[3] This does not mean that metaphor is entirely independent of "what is said." Camp argues that Cappelen and Lepore's (2005) appeal to nonliteral meaning is only an *ad hoc* mechanism to ground their speech act pluralism. When Cappelen and Lepore introduce the three tests regarding contextuality, they only apply them to intuitive facts regarding utterance-truth *per se* since they are only interested in the truth of indirect reports regarding what a speaker has said. According to Camp, their mistake is treating as equivalent verbs such as "to say," "to inform," and "to assert."

The tests should work when addressing what a speaker affirms or asserts as well as when she says it.

Nonetheless, even though when applied to metaphorical statements with verbs "to inform" and "to assert" speakers also pass the tests; the evidence is weaker when her statements include the verb "to say." Therefore, Camp claims, Cappelen and Lepore need to choose between a reduction of metaphors to semantic content and a distinction between the meanings of the three verbs above-mentioned. In other words, it cannot be true at the same time that all meaning is invariant and truth-conditionally dependent and that the same verb accomplishes different speech acts.

Camp believes that we cannot have it both ways. If metaphors pass the context-sensitivity tests, they must be contextual while reducible to semantic content. We cannot exclude them, as Cappelen and Lepore do, from context-sensitive semantics. The price to pay, though, is that the verbs "to say," "to affirm," and "to assert" have different meanings since speakers perform different speech acts with them. Even though Camp considers metaphor dependent on semantic content but contextual, she does not acknowledge a total reduction. For Camp, a connection between semantic content and speech acts is evident, which indicates that it must include both conventional content and a cognitive element (cf. Camp 2016b).[4] Therefore, Camp accepts the distinction but also an interaction between semantics and pragmatics, given the fact that when a metaphor is uttered, audiences must keep in mind both what the speaker says and what the speaker means to make complete sense of her words.

Camp privileges the semantic contextuality of an utterance, since when a speaker says something, she compromises "what is said," with the propositional content her words carry and that many believe, including the speaker. When asserting, therefore, a speaker is saying that she believes what she says to be true. She takes responsibility for the truth of what she says and somehow could retract it if it were false (Lewis 1979; Brandom 1983). In contrast, when someone informs, even indirectly, by reporting what others said, one communicates some information, but a compromise requirement is not in place. The speaker does not need to believe what others say when reporting it since that is not what is at stake. Therefore, it seems proper to conclude, according to Camp, that in indirect reports, the responsibility of what is said falls upon the original speaker (the one that said what the report informs about), and the reporter should be somehow exonerated.[5] This is the main reason, she believes, semantic content is invariant but context-sensitive.

In the same way, when a speaker employs a metaphor, she is not asserting anything. When Romeo says "Juliet is the sun," he is not asserting that Juliet has properties x and y. Romeo invites us to perceive Juliet from a particular perspective. Romeo is not saying that Juliet is literally the sun. He is not describing Juliet as having the sun's features, even though Romeo could not retract that what he indeed said is that "Juliet is the sun." Romeo did not assert that Juliet is the sun. He is telling us to see Juliet as he does, to wear his shoes and take Juliet as the center of his life, the light that feeds him, or something similar. This is why Romeo could retract what he said by explicitly canceling its literal meaning. By rejecting that when he uttered "Juliet is the sun" he did mean it at face value (Camp 2020). (Camp understands sarcasm under the same analysis.)

As mentioned, Camp considers that some linguist phenomena acknowledge the distinction between conventional meaning and speaker's meaning and that linguistic content is part of meaning-fixing but only if taken in context. This does not mean that Camp defends a contextualist position though. Contextualists believe that semantic content is incomplete and always requires some pragmatic process of enrichment and completion. In contrast to semantic accounts that consider sentences the minimal unit of meaning, contextualism understands that only utterances (sentences in contextual use) have meaning. Therefore, meaning-determination does not depend upon what is said but on the speaker's meaning alone. In this view, literal readings are hard to digest. Think about metaphor, for instance. A literal reading of a metaphor is absurd. Therefore, an interpretation that considers intentional exploitation of conventional and conversational maxims better accounts for meaning.

For instance, according to Grice (1989, 87), what is said by an utterance depends on "the meaning of the component elements of the sentence, on their order and syntax." This interrelation between the conventional meaning (the semantic content attached to a phrase) and what the speaker means establishes a two-step connection between semantic and pragmatic elements while preserving the compositionality principle. For Camp, this is a good thing because such a principle encourages a general explanation of human communicative skills, and the two-step process indicated better accounts for normal linguistic exchanges.

Nevertheless, according to some contextualist positions, this view is simplistic. Linguistic reality is much more complex than the Gricean image entertains. Expectations and assumptions interact in such a way that conventions always require the specification of some contextual aspects *de facto*. Often, speakers use words to express thoughts that go far beyond what a conventional understanding allows. Often, speakers talk indirectly, or they lie. This jeopardizes a plain Gricean analysis since appealing to pragmatic resources to close the gap between what is said and what the speaker meant (convention and speaker's meaning) seems *ad hoc* (cf. Levinson 2000).

Contextualism then argues that context and the speaker's meaning invade and even replace semantic content. In other words, there is no semantic content as such but only contextualized speaker's meaning. Properly speaking, there is no what a sentence says, but only what a speaker means with an utterance of a sentence on a particular occasion. Meaning is therefore reduced not to semantic content (as semanticism defends) but to the concrete occasions in which a sentence is employed and, then, to what the speaker performs with such a particular utterance of such a sentence on a concrete occasion. As revisionists of the Gricean program, contextualists usually reject implicatures (or reduce their existence to a minimum) because they believe that what a speaker wants to say, what she means, can directly and explicitly be said.

3.2. CONTEXTUALISM AND METAPHOR

Regarding metaphor, some contextualists believe that they express *ad hoc* concepts (cf. Carston 2002) and, hence, are part of what a sentence says. It is part of what intentionally a speaker says when uttering a particular sentence in front of a specific audience in specific circumstances. As mentioned in the previous chapter, Carston offers some criteria to prove her point. Nevertheless, Camp (2006a, 284–299) considers that at least four of these criteria do not accomplish the role contextualists believe because they still reinforce a Gricean image of metaphor. That image, remember, considers that, when a speaker talks metaphorically, she only says something literally with the intention to say something else. Therefore, there is a two-step process: the speaker's meaning is triggered after the absurdity of the literal understanding of the sentence's meaning.

The first criterion is that, when speakers talk metaphorically, they figuratively mean something that is not the conventional meaning of what is said. Briefly, "what is said" and "what is meant" are often confused. Therefore, there is a certain ambiguity in the verb "to say," for its scope is too broad to keep the distinction. Myriad examples prove that, even though contextualism is correct in saying that audiences usually entertain the speaker as meaning something other than what she says, this is not because the speaker conventionally says something that taken literally is absurd. Audiences exploit a natural resource, conventionality, to say what they mean. If this is correct, then an indirect report of the speaker's meaning will explicitly individuate the specific speech act that the speaker implicitly performs with her utterance.

According to Camp, though, "what is said" and "what is meant" coexist in metaphor. Therefore, it is not possible to reduce metaphor to indirect reports that explicitly indicate the speaker's meaning. There are examples where it is not possible that a speaker communicates what she meant if it is not possible to distinguish it from what she says. Camp points explicitly to poetry. One cannot speak about the poet's meaning/intention without making explicit that this is different from the literal meaning of the sentences she wrote. First, even though one can say that perhaps the poet meant her words literally, it is always possible that the poet really meant to say something else than what she wrote. Second, it does not seem adequate to say either that the poet describes a fact or predicates some properties of the world because given the elusively intentional nature of poetry, it is always possible that the poet meant something else. Third, even though it is possible to take what the poet says at face value, it is still possible that different audiences interpret the poem differently, different even from the original poet's meaning, because poetry is usually written for a generic audience with the intention that the poem could be experienced and interpreted differently (cf. Camp 2015). Fourth, even though it is always possible to literally interpret a poem, as important as what the poem says is how it says it: the poem itself. Therefore, this criterion helps distinguish between "what is said" and "what is meant," against Carston's intentions.

Another criterion employed by Carston and contextualism to blur the conventional/speaker meaning dichotomy is that metaphor is a direct linguistic phenomenon. As Bezuidenhout (2001) and Recanati (2004) claim, unlike other indirect expressive phenomena that require a two-step interpretative process, figurative meaning is the first thing that comes to mind when interpreting a metaphoric sentence. Briefly, metaphoric content is transparent and, therefore, part of what the speaker says, as section 2.1 mentions. This transparency is due to an accessibility or expressivity or relevance principle that points directly to the metaphorical content as available to any competent speaker. The problem with this principle is that speakers often exploit conventional meanings because they usually imply metaphorical contents, which indicates that metaphor is a two-step process. When the direct content, the literal and absurd conventional meaning of what is said, fails to be recognized, the audience seeks a secondary reading that triggers the implicit, indirect metaphorical content, the one the speaker meant. Again, the contextualist criterion fails, not only because it is counterintuitive but also because it reinforces the opposite point that contextualism wants to prove. Therefore, convention and the speaker's meaning are separate but interconnected parts of the communication process.

Carston's third criterion is that metaphors trigger implicatures and sarcasm, but not the other way around. Carston one more time tries to prove that the metaphorical reading is intuitively prior to the literal reading. This time, though, she does not appeal to any accessibility or transparency principle but the supposed intuitive expressivity of language. For instance, for Bezuihendout (2001), sentences such as "Our piggy is all dirty" (when someone says to their partner that their offspring is covered in mud) and "She is the Taj Mahal" (metaphorical phrase employed sarcastically to refer to someone that is not so pretty) can be interpreted metaphorically according to the two-step process described above. Otherwise, they will make no sense.

Nevertheless, a direct reading according to the display of expressive or sarcastic content would fail. As Camp says, an interpretation that departs from other plausible interpretations is not enough to distinguish what is literally said, at least here, since an implicature can perfectly do so. The question now is, when does an indirect interpretation suppose implicature? One requires an explicit expression of the speaker's intentions, what Bach called an "explicature," and not merely implicit and hidden in the phrase (cf. Camp 2018a). Given that implicature and sarcasm can also do so, contextualism still needs to explain why these interpretations are part of the sentence's meaning and how they are interconnected. As Camp argues, metaphor is a function of the content and is in play when any possible other interpretation fails.

The fourth criterion is that metaphoric content is often explicit since other speakers can repeat it or answer it directly, appealing to the original speaker's meaning. Since the words employed carry such metaphoric content, any other instance of such words would carry it, even though it is taken *ad hoc*. Nevertheless, Camp disagrees because this is neither unique nor definitory of metaphor. Think again about Romeo when he says, "Juliet is the sun." Someone can say that that is absurd. Romeo's answer could be, "No, it is not absurd" or "Yes, she is."

Nevertheless, that would be to accept that Romeo literally means what he said that Juliet is the sun. However, this is not the case. What Romeo says is that we, metaphorically, should take Juliet as an (if not the more) important part of his world, to adopt his perspective over what he said about her. Therefore, a more reasonable response would be, "No, I do not mean that she is literally the sun but that she is the most important thing in my life." This cancels the other reading, and, therefore, contextualists are mistaken when claiming that metaphorical content is directly and explicitly contained in the audience's response since examples like this would be confusing if one would claim that the audience takes it literally. In other words, precisely because Grice's cooperative principle works here, contextualism is wrong and the audience would always tend to reject the literal reading for absurd, seeking a more caritative interpretation of what the speaker meant. One could even imagine Romeo employing a language lacking expressive content. Besides, the proper interpretation would explain Romeo's words in the simplest possible terms to include his perspective about Juliet, perhaps paraphrasing what he said to entertain what he meant. This is so because one can retract, as above, what one said when expressing metaphors without necessarily retracting what she meant. This is only possible because who expresses metaphors neither asserts nor compromises to "what is said" but only to "what is meant."

If this criticism is correct, the distinction between "what is said" and "what is meant" (between sentence and speaker's meaning) is real and must be kept. In metaphor cases, speakers communicate implicit content that cannot be communicated in a literal or explicit manner. Therefore, the contextualist's claim that what a speaker means can be directly said or that content can be reduced to the speaker's meaning is mistaken (cf. Camp 2006b, Reimer and Camp 2006). What is the alternative?

3.3 CAMP'S PERSPECTIVISM

Unlike minimalism and contextualism, Camp defends the classic distinction semantic/speaker's meaning. In metaphor, the distinction is clear. When a speaker says something, she does it because she knows that when she says it, the audience will interpret it as literally absurd, which will trigger the secondary metaphorical reading. According to Camp (2016b), metaphors provide unique cognitive access to objects' properties that a literal interpretation cannot. Metaphors provide a *perspective* that indicates how to interpret the surrounding world. Metaphors provide access to the speaker's point of view. They offer unique access to new structures and thought processes (new concepts and thinking). Contextualism is wrong when considering metaphors in terms of loose talk or vague language. Metaphors are not that. They are perspectives that offer new ways of thinking about the world (Camp 2008). Therefore, metaphors often presuppose complex open and holistic perspectives. They are often highly imaginative and emotionally charged, like in poetry. Other times, they are less specific. Even though literal interpretation can sometimes work to interpret metaphors, often it falls short because it cannot move between perspectives, given the purely descriptive nature of literal content. It is, therefore, the combination of perspectives and properties (description and prescription) that provides metaphor its rhetoric force. Metaphors are then perspectival thinking and must be distinguished from other forms of poetic language, such as juxtaposition, analogy (cf. Camp 2020), and other types of expressive language.

For Camp, sarcasm operates as a metaphor. For contextualists like Recanati and Bezuihendout, sarcasm (and metaphor) are part of "what is said." They are a pragmatically enriched part of the literal content. Therefore, the expressive content is always directly accessible to the audience. As seen, Camp demonstrates that this is not always the case. In sarcasm, for instance, a speaker says something to mean precisely the contrary. A literal reading then would fail, which will trigger the secondary reading. The difference between another type of metaphor and sarcasm is that, in sarcasm, the second reading will always be the contrary to what has literally been said (Camp 2012). In metaphor, the second reading is triggered as an invitation to take a perspective from where to interpret the words differently. In sarcasm, the second reading invites to take the contrary perspective of "what is said" in the same way. Therefore, it seems that sarcasm is purely conventional since it responds to semantic mechanisms, and even the so-called "like-sarcasm" functions in purely syntactic terms (cf. Camp and Hawthorne 2008).

However, this strategy does not explain a special case of sarcasm: irony. Irony is not always the negation of what is said. Irony sometimes functions this way. One can say "This is great" to literally mean the opposite. Nevertheless, other times a speaker employs irony to express a negative attitude toward something. Some believe that irony contains an intrinsic critical component (cf. Garmendia 2010). The proof is that the contrary is not possible. One cannot ironically express a negative attitude toward something to express a positive attitude. If this were true, speakers would just exploit conventional meaning to communicate. Moreover, this seems to be true of other cases as well.

Think about pretense: when a speaker wants to pass as true something that is not, and vice versa. Pretense is not the same thing that lying. It will be the linguistic equivalent of what an actor performs in a play or a movie. In a case of pretense, the speaker is trying to make the audience believe something different from "what is said." Camp (2009) considers pretense as the other side of metaphor. They are similar phenomena that differ in terms of their direction,[6] interpretation, and phenomenology. Pretense involves a process of manipulation from imagination to alter the state of affairs. Metaphor reconfigures how to think about such a state of affairs. Nevertheless, this seems to jeopardize Camp's theory. For Camp, fiction and poetry provide "metaphors for life" because they invite us to imagine different scenarios as conceptual frameworks from where to interpret our own vital experiences (cf. Camp 2005, 2012). If this is the case, it is awkward that Camp does not simply admit that pretense is nothing else than a special case of metaphor that provides a different perspective about the world, since, in pretense, the speaker invites to see the surrounding world through a new conceptual model that will reconfigure our ways of thinking about the world.

Even though I cannot entirely agree with Camp about how to interpret irony and pretense, I agree with her that we should keep the distinction between convention and speaker's meaning. Even though speakers often do things intentionally, it is not always clear that such intentions are transparent. Therefore, accessibility principles are not always operating in the background. In other words, it is hard to digest that, as Brandom (1998) demands, we can always explicitly articulate why a speaker says what she says. As Lewis (1975) suggests, speakers' actions are usually rational and can be explained by their beliefs, even though the individual speaker had not, at least not consciously, access to the beliefs that caused her behavior.

Nevertheless, this does not mean that speakers cannot have access to such reasons. These reasons are available because they are part of the speech community that created and sanctioned the ways things can be said and done, and, somehow, competent speakers have learned with language. The speaker's responsibility is to be aware of them when she says what she says because her words have personal and social consequences. It is true that sometimes the reasons why she says and does what she says and does may not be entirely hers but are of the speech community (as a part of the shared common ground). Nevertheless, they still are *her* reasons because they are part of the internalized normativity that came with language. This is what Grice defends since language is a rational process guided by reasons and is what allows cooperative communication in the first place.

The additional problem is that Camp theory seems to fall in solipsism. Camp defends that cases such as metaphor demonstrate a cognitive perspective behind meaning-fixing. If this is the case, the primary role in determining meaning falls onto the speaker, who invites others to take a particular perspective from where to see things. If the individual speaker does this, is not this meaning somehow disconnected from the world and her words? Is not the speaker who seems to create the world? Camp seems to fall in the same disconnection that she criticized in Davidson's holism since the context where meaning is fixed seems to be only the speaker's.

This is not particularly problematic if, instead of prioritizing the speaker's cognitive perspective, one prioritizes the conventionality established by the speech community. Then, the conceptualization the speaker invites us into shifts from a solipsistic speaker's viewpoint to a communal speaker's viewpoint, as the Interactive Theory defends. What I propose is, therefore, to understand conventionality as normativity. Different perspectives are operating in the background and common ground that speaker and audience share (in terms of rules, norms, meanings, attitudes, beliefs, etc.) that are always available to them but not always consciously. Sometimes such perspectives are restricted for special or specific purposes, so they can be hyperlocal and even inaccessible to some since they may lack the adequate vocabulary to access it. Other times, such perspective is common and shared by all, facilitating communication. Sometimes, speakers must find common ground first before being able to do so. Because communication is supposed to be cooperative, convention and the speaker's meaning are related. Therefore, a link between them is always possible (even though sometimes it is hard to find), and their distinction still holds. In other words, it is necessary to include in the notion of convention all the mechanisms that allows speakers to exploit the tools the speech community they belong creates for cooperative communication. I believe that Austin's (1962) classic trichotomy between locutionary, illocutionary, and perlocutionary acts helps in doing precisely this. In fact, as Camp (2006a, 302) recalls, what a speaker says is a locutionary act, and that she asserts something with it is an illocutionary act that has specific consequences (perlocutionary act).

3.4 SPEECH ACTS, UPTAKES, AND LANGUAGE LOSS

Nowak (2020) argues that language loss always supposes illocutionary silencing. I believe that Nowak's conclusion is correct. Nevertheless, clarification of some of the arguments that support such a conclusion is required. This section examines Nowak (2020) and explains why, when a language disappears, "speakers lose . . . their standing as fully empowered members of a linguistic community" (Nowak 2020, 831).

This is the argument. Based on an unexamined lexical theory of slurring words, Nowak (2020) claims that the audience's uptake often depends not on what is said but on how it is said. In the same fashion, the speech acts a speaker can perform often depend upon how such acts are performed, which can be highly idiosyncratic. Therefore, Nowak continues, when a speaker can no longer speak her language (because it is lost or she is cut off from the speech community), the speaker no longer has access to all the required linguistic and extralinguistic elements that embody such language, which consequently supposes the loss of her communal and individual identity. This is nothing else than the illocutionary silencing proper of any disempowered speech community.

As I said earlier, the conclusion Nowak reaches is sound, and I believe that it holds. It is somehow evident that, when a language vanishes, all linguistic actions that a hypothetical speaker could perform are no longer available. This is not only because there is no individual speaker who can lexically reproduce any meaningful sentence from such a language. Nor can it either only be that there is nobody else that could make sense of what the speaker says. This is somehow trivial. Nowak says that, in language loss situations, there is no longer the metasemantic infrastructure grounding what illocutionary act is performed with what and how a speaker utters any potential well-formed sentence within such a language. Briefly, even though the locutionary act and the illocutionary force of an utterance are still potentially available to anybody who might be capable of somehow reproducing such sentences, there is no feasible audience capable of adequately entertaining (deciphering, if you want) all that is going on as triggered by such occasional utterance. However, this is not because there is nobody to listen, but because nobody can engage with the social practices required to make sense of what is going on with what and how the speaker says what she says (the illocutionary and perlocutionary acts).

This section briefly focuses on only two different but related points, which will provide caveats that the Interactive Theory integrates into the subsequent chapters. First, it discusses how better to understand Nowak's use of the notion of uptake. Second, the section also distinguishes different situations of language loss to identify which of them Nowak's conclusion applies to. Unfortunately, when properly understood, not all situations of language loss necessarily suppose identity dispossession, which obligates slightly modifying Nowak's conclusion.[7]

Many times the notion of uptake is interpreted as having limited scope, primarily when taking for granted the classic Strawsonian interpretation of uptake as the understanding of what someone is doing with words (cf. Austin 1962, 117; Strawson 1964; Nowak 2020, 833, 837, 848). I do not mean that such understanding is not many times necessary for the illocution to take place. I am saying that the notion of uptake includes much more than understanding, and often one finds cases where something else than understanding is required for the illocutionary act to hold.

The notion of uptake first appears in Austin (1962, Lecture IX), when he presents the distinction between illocutionary and perlocutionary acts. There, Austin claims that what allows differentiating one from the other is that illocutionary acts are conventional in a way that perlocutionary acts are not, since the second suppose a specific causal effect that the former lack. In Austin's words: "We must then draw the line between an action we do (here an illocution) and its consequences" (Austin 1962, 111). The point to understand the distinction supposes to acknowledge that there are three types of "effects" that belong to the illocutionary act but are not a part of the perlocutionary act because otherwise, the illocution would not hold. Austin says that an utterance must grant certain *uptake* to be an illocutionary act. The audience must take such an utterance as a concrete type of action because the speaker seeks that the audience understands the utterance as such. Austin offers the following example: "I cannot be said to have warned an audience unless it hears what I say and takes what I say in a certain sense" (Austin 1962, 116).

As mentioned, Strawson (1964) employs the Gricean speaker's meaning to define the notions of uptake and illocutionary act. For Strawson, the type of illocutionary act a speaker performs depends on the speaker's intentions. Therefore, the only requirement for uptake is that the speaker must make sure that the audience adequately understands her intentions. Otherwise, the act will not succeed.

Nevertheless, two other types of effects belong to the illocutionary act and must be taken into account when evaluating illocutionary acts. One often-neglected type of effect is that "many illocutionary acts invite by convention a response or sequel" (Austin 1962, 117). Austin offers commands and promises as examples but clarifies that the speaker's intentions may have nothing to do with the success of these acts because their fulfillment requires certain reciprocity. This is the case of swearing, insulting, and betting as contraposed to unidirectional acts such as commands and assertions.[8] Austin also mentions that sometimes "the illocutionary act 'takes effect' in some ways" (Ibid.) This type of effect is different from the consequences one should expect from the performance of a perlocutionary act. As Austin puts it: "[these are] distinguished from producing consequences in the sense of bringing about states of affairs in the 'normal' way, that is, changes in the natural course of events" (Ibid.)

As Marina Sbisà (1984) describes it, illocutionary acts often change the deontic status of those involved in a linguistic exchange. Therefore, illocutionary acts have a lot of conventional. However, they are not conventional regarding the linguistic ways speakers may decide to communicate and perform illocutionary acts since they may vary and often are implicit and dependent on pragmatic inferences. For Sbisà, these effects are conventional because they depend on the stances that the speaker and audience share and the attitudes and assumptions that push for certain dispositions (similar to the common ground described by Stalnaker). This must be taken as a different type of uptake then. Sometimes the audience does not need to understand anything the speaker has said for the illocutionary act to hold. Sometimes the audience (and everybody else) must simply accept what the speaker performs by saying what she says because the speech community sanctions such.[9]

If what this section has so far explained holds, hence what one requires to adequately address the question of what is lost when languages disappear is an adequate explanation of how uptake (effect 1) and the constitutive conventions (effects 2 and 3) that conform any illocutionary act come together without making them dependent on the speaker's intentions. The reason why is that if one tries to answer that question using only an intentional interpretation of the uptake (effect 1), then it does not matter what language the speaker talks but only that what she says is understood as performing a specific act: the act intended by the speaker. This is an implausible scenario primarily because whether, as Nowak claims, what matters to entertain certain utterance as performing such-and-such act is just how the speaker says it, many acts would depend on something else. Second, this then would not be different from an implicature. Nevertheless, as seen, these uptakes are not implicatures. After analyzing Austin's treatment of the notion of uptake, one must also accept that there are conventional answers to ways of saying things that will trigger a certain act, as well as there exist many stances that will predispose the speaker and audience to certain behaviors. Therefore, an adequate account needs all three effects, which explain how the social dynamic practices speaker and audience share produce the acts such language can produce. In agreement with Nowak (2020), though, what a speaker and speech community lose in language loss situations is the ability to perform the locutionary, illocutionary, and perlocutionary acts associated and proper (idiosyncratic and definitory) of such a language.[10]

NOTES

1. Morris (1938) distinguishes between syntax, semantics, and pragmatics. Syntax is the branch of semiotics (the science of language and signs that make communication possible) dealing with signs in their relationship with other signs. Semantics is the branch of semiotics that analyzes the relation between signs and their *designata*: their reference and propositional content (as established by their truth conditions). Pragmatics is the branch of semiotics that explains signs in relation to their users and interpreters. As Gazdar (1979) states, pragmatics is the quest for meaning without truth conditions. As seen, the three are different and devoted to distinct matters. Of course, the trichotomy is dynamic, and many cross it freely.

2. By the way, "snow" in Pig-Latin is "owsnay."

3. Stern (2000) claims that a metaphor operator 'Mthat' allows a semantic analysis of metaphorical content, similar to how Kaplan treats some demonstratives. Camp (2005) correctly argues that some of the semantic limitations Stern's analysis encounters can be solved should we keep some pragmatic mechanisms of generalization and accommodation regarding shared knowledge between speaker and audience.

4. Donald Davidson believed that metaphorical content could be reduced to literal meaning. Camp (2013a) claims that his position is inconsistent. While Davidson (1978) argues for a noncognitivist approach to literal meaning, Davidson (1986) applies some of his prior arguments against metaphorical content. Therefore, Davidson's position seems to have shifted. If before semantics operated over all language, as Camp (2016a) says, now Davidson believes that semantics can be reduced to the more local of all possible contexts: the utterance of a sentence by a particular speaker on a specific occasion (the Gricean speaker's meaning). Camp argues that such hyperlocalism does not explain the systematicity of semantics, which is crucial to Davidson's holism and the distinction between sentence and speaker's meaning (cf. Reimer and Camp 2006).

5. Other examples of expressive sentences are different. Somebody could metaphorically employ a sentence to insult by inviting to observe the target under a particular perspective, saying something like "you are a pig." Offering an indirect report of what the speaker said is not necessarily asserting or compromising to such metaphorical content. For Camp (2013b), it is even possible that the original speaker retracts the insult when she realizes that it is mistaken to refer to somebody that way or because she repents. However, this is not possible with slurs. Unlike other insults, first, slurring words do not insult individuals but are used to belittle the group of individuals to whom the target belongs, supposedly because they share the characteristic

that is pejoratively highlighted. Second, in slurring sentences, it is not clear that there is descriptive content since it never seems to be a context where what is said is true. Third, speakers cannot simply retract what they said since, in the use of slurs, the speaker both says and asserts what is conventionally said and what she means by saying it. In other words, since slurs derogate, one cannot take the offense away by merely retracting the words. That supposes adding injury to harm. Fourth, even though a speaker is indirectly reporting what other speakers said by using a slurring word if reproduced, such another speaker would repeat the original derogative action (cf. Camp 2017b and 2018b). Colomina-Almiñana (2014) offers a dichotomy of slurs. Cases of whistleblowers can be analyzed in similar ways.

6. Camp (2005) claims that metaphor and pretense differ in the level of required attention and direction. Metaphor *requires* attention about concepts because it establishes how we conceptualize the world. Pretense *is about* concepts because it "fixes" the world by altering the perspective employed to conceptualize it.

7. Section 5.4 criticizes the lexical theory of slurs.

8. In my view, these cases are not so clearly unidirectional. In previous work I have addressed this regarding commands, and have expanded on the notion of uptake in Austin and Strawson. Section 8.1 expands a bit upon the notion of assertion.

9. Sbisà (2006) applies her conventionalist model to national identity. Sbisà (2014) applies it to aesthetic and moral judgments. Blanco Salgueiro (2021) is the only analysis I know that explicitly acknowledges the importance of the distinction between these types of uptakes. He calls them uptake-as-understanding (uptake 1) and uptake-as-acceptance (uptake 2). My position also considers the existence of a hybrid uptake: an uptake that requires both conventionality and understanding by the audience (uptake 3). My guess, though, is that there are other potential types of uptakes. The chapters ahead build an account of metasemantics taking upon all these types of uptakes.

10. When a language dies, it seems obvious to say that any possible locutionary act dies with it. Since there is no way to reproduce how that language might have sounded correctly, there is always the possibility that what a potential new speaker says is not actually in the dead language since the attempt will suppose the creation of a different language. This must be distinguished from speaking a language with an accent, but I will not go deep here. It is also necessary to highlight that the only illocutionary acts that will disappear are those that do not coexist within other languages, which can only be performed *in* (virtue of speaking) the lost language. Something similar occurs with perlocutionary acts.

Chapter 4

The Interactive Theory

The end of chapter 1 introduced P. Strawson's theory on referring. Referring is nothing that words do, but what speakers employing them can do.[1] Strawson criticizes Russell's approach to proper names and definite descriptions as denotational terms, which is at the core of the Traditional View. This classical view considers that many linguistic items occupy a two-place semantic relationship with the world. Words refer and designate (and are significant) because they stand in language for objects of the world. Nevertheless, this well-accepted view suffers from a widespread disease that Kent Bach dubs "linguistification." This is the tendency of "attributing linguistic properties to nonlinguistic phenomena" (Bach 2013, 1), like when we say that referential terms refer. This concept is at the core of Strawson's critique. It is also an idea defended by John L. Austin and Paul Grice, for whom language is not a mere descriptive tool of reality but a type of action and a well-regulated human behavior.

As chapter 2 demonstrates, I am highly skeptical that the only purpose of language is to describe the surrounding world and, even more, that in determining the reference and meaning of natural language, only semantic processes have to be considered. I believe speakers' intentions and hearers' uptakes are essential in determining meaning. Nevertheless, as chapter 3 warns, one should be cautious when accepting that all that is required for determining meaning is the speakers' mental states since the conventions built by speech communities have a crucial role. Then, a good part of what language is about has to do with the external, normative set of rules that the speech communities build.

This chapter proposes a new theory of meaning: The Interactive Theory. Two distinct but related ideas form the basis of this theory. On the one hand, a multidimensional conception of language claims that communication cannot be the proper function of language. Communication is, of course, one of its functions, but neither the only nor necessarily the most important. On the other hand, a pragmatic understanding takes language as human behavior, a type of action. Based on these two interconnected ideas, the Interactive Theory claims that the meaning of our natural language is grounded on the interface of three items:

1. The conventions constructed by our speech communities and that constrain our ordinary ways of speaking
2. The speaker's intentions when making statements
3. The audience's possible uptakes of such statements

The Interactive Theory departs from the classical view. This new theory raises caution about purely semantic strategies. Assuming the existence of a unique, literal meaning in each sentence, besides its apparent context-sensitivity, internally determined by the semantic content of its components, it eliminates any role speakers and audience have when determining meaning. Given the risk of psychologism that any theory based on the speaker's intentions carries, skepticism toward personalist/intentionalist and relativist positions is also crucial. The Interactive Theory proposes a solution favoring contextual, conventional nonlinguistic elements that provide the appropriate truth conditions for each utterance of the sentence in question. My theory, therefore, embraces the existence of "unarticulated constituents" based on an externalist but pluralist explanation supported by pragmatic presuppositions, which preserves the speaker's epistemic relevance in language while explaining the externalist and conventional nature of language and meaning. The conclusion is that speakers mean things with the words they employ and not words by themselves because speakers display the values and interests of the concrete speech community they belong to and endorse when they say what they intend to say.

4.1 PRELIMINARIES

Usually, speakers employ an expression to talk about some objects of the world and their properties. Language has a cognitive role and can identify certain entities in this case. Language is employed referentially. There are several different devices that speakers may utilize to exploit this function of language, from demonstratives and indexicals to proper names and definite and indefinite descriptions, which capitalize on the truth-conditional content of these linguistic elements. Some of these linguistic mechanisms determine truth values for one and all occurrences of the sentences where they appear, through what Mill referred to as the method of "concomitant variation."[2]

There are other cases, however, where intention in referring to an object and its properties may exist, nonetheless the speaker does not employ any of these mechanisms, or instead, there is no explicit word to determine the actual referred object, and meaning should be inferred from the context of utterance: the so-called background. These instances are called "occasion sentences,"[3] since their truth value may change and would depend upon the particular circumstances of, as Quine (1977, 178) said, "what is going on in the neighborhood." The current non-Gricean preferred solution to this kind of sentence's truth value determination problem is based on "unarticulated constituents." With highly sophisticated proposals in favor and against, with many linguists and philosophers of language have made distinctive contributions to the topic to deepen and sharpen the understanding of this phenomenon and its consequences for truth and meaning.

As stated before, the discussion about unarticulated constituents is placed in a broader polemic concerning the meaning of "occasion sentences." An occasion sentence includes, for instance, an indexical expression. Examples of indexical words are "I," "this," and "now," and sentences including them are context-dependent. "I" contrasts with the other indexical items in the sense that it is considered an automatic (Kaplan 1989) or essential (Perry 1979) indexical because any occurrence can only refer to the speaker. Nevertheless, it is also apparent that "this" and "now" refer to the intended object and the moment of utterance, respectively, even though this is a more controversial issue. Since at least Charles Sanders Pierce's works, many indexical expressions are considered "words or sentences which reference cannot be determined without knowledge of context of use . . . [they] cannot be considered either true or false independently of the context of use" (Montague 1970, 142). Nonetheess, as Carnap (1937) states, indexical sentences may show transformability. It is always possible to rephrase indexical sentences into a context-invariant form without loss of information.

The problem with this last point is, however, that it cannot be assumed, for example, that sentences including psychological verbs (or, as are commonly known, propositional attitudes, such as "I believe that . . .") indicate a fixed relation between a subject and a proposition, understanding the latter as the bearer of truth conditions. The same holds for sentences containing purely indexical words. If this is so, sentences with such expressions must covertly include variables in their logical form that, once semantically determined, will provide the literal meaning for such a sentence. The reason is that if Carnap is correct, one and only one single proposition is contained in any sentence, and this literal meaning can be grasped by purely semantic mechanisms independently of the context of utterance, given the compositionality principle. However, since propositions are individuated only according to their truth conditions, it seems implausible to claim that a unique proposition is in place at all times in indexical sentences. Given that they would lack truth value until completed, only a contextual determination of the indexical word's proper reference will provide the appropriate and complete sentence's truth conditions. A further quandary is that if Carnap's theory is correct, some propositions shall often contradict the facts of the matter.

To exemplify this issue, consider, for instance, the following sentence (from Perry 1979, 3): "I am making a mess."[4] The truth conditions of this sentence are indexically articulated by the reference of the articulated constituent "I," independent of one's beliefs. Its truth conditions vary across contexts depending on which person utters it and to whom that instance of "I" refers. Besides the fact that the sentence will always refer to the speaker and not necessarily to who is making the mess, this example shows that the speaker believes that he is the one making the mess, which modifies the whole situation, including the speaker's behavior. This is why Perry considers "I" an essential contextual linguistic item since only the nonlinguistic context can provide the reference, which completes the thought expressed by the occasional utterance of a sentence. (See Spencer 2007 for a defense of the opposite view.)

Perry (1986) introduces the notion of "unarticulated constituents." He argues that the content of "selfless" thoughts must accommodate elements that are not and could not be represented in the vehicle of thought itself. Accordingly, the constituent elements of a sentence expressing that type of "selfless" thought does not and could not represent everything that the speaker could say with such a sentence either. Consequently, the truth conditions of any sentence utterance motivated by such thoughts require contextual nonlinguistic element composition to complete what is said.[5] Consider the thoughts expressed by the following two sentences: "The book is to *my* right" and "The book is to *the* right." Both share the same truth-conditional content, one that involves the agent/individual thinker, but both do so differently. The former does it to represent the self (articulated), and the second does it without such representation (unarticulated).

If this is correct, then the notion of unarticulated constituents explains the variation presented by the particular case of occasion sentences. The reason why, as Recanati explains, is that an unarticulated constituent is an element

> of the truth-conditional interpretation of an utterance which is not syntactically articulated in the sentence, yet cannot be disregarded without making the utterance semantically unevaluable, [t]he contextual provision of such a constituent is therefore semantically mandatory even if it is not triggered by some constituent in the sentence. Without such a constituent, the sentence, though syntactically complete, would not express a complete proposition. (Recanati 2002, 310)

Instances of this particular case of occasion sentences are the following:

(1) It is raining (in time *t*).

(2) It is 9 a.m.
(3) In the second drawer.
(4) Everyone is having fun.

Sentence (1) does not explicitly mark the raining location to provide tips on completing the sentence's proposition. Even though the verb explicitly provides the required relational and temporal arguments to determine the proposition functioning behind the scenes, the sentence is syntactically complete. However, there is no specification of where it rains, and, as a consequence, the contained proposition remains incomplete. The same applies to sentence (2), where one must assume that the time zone is where the speaker is situated and determines the sentence's truth conditions.[6] As Zeman (2012, 617) correctly points out, there is "a gap between the truth conditions of the sentence taken independently of any of its uses in a context and the truth conditions of an utterance of that sentence in a context." If this is the case, one should assume a covert element that indicates the raining location and the appropriate time zone respectively, depending on the context of utterance. Therefore, "the place of utterance is an unarticulated constituent of the proposition which the utterance expresses" in these scenarios (Recanati 2002, 310), which makes indeterminate the proposition expressed by any utterance of such sentences until the truth conditions are completed through nonsemantic mechanisms.[7] Alternatively, by appealing to nonlinguistic elements placed in the nonlinguistic context of utterance. Once the audience realizes which unarticulated constituent completes the utterance's truth conditions, which the speaker would have in mind and intend to state, one can individuate the proposition expressed. (Taylor 2001 also defends a similar approach.)

This solution seems sound. Nevertheless, I want to argue in favor of an alternative view based on pragmatic presuppositions, as defended by Stalnaker, and Quine's notion of "observational sentences."[8] This novel solution neither relies on psychological elements, such as speaker intentions or individual beliefs and the audience's myriad possible uptakes, nor semantic elements articulated in the sentences in isolation. The remainder of this chapter demonstrates that these elements always work in interaction.

A presupposition is a bit of information whose truth is taken for granted because it is implicitly embedded in discourse instead of being part of the propositional content of an utterance. Such information must mutually be recognized as truth by speaker and audience or at least has to be assumed as trustworthy by both as part of the context. Presuppositions' main characteristic is their projection. A presupposition triggered by a part of a sentence will expand to the information presupposed in the sentence. A trigger is whatever linguistic item induces the presupposition (the bit of relevant information embedded in discourse). According to classical understanding (Karttunen

1974; Levinson 1983; Huang 2006), definite descriptions, factive and implicative verbs, iteratives, temporal clauses, counterfactual conditionals, and so on, function as presupposition triggers. When a presupposition does not project, that is, when the presupposition does not carry over to the sentence as a whole, the presupposition is canceled. Typical cases include, but are not restricted to, occasions where the presupposition in one of the units is directly denied by the sentence taken as a whole.

According to the Traditional View, presupposition is a semantic phenomenon. Whatever presupposition is part of a sentence must also be a part of such a sentence's determination conditions. Presupposed contents must be, then, part of the sentence's truth conditions. Otherwise, the sentence would lack truth value. For this reason, whatever the truth value of a sentence could be, the presupposed sentence must always be true. However, sentences such as "The king of France is wise" exemplify that when a presupposition fails, a semantic catastrophe occurs. The presupposition in a sentence such as "There is a king of France" is false because there is no referent in the present time who fulfills the definite description "The king of France." Hence, one must accept that the sentence lacks truth value (Frege) or is false (Russell), and therefore meaningless. However, and this is the crucial piece here, the sentence demonstrates that not all presuppositions are semantically embedded.

Robert Stalnaker proposes at least two different approaches to presuppositions as a pragmatic phenomenon. His primary purpose is, particularly, to rescue meaning from presupposition failure by considering not what words presuppose but actually what people presuppose with the use of their words in a communicational exchange. On the one hand, Stalnaker (1974) explains pragmatic presupposition in terms of beliefs. Under this interpretation, no requirement of truth is expected from the presupposition, alleviating the necessity for the whole sentence to be always true in examples like the above. A particular coincidence between the communicational exchange parts is required to believe that the sentence is true about the presupposed information. On the other hand, Stalnaker (1984) defines pragmatic presupposition in terms of iterative propositional attitudes and acceptance "for the purposes of the conversation" (Stalnaker 2014, 4).[9] Under this interpretation, no requirement is demanded from the sentences either. However, instead of a coincidence in individual beliefs, pragmatic presupposition assumes an endorsement and agreement in attitudes (even though merely unconsciously) regarding such a presupposed content. Neither option, though, demands anything at all from the world.

My approach aligns with the second option, understanding pragmatic presupposition in terms of propositional attitudes and acceptance. The information presupposed by a sentence must be, under normal circumstances, part of the occasional utterance's contextual common ground, and, at least in nondefective scenarios, both are coextensive.[10] The information bit carried by a presupposition is, in part, shared knowledge that both the speaker and the audience have, at least if one wants for such a sentence to be felicitous, without depending at all on the subjective beliefs of the speaker and audience. Therefore, the Interactive Theory this book presents incorporates Stalnaker's (2014, 122) notion of common ground as "the information shared in common between a group of *n* individuals . . . there will be *n* individuals at the center: the individuals that they all presuppose themselves to be."[11]

As I understand it, this coincides with a broader notion of presupposition based upon speech communities and their viewpoints, always taken under maximally local contexts. To illustrate this alternate account, consider the following situation:

(3) {Ausiàs cannot find the train engine he got for his birthday. After looking for it for a little while, he loses his patience. Nicole, his mother, utters:} In the second drawer.

As pointed out before, sentence (3) is syntactically and truth-conditionally incomplete. However, Ausiàs seems to fully understand what Nicole told him since he could compose himself, walk to the credenza in our living room, and open the second drawer, where he finally finds his train engine. It is sound to assume that this concrete utterance of (3) has been understood as: "Your (Ausiàs's) toy (the train engine you got for your last birthday) is stored in the second drawer of the credenza (the one we have in the living room of our house, where we are now)." As we have learned from both the Stalnakerian notion of pragmatic presupposition and the Quinean notion of observational sentences, the best explanation for Ausiàs's interpretation of Nicole's utterance of sentence (3) can only be that Ausiàs and Nicole share a common ground.[12] Moreover, specific training that Ausiàs previously acquired allows him to learn that what has been said in such circumstances must be understood as such-and-such and not otherwise. Only a maximally local contextual determination of a sentence's truth conditions could provide the real expressed proposition for such an utterance if this is the case.

The same analysis applies to all other sentences mentioned here. For instance, a particular utterance of (4) must be understood under the common ground that applies to that and only that context. It refers to those individuals having fun in the circumstances presupposed by the background and under such and such circumstances, which I suggest are a part of the ways we have normatively learned to use such sentences, and not others, under such circumstances, etc. Think about the following situation:

(5) {You are seated on a table inside a diner, and you hear a waitress telling the manager:} The ham sandwich left without paying.

It seems evident that she is not talking about any sci-fi-like scenario happening where a sandwich was the customer. She wants to communicate to the manager that a specific customer (the one that ordered a ham sandwich not long ago, today, at that diner, during her shift, and to whom she provided service, etc.) left without paying for his meal. This information is pragmatically embedded in the common ground that both waitress and manager share, and it is communicated not by the words employed, but because both have learned that in certain circumstances you would employ some words in a specific order, but not other, to communicate that and no any other thing.[13]

As it is clear, all these common ground nonlinguistic elements are unarticulated constituents required to understand the previous utterances. How and when to use what linguistic element in which circumstances we learned from and because we, as competent speakers, belong to specific speech communities. They tell and teach us how to correctly employ them under adequate circumstances. After all, this is what language acquisition is all about. The Interactive Theory then concurs with Stalnaker's thesis, pace Lewis (1979), that common ground and presupposition are independent of a natural language's normativity, and that the process of accommodation identified by Lewis (remember, the acceptance as true of the presupposed sentence besides lacking enough evidence to assert its truth) is the result of the speaker and audience's rational activity during a conversation.[14]

4.2 EXTERNALISM, PRAGMATICS, AND COMMON GROUND

The previous section overviewed Stalnaker's notions of pragmatic presupposition and common ground and its relation to Quine's observation sentences and introduced Perry's notion of unarticulated constituents. These notions express the core of what has been called truth-conditional pragmatics (TCP). TCP accepts the role of nonlinguistic elements situated in the context of utterance in determining a sentence's truth conditions, besides purely semantic factors. Under this strategy, the audience realizes which elements the speaker has intended to communicate, or "has in mind," when uttering a particular sentence in a concrete moment. Therefore, certain utterances of a sentence require unarticulated constituents to complete the truth conditions of the expressed proposition, independently of its apparent grammatical correctness. Some (utterances of particular) sentences have no truth value until these nonlinguistically articulated elements are specified to complete the sentence's truth conditions through purely pragmatic mechanisms.

I agree with Perry and others that unarticulated constituents are fundamental and, actually, necessary for the completeness of the truth conditions of the proposition expressed by some utterances of specific sentences. I cannot entirely agree with how these nonlinguistic elements are individuated. However, if Stalnaker's and Perry's theses are correct, variation in meaning follows. Since a particular sentence is uttered, the audience has to look for the unarticulated constituents located in the context of such utterance (the common ground) to complete the proposition and find the speaker's intended meaning. Multiple meanings may be identified on different occasions and even for different audiences, violating the principle of linguistic parsimony (what Grice called the "linguistic Ockham's razor").[15] It is for this reason that, contrary to the previous view and based on Carnap's claim previously stated, one finds truth-conditional semantics (TCS): The idea that there is one and only one unique, literal meaning in each sentence, and that such content is sufficient and necessary to determine the truth conditions of an utterance of a sentence in a given context. This is an evolution of the Traditional View. It argues that, in contrast to TCP, the place where it rains (in a sentence such as "It is raining") is embedded in the logical form of the sentence itself, and proper scrutiny will make it surface. According to TCS then, sentences such as the above one include complete propositions because "any contextual effect on truth conditions that is not traceable to an indexical, pronoun, or demonstrative must be traceable to a structural position occupied by a variable" (Stanley 2000, 401). Cappelen and Lepore (2007) agree with this analysis and consider that any element supplied by context for a given sentence's truth conditions has to be a covertly functioning variable at the logical/syntactical level of the sentence. The main reason is TCP's obvious risk of reproducing psychologism and relativism, as will be explained later.

Given the rigidity and dangers of TCP, some advocate for a middle ground (Martí 2006, for instance). This intermediate position claims that the truth-conditional effects of nonlinguistic contextual elements should only be traced throughout a contextual variable placed within the logical/syntactical form of natural languages, which is always optional.[16] Both accept the existence of embedded variables in the sentence's logical form, but the difference with TCS, of course, is Martí's criterion of optionality regarding the existence or inexistence of these embedded variables in the logical/syntactical form of sentences.[17] Besides embedding in the sentence's logical/syntactical form, these variables can be or cannot be available depending on the context of utterance. Besides the fact that I applaud this third option for escaping both the frustration TCS creates when confronting the intuition that no single and unique strict and invariant, literal content is contained in any sentence and at the same time offers a solution to the undesirable proliferation of meanings and contents and the illusion that may be individuated by the speaker's and hearer's inner mental life, like TSP promotes, this middle ground is still problematic.

The quandary is the following. On the one hand, even though optionality is sound here, if one accepts the existence of embedded variables operating at the logical/syntactical level, their functionality cannot be optional but necessary since it still seconds the idea of the compositionality of meaning. On the other hand, besides the problems raised by psychologism and internalism, examples like the previous ones where the speaker becomes aware of some extra knowledge are the mainstay for completing these sentences' truth conditions. Therefore, an account as the Interactive Theory based on pragmatic presupposition and observational sentences is the answer since it follows this two-fold criterion. On the one hand, it proposes a contextualized and pluralist approach to meaning. This necessarily rejects invariant content in each sentence (essentially fixed truth conditions) that determines meaning since these will only be completed context-by-context. Hence, the Interactive Theory negates TCS's plausible hypothesis: words mean nothing since there are speakers who create and re-create meaning with words.

On the other hand, the Interactive Theory is externalist and conventionalist, since it argues that both the speaker intentions and the audience's possible uptakes of the epistemically relevant elements for completing the sentences' truth conditions do not depend on their respective mental, inner lives (individual beliefs and other mental states), but on shareable, accessible knowledge in the context of an utterance that speakers learn to employ when acquiring the ways speech communities codify their meanings and values. In short, it depends upon specific agreement in attitudes toward the common ground. My primary purpose is to return control over truth and meaning to speakers and audiences as part of the speech communities that create and re-create them.

Recanati's approach is concerned with the behavior of verbs such as "eat" and "rain." Sentences including "rain," for example (1), have a covert specification of the location where it rains. Sentences including "eat" have a covert specification of the object eaten. Besides the fact that these locations are covert, Recanati's approach reveals *salience*: what is said by an utterance of a sentence usually is identified with the first meaning normal interlocutors would consciously understand to be presupposed in an everyday context.[18] Independent of the syntactic and semantic assumptions made that establish truth conditions of sentences with "rain" and "eat," according to Recanati, any possible interpretation of this sentence type should take place in a purely pragmatic and nonoptional free enrichment process, one that includes some sense of elaboration, or extension. By definition, this process cannot merely be linguistically controlled. What we have here, Recanati says, are three possible interpretation scenarios that are always going to take a covert but salient place and object, respectively, which are relevant to interpreting the sentence in question. According to Recanati, there is a metaphysical necessity behind the existence of unarticulated constituents because it is metaphysically necessary that every time it rains, it rains somewhere. It is also necessary that when someone eats, something is eaten. However, independently of the necessity of this fact, we can also say that although one refers to a concrete state of affairs when uttering "It is raining," which is bounded to necessarily involve a place, this place is not articulated in the sentence. The bounded place should be interpreted as a metaphysical unarticulated constituent of the interpretation of the sentence (Recanati 2002, 306).

Nevertheless, like Perry's approach, according to Recanati, the concrete place where it rains and the concrete object eaten should be epistemically relevant to the speaker, like his Availability Principle advocates. I partially accept this position, even though I argue that some elements are not always explicitly available or are mentally and internally accessible only as they are a part of the common ground speaker and audience inhabit because they belong to the same speech community. If these have a crucial role in meaning determination, it may be illusory, and a deeper analysis should be conducted.

Coming back to the three scenarios highlighted by Recanati, one can insist that the preceding context makes salient the concrete place and the particular objects sensitive to "rain" and "eat," respectively. Consider the following scenarios:

(6) {While planning a little trip to the lake, Nicole says to Ausiàs:} It is raining.
(7) {James, Domino, and Ewan are in the kitchen arguing about the potential poisonousness of the mushrooms they gathered. James exclaims:} He is eating.

According to Recanati, although the place is not articulated, we should interpret (6) as claiming that it is raining at the lake because the salient place of "rain" in this context is where they are planning to go. Similarly, even though the thing eaten is not articulated, (7) should be interpreted as referring to the gathered mushrooms because they are contextually salient.

The second scenario says that sentences including "rain" and "eat" can have a meaning with some existential relevance even if the location and the object eaten, respectively, are covert in the context. Examine the following situations:

(8) {Rain is something rare in the Mojave Desert. A scientific team is analyzing the weather data relative to rain there. They place several rain detectors in the area—a single bell on a single monitor rings when a detector is triggered. The bell rings, and someone says:} It is raining.

(9) {Because of his illness, John rarely eats. John enters the kitchen, takes something nobody sees, and bites it. His father says to his mother:} He is eating.

Even though in (8) the Mojave Desert is significant, given its vast size, the concrete location of the rain is not precise enough. One could say that (8) has no contextually explicit salient place, beyond the fact that the audience would consciously recognize that the place where it rains is somewhere in the Mojave Desert. However, this is unfortunate since one can still say that the speaker means that it is raining in some concrete point within the Mojave Desert. Similarly, in (9), one can argue that even though the speaker does not precisely know what John is eating because the object does not seem salient in the context, she still means that John is eaten something. However, pace Recanati, such a thing eaten must be something that the speaker and audience must agree, even though they are not epistemically aware of what may be. Therefore, besides the fact that the salient place and the salient object eaten are covert in the sentence and not explicitly salient, they are still at hand to both speaker and audience because such location and object would be part of the information interlocutors share.

However, and this is important because it differentiates the Interactive Theory from Recanati's moderate contextualism and Martí's middle ground, the fact that the place where it rains and the object eaten are covert and not explicitly salient in the sentence does not mean that speaker and audience must be necessarily aware of the whole situation involving raining and eating. There is a salient place where it rains and something eaten, respectively, that necessarily accomplishes a specific role in determining meaning, besides the awareness requirement claimed by salience, since such shared information is what completes the uttered proposition. While Recanati's (2004) Availability Principle claims how what is said should be available to the participants of communicational exchange intuitively and cognitively, other pragmatic processes may also complete the sentences' truth conditions presupposed in the context.

Nevertheless, and this is what explicitly distinguishes the Interactive Theory from Recanati's position, such availability is external to both speaker and audience since it depends upon the presence of a pragmatic presupposition and not on what Recanati (2013) calls mental files.[19] Thus, these metaphysical conditions should be taken as a quantificational scenario embedded in the common ground: the relevant place and object eaten are the concrete place x and object y where it is true that it rains in x and y is eaten, respectively. However, they are not explicitly articulated in the sentence, nor are interlocutors necessarily epistemically aware. However, these are unarticulated constituents when these variables are not located in the logical/syntactical form of the sentences. They are nonlinguistic elements situated in the context, they are a part of the common ground (the background, if you prefer, are part of the complete speech situation), and by definition, an externalist account must grasp their details and how they function in the process of propositional completeness.

The third scenario says we can also interpret sentences with a covert specification, including a bound variable reading. Consider the following sentences:

(10) Every time John lights a cigarette, it rains.
(11) Even though John does not like fish, he always eats when his wife buys salmon.

We can interpret (10) as including a quantifier that binds the silent location of "rain" to every place where John lights a cigarette. In the same way, (11) says that John's eating should be relatively applied after the fact that his wife buys salmon, and the thing that he eats is the salmon his wife bought. From Recanati's view, one should consider the sentences' meaning under this reading as relative to the pragmatic conditions completing the adequate uttered proposition. Hence, free enrichment takes the salient object from the context to accomplish the concrete characteristic that determines the sentence's truth value. Briefly, truth value is relative to truth-utterance.

In contrast to TCP, or at least Recanati's version defending unarticulated constituents, Martí (2006) takes semantics as a separate module from pragmatics, insisting that the sentence, including indexical expressions, must be explained only within syntactic and semantic characteristics. She departs from the idea that sentences with covert locations and objects have, as Recanati says, free variable-like and bound variable-like readings (Martí 2006, 139). According to Martí, these readings can only be optional.[20] In other words, since salient variables are adjuncts but not arguments, they can but do not have to necessarily be generated within the sentence's syntax or be contained in the sentence's logical form. When generated then, on the one hand, like in scenarios one and three in Recanati's analysis, they must be treated as articulated variables embedded in the sentence logical/syntactical level. Therefore, one should appeal to a weak reading of the indexical. One should appeal to a robust metaphysical reading when not generated, like in Recanati's second scenario.

According to Martí, then, both phenomena can be explained only by appealing to Gricean mechanisms, and the completion of a sentence proposition depends on the appropriate reference determination for each articulated variable embedded in the sentence's logical/syntactical form. Think about (8) and (9) again. According to Martí, since no variable is generated next to "rain" and "eat," there is no contextual requirement. When this happens, nonlinguistic reasons metaphysically imply that all rain happens somewhere and all eating requires a thing to be eaten. In other words, because of the way "rain" and "eat" function in a sentence, one knows that when someone eats, she has to be eating something, and when it is raining, it must rain somewhere.[21] Hence, Martí concludes that no variable is generated next to the predicates, but the salient place of rain and the salient object eaten, respectively, are metaphysically induced by implicature, recognizing the context of the utterance (Martí 2006, 145).

The main difference between Recanati's and Martí's proposals resides in the epistemic scope and extension of their respective theories and the rigidity both employ to identify truth conditions and how they are obtained. On the one hand, Martí claims that Gricean mechanisms are continuously operating, and an implicature always induces a metaphysical requirement within this kind of scenario. This sentence type existentially appeals to the place where it rains and the object eaten, respectively, wherever and whatever they are. Since variables are optionally generated in the syntax of sentences with "rain" and "eat," one can only existentially interpret the sentence where they are not generated. Thus, the proposition uttered is unavailable to both speaker and audience. This interpretation, according to Martí, is forbidden in pragmatic readings because the context determines the derivation of the variable.

Nonetheless, as Recanati correctly demonstrates, pragmatics does not necessarily trigger a variable in a sentence's logical form. Thus, unlike Recanati, Martí is obliged to claim that an implicature must always be covertly operating behind the scenes. When required, this implicature would determine the articulated variable in the logical/syntactic level and provide the appropriate reference to complete the uttered proposition semantically. In my view, the main consequence of this thesis is that no availability, or relevance, is required to determine what is said. Martí's conclusion is psychologically unrealistic because the speaker and the addressee have no role in meaning determination. Since truth conditions can be determined only from the logical/syntactical level, Martí's theory makes the speaker and the addressee irrelevant in determining utterance-meaning, besides that conventional implicatures may contextually condition them. Nonetheless, as the Interactive Theory proposes, we speakers are the ones that mean things with words, and not words by themselves.

On the other hand, according to Martí, when the variable is available, different derivations are possible until one is successful. Moreover, success implies an articulated variable that binds "rain" and "eat" at the logical/syntactical level with the concrete place and the specific object eaten, respectively, wherever and whatever they are. For Martí, this is a technology that pragmatics does not have because it would always require some cognitive or epistemic salience that would put the analysis of language dangerously close to subjective relativism, as Martí asserts. After all, with the constant presence of this implausible epistemic requirement, we must agree that "there is no process of free enrichment" (Martí 2006, 150). However, besides Martí's insistence that contextual relevance and not subjective salience play a crucial role, her theory does not leave room for optionality. Given natural languages' rigid logical form and the mechanisms that govern Gricean implicature, truth conditions become semantically invariant across contexts.

Even though one may cite the existence of variable terms, once the truth conditions are conventionally established (when the concrete reference is causally made explicit by the implicature), the speaker's utterance (what is said) should be interpreted according to the implicated meaning. This invariantly determines the sentence's truth conditions and, hence, the secondary interpreted content (what is meant). One can still reject my criticism by appealing to Martí's defense of Gricean implicatures based on contextual assumptions: "There are two properties of [the relevant sentence] that are important: (i) nothing in the context suggests that Andrew's eating of just anything is something that could surprise Luisa, and (ii) something in the context suggests that Andrew's eating of poisonous mushrooms is something that could surprise Luisa" (Martí 2006, 15). However, this only reinforces my claim that, besides the relevance and the role that it could have in her theory, Martí's endorsement of Gricean implicatures eliminates any possibility of optionality. Let me explain why.

According to Grice (1975), in cases of what he called conventional implicatures, such as his classic example, "He is an Englishman and he is, therefore, brave," a certain entailment holds its implication. Meaning here is somehow conventionally linked to what is said. Nevertheless, the former is neither part of the propositional content of the main sentence nor its truth or falsehood affects the main sentence's truth value. Independent of problems regarding the two previous requirements (see primarily Bach 1999 and Potts 2005), it is assumed that conventional implicatures are true only if all their parts are also true. If one cancels the implicature (by, for instance, challenging the truth of the main sentence or explicitly saying what was meant), that will take away from the main sentence whatever implicated content. However, if this is the case, "what is meant" must be a part of the main sentence's truth conditions ("what is said") and, therefore, such content must be something that is causally entailed by such sentence. If one can reduce implicatures to logical entailment, then there is no optionality, and every conventional content is necessarily linked to its preceding sentence entailment relation.

However, as Pavese (2017) correctly suggests, what is meant is still trackable since linguistic context is inferred as the antecedents of conditionals. Implicature would behave more like a presupposition than as an entailment "because it can project out of these embeddings" (Pavese 2017, 90). If Pavese is correct, the fundamental, irrefutable advantage of considering "therefore" as a presupposition trigger instead of the mark for an implicature is that the preceding sentence does not need to be true in order for the presupposed content to be true. The presupposition analysis provides a natural way of predicting the contextual content embedded in this kind of sentence. Moreover, the classical presuppositional analysis (Heim 1983; Karttunen 1974) is more appropriate for predicting context-sensitivity patterns than implicatures. As the Interactive Theory argues, presuppositions can only be felicitous when considered relative to maximally local contexts, which are the scenarios where utterances occur.

On Martí's analysis then, I conclude, there is no real optionality after all. If the logical/syntactical level determines a variable's reference through mandatory implicatures, then all truth conditions are established by logical entailments. Meaning becomes invariant even though contextual. Therefore, we lose an intuitively important aspect of context-sensitivity: the possibility that the speaker expresses meaning differently since both speaker and audience lose control over it. Moreover, if this is true in cases where conventional implicatures occur, it may not be a bad idea to change how we think about them, as Pavese (2017) correctly proposes.

Martí's position has, nonetheless, other undesirable consequences. Because she defends free variable-like and bound variable-like interpretations and metaphysical implicature, Martí should reject that there is no contextually salient concrete place in examples like (10). Furthermore, she would also have to negate a concrete contextually salient, relevant object in examples like (11). Contrarily, Martí must accept that place and object are contextually implied, although they cannot be concretely specified: the territory-where-it-rains and whatever-is-eaten, respectively. Hence, Martí's expectations for "rain" and "eat" do not create existential implicated interpretations but only, at best, empirical generalizations. To prove it, suppose someone utters the following sentences:

(1) It is raining (in time t).
(12) She is eating.

A possible interpretation, if one follows Martí's middle ground thesis, is the following:

(1′) It is raining somewhere in the territory (wherever that place is).
(12′) She is eating something (whatever that thing is).

However, this sounds counterintuitive. To see why, think again about sentences (10) and (11):

(10) Every time John lights a cigarette, it rains.
(11) Even though John does not like fish, he always eats when his wife buys salmon.

If interpretations of (10) and (11) always involve Gricean mechanisms, as Martí insists, then several situations allow these sentences to be true. Nothing in their context suggests that John's lighting a cigarette causes the rain and the fact that John's wife buys salmon causes John's eating, respectively. According to the implicature strategy, the context only suggests that the fact that it rains and John eats are relevant to interpreting the existential implicature. Remember that, for Martí, the generation of variables is optional, but the metaphysical implicature is mandatory. Therefore, in my view, the only interpretation here is not the existential/causal one outlined by Martí but the generalization of the bounding, acting as a strong pronoun. If that is the case, such bounding will induce the always required implicature that there is a place where it rains and the eaten object exists, respectively. Alternatively, in Martí's own words, it seems necessary and not an option that "a variable is always generated in sentences where the location is silent" (Martí 2006, 158).

The Interactive Theory argues that because "rain" and "eat" are no zero-place and no zero-object predicates, an entailment-like mechanism would also be necessary whenever the variable is unavailable, which contradicts Martí's account. According to Martí, though, contextually provided linguistic constituents should be semantically bound in the sense that, always when it rains and someone eats, a place where it rains and something eaten is required. These are the only contextually relevant facts. The specific place where it rains and the specific thing eaten are just optionally specifiable. Therefore, an overt or a covert place and object are necessary because, as Taylor (2001, 53) says, "rain" and "eat" have a "lexically specified argument place," but nothing in the sentences' logical form asserts what they are. Martí's conclusions, then, provide important information about the behavior of verbs such as "rain" and "eat."

Nonetheless, her interpretation of sentences' meaning including covert indexical expressions is not tenable because it derives odd readings. To determine the reference of linguistic items like "When John lights a cigarette" and "What John eats," it is necessary to provide the concrete place where it rains and the concrete object eaten, respectively. It necessarily requires the specification of the concrete place where it rains (where John lights a cigarette at time t_n) and what John eats (the salmon his wife bought). Any other interpretation, such as saying that these sentences only existentially or causally implicate a place where it rains and a thing eaten in broad and general terms, as Martí claims, provides another reading where the proposition uttered remains incomplete.

Consider examples (10) and (11) again. According to Martí's analysis, several different situations may make them true, in the sense that the only semantically induced implicature asserts that a place where it rains and an object eaten is required. However, the specific place where it rains and the specific object eaten are optional arguments provided by a variable when available. For instance, one can say that (10) indicates that in some instances, when John lights a cigarette, it rains where John lights the cigarette, but other times it rains in another place or does not rain at all. Furthermore, (11) says that in some of the instances when John's wife buys salmon, John eats the salmon she bought, but other times he eats lasagna, or a steak, or shrimp. However, these are bizarre readings since their interpretations are sensitive to that specific utterance's local context.

A more intuitive interpretation, like the Interactive Theory proposes, makes explicit that when someone utters (10) and (11), she means something like the following:

(10′) All times t_1, t_2, t_3, t_n at which John lights a cigarette, it rains at x_{t1}, x_{t2}, x_{t3}, x_{tn} (where x is where John is and t is the time when John lights the cigarette).

(11′) Every time John's wife buys salmon, John eats the salmon his wife bought.

Read this way, sentences (10) and (11) only make sense if one assumes that they refer to some element that is not explicitly articulated in the sentence but maximally locally presupposed in the context of utterance, requiring the common ground to complete the utterance of such sentences' truth conditions. This unarticulated constituent may appeal to the relevant concrete place and concrete thing eaten to which the sentence refers, and from this information, one can find common ground that both speaker and audience share. However, these must be salient to the context of the utterance itself and not part of either speakers' or audience's mental lives.

Specifically, the Interactive Theory argues that in sentences containing covert indexical expressions, these sentences pragmatically presuppose the quantificational domain that the speaker is talking about, some kind of restriction in scope. This domain is intuitively and cognitively overt and at hand since it is part of how speakers learn to communicate and is epistemically shared by speaker and audience. The examples above directly appeal to the actual place where it rains and the real object eaten. Both are then part of the common ground that makes the extension of this domain feasible. At the same time, sentences' truth conditions are maximally locally determined since they only refer to the concrete place and the concrete object eaten any time where John lights a cigarette and John's wife buys salmon, respectively. All interlocutors share this information in any communicational exchange where they occur because it is part of the common ground where they stand.

4.3 COMMON GROUND, SPEAKER'S INTENTION, AND RATIONALITY

This section refines the Interactive Theory, further detailing how the approach is novel and how it differs from current alternate accounts to context-sensitivity. It delves into the groundbreaking nature of some implications and also anticipates and responds to some possible objections and criticism.

Consider the following sentences:

(13) John believes that his cello is broken.
(14) If dinosaurs were not extinct, I would get a T-Rex.
(15) When the opportunity is gone, it is gone for good.
(16) The judge banned Tonya Harding from ice-skating competitions for life because of her involvement in the Kerrigan incident, but she had nothing to do with that at all.

According to the Interactive Theory, one should look for the unarticulated constituents placed in the context of utterance to complete the proposition the speaker intends to convey. These unarticulated constituents, as stated before, are placed in the context of utterance and are part of the common ground that speaker and audience share, understood in maximally local terms. They are a piece of the common ground within the speech community to which both speaker and audience belong. Interpreted this way then, the previous sentences could be read as follows:

(13′) John owns a cello, and that cello is now broken.

(14′) Dinosaurs are extinct now. If there were dinosaurs still around, I would buy myself one, for sure, and that one dinosaur that I would buy would be a T-Rex.
(15′) When you have a good chance to do or get something good, better do it or get whatever that something is in that moment, because you do not know if you will have another chance to do or get it.
(16′) Besides the fact that the judge condemned Tonya Harding to be banned for life from ice-skating competitions for being involved in the beating of Nancy Kerrigan's knee before the 1994 US Ice-Skating Championship, she was wrongly convicted since she had absolutely nothing to do with such incident, or at least that is what she claims.

In the previous cases, the presupposition projects. The presupposed content binds to the sentence as a whole, and it is so induced, initially, because some trigger is present, leaving the presupposition itself somehow undetermined. For this reason, given the presuppositions' highly contextual sensitivity, even though the apparent incongruity, inconsistency, or contradiction of some of them, speaker and audience tend to agree upon some nonexplicit information to resolve apparent conflicts. The presupposition sentence is always understood under some rationality that explains such conflict.

One usual objection to pragmatic accounts is the so-called puzzle of belief reports. The puzzle states that psychological verbs do not modify the truth conditions of the sentences where they appear. Think again about (13). According to a widespread interpretation, that John believes that his cello is broken does not impose any conditions onto the world. Whether his cello is broken or not is independent of John's belief since our semantics cannot guide our ontology. Therefore, whatever is meant by (13), the proposition it expresses depends on the semantic relation between the sentence and its content. Normal interlocutors will take John as a rational being whose beliefs are perfectly coherent and consistent with reality. The difference with a semantic proposal is that one does not need to believe that the expressed proposition reinforces the triggered presupposition because of the linguistic marker. The entire proposition indeed comes to us because of accommodation. This process is achieved through pragmatic means. For instance, under ordinary circumstances, participants in a conversation are rational agents whose belief system is coherent, consistent, and contradiction-free. They share the same space of reasons, which also is part of the common ground. The Interactive Theory substantially endorses the pragmatic spirit by taking this notion seriously, without endorsing the awareness component included in a position such as Lewis's or Recanati's as seen before.

Another potential objection to the Interactive Theory endorses a notion of common ground based on individual beliefs, or even senses, instead of agreement in propositional attitudes. To see what I mean, think about the following scenario:

(13) {John pawned his cello a few months back. John and a group of friends encounter this guy on the street playing what seems to be John's old cello. It is evident that the cello is worn down, it has some stickers here and there, and it even sounds different. Looking at John's horrified facial expression, somebody states:} John believes that his cello is broken.

If we take the Fregean solution at core, appealing to modes of presentation reconstructing the believer's mental life, as Recanati (2013) does, we must consider all relevant cognitive effects and efforts to determine what the speaker means. Since these considerations may drastically vary among all the parts involved in the conversation, it is not entirely clear the believer's proper mental life. The Interactive Theory employs the notion of common ground understood in propositional attitudes endorsement to amend this confusion. This way, the reconstruction of the believer's mental life is not taken as individual beliefs but as the agreement in attitudes with others belonging to the same speech community or sharing the same viewpoint. Interpreted this way, John is taken as a rational being speaking about his previously owned cello, which is understood from the point of view (the common ground) of those who share some particular understanding of what a cello should be, or should sound like, or even what music should be. This contrasts with an account that considers individuals' concrete particular psychological life, which may differ and change across speakers, dangerously leading to subjectivism and relativism. The completion of the presupposed proposition, then, depends on the scope of the implicit quantifier that tracks down the cello that somebody is playing as the cello once owned by John and that, given the awful appearance and sound of such instrument, all participants in the communicational exchange must agree that it is "broken."

One can interpret (14)–(16) similarly. All the conversation participants can understand that who states (14) is speaking in conditional terms and not as a lunatic, that (15) is a conventional way to state the old Stoic *Carpe diem* lemma, and that (16) is not part of a conspiracy theory statement but part of a view that many people share. As stated earlier, employing a language or speaking is something we do without putting too much effort into it. Therefore, the Interactive Theory gains parsimony since it requires less than a Gricean strategy, even though the latter is based upon the so-called Modified Ockham's Razor.

An additional possible objection to the Interactive Theory is that this theory does not consider how the notion of intentionality underlies pragmatic presupposition. If the objection states that taking presuppositions as interpretable using unarticulated constituents from the common ground is a problem for the Interactive Theory because it does not argue for the completion of the presupposed proposition through strong Gricean intentions, that is correct. However, the fact that the Interactive Theory does not support that the speaker's intentions and individual beliefs are at the core of presupposition determination does not mean that intentionality is not part of the equation. As stated earlier, the Interactive Theory economizes some elements to complete the presupposed propositions. For this reason, the notion of intentionality in the Interactive Theory is derived, one where what is meant is part of the speech community we inhabit, as chapter 5 further elaborates.

4.4 RECAPITULATION

Wittgenstein (1953, §371–2) introduces "the autonomy of grammar": grammar is the totality of arbitrary and contextual rules and necessary principles that explain a community's linguistic and behavioral patterns. In my view, this is in concordance with what Sellars (1956) calls "the logical space of reasons."[22] It is a human characteristic that language re-creates all features of our nature, and it is logical that someone's labor analyzing the nature and structure of language does so by explaining the speaker's knowledge of meaning and how to produce it.

Nevertheless, this conception of language contains a conundrum, at least in its current form. Phrased as it is, language and communication are the products of somebody's intention to say something and the audience grasping what is said via inference. However, one necessarily has to employ the set of sentences that our community builds for that purpose to do so. Meaning, after all, is not something that any speaker produces in isolation but something that the grammar of our natural language contains. The speaker simply borrows it when uttering any sentence. This creates some of the most fundamental problems presented in this book. How is this possible?

The above-mentioned Gricean notion of grammar is based on the idea that language contains and exemplifies the *normativity* that governs meaning and rationality, from language to logic, in a given society. These are the rules of inference that any speaker and audience must know to be a competent speaker or member of society. The second notion of grammar, as detached from any speaker intention, considers grammar as the set of linguistic rules that determine the structure of a natural language and that it is also grounded upon a very different conception of the nature of language itself.

Given that languages are not simply repositories of their speakers' cultures and views but rather express intentional social relations, natural language cannot merely be the means for communication and description of the world. It provides recurrent forms of social behavior to represent speakers' interactions and novel ways of vindicating social identity and belonging. Thus, as chapter 5 proves, the Interactive Theory demonstrates how language influences the speakers' understanding of the world to a certain extent. It codifies in its grammar its society's distinctive normativity, that is, the explicit and implicit rules governing such society's nature and structural relations, its rationale. If this were the case, as I argue, then different languages and their diverse lexical and grammatical patterns represent different and distinctive patterns of social behavior and interaction. These differences necessarily show up in the ways they convey meaning, their semantics, and their distinctive linguistic habitus and institutions, which express their respective interests and even the ways they structure reality.

This chapter introduces the Interactive Theory. It argues for an interpretation of occasion sentences based on speaker intentions and the audience's possible uptakes, and the conventions established by our speech communities. After documenting potential counterarguments about the existence of invariant truth conditions for every sentence of our natural language, alternate pragmatic positions siding with extreme appeals to unarticulated constituents are discarded because of their proximity to relativism and psychologism. Nevertheless, unarticulated constituents can be part of a pragmatic solution to meaning-determination of covert indexical sentences. The way is to understand such elements externally, in terms of quantificational domains governed by pragmatic presuppositions and observational sentences with an expanded notion of common ground. This approach reveals epistemically relevant elements in the context of utterance that both speaker and audience share without being necessarily conscious about them. This completes any sentence's truth conditions when taken as part of the maximally local context of utterance. This is, of course, part of the common ground (the total background accompanying any complete speech situation) that speakers and interlocutors share and have learned from the speech communities to which they belong. As such, they must be distinguished from the set of rules that normatively govern them.

The Interactive Theory argues then that empirical generalization is not enough to capture the metaphysical necessity created by the previously analyzed scenarios. Many attempts fail to capture the overt character of utterance context. One needs to determine context-sensitivity in natural language for content to be contextually manifest and part of the context and background of utterance in a maximally local way. This cannot simply be reduced to implicatures but requires a situational proposal based on pragmatic presuppositions considered under conventional and rational understandings. In my view, the appeal to rationality has certain similarities to the core of a true Austinian position more than to Gricean ideas. After all, Grice (1969) explicitly linked conventional implicatures and intentions to meaning determination of occasion sentences. This, of course, indicates the existence of a rational framework to which speakers and audience refer, making sure their communicative intentions are properly understood: that is, to determine what they meant by saying what they said. Nevertheless, as Austin (1956, 195) states: "However well-equipped our language, it can never be forearmed against all possible cases that may arise and call for description: fact is richer than diction." Adequate attention to conventions and not only intentions is, therefore, required.

NOTES

1. "Referring is not something an expression does; it is something that someone can use an expression to do" (Strawson 1950, 326).

2. "Whatever phenomenon varies in any manner whenever another phenomenon varies in some particular manner, is either a cause or an effect of that phenomenon, or is connected with it through some fact of causation" (Mill 1843, 470).

3. There are at least two different conceptions of the notion of "occasion sentence." The first one is due to Grice, who claims that the meaning of a sentence is determined according to the specific intentions of the speakers on the specific occasion of the utterance of a sentence. This is a causal interpretation of "occasion sentence" since "what is meant" will be determined depending on "what is said." The second conception of the notion of "occasion sentence" was championed by Quine, who established a behaviorist interpretation in which the meaning of a particular (utterance of a) sentence depends upon the "expressions that we have learned to associate with publicly observable concurrent circumstances" (Quine 1977, 178). As it will be shown, my alternate view grounds upon the Quinean more conventionalist notion of "observation sentence," even though Grice's could also be considered somehow conventional.

4. "I once followed a trail of sugar on a supermarket floor, pushing my cart down the aisle on one side of a tall counter and back the aisle on the other, seeking the shopper with the torn sack to tell him he was making a mess. With each trip around the counter, the trail became thicker. However, I seemed unable to catch up. Finally, it dawned on me. I was the shopper I was trying to catch. I believed at the outset that the shopper with a torn sack was making a mess. And I was right. But I didn't believe that I was making a mess. That seems to be something I came to believe. And when I came to believe that, I stopped following the trail around the counter, and rearranged the torn sack in my cart. My change in beliefs seems to explain my change in behavior" (Perry 1979, 3). As it is evident, the epistemic relevance of the speaker's realization that "he (John Perry)" was making the mess is crucial to the completion of the proposition contained in the example "I am making a mess." This element is of crucial importance in the account this chapter defends.

5. I want to emphasize that failing to notice that Perry's original notion does not apply to utterances but "selfless" thoughts is an extended error. Unfortunately, this lacuna is not uncommon amongst the humongous literature on the topic. In my view, it is the source of many misunderstandings about Perry's thought, and it has gone so far that the notion of unarticulated constituents has even been dubbed a "myth" (Cappelen and Lepore 2007).

6. Utterances of sentences (1) and (2) are examples of the second type of unarticulated constituents identified in Korta and Perry (2011, 104–109): those utterances of sentences that are grammatically complete but truth-conditionally incomplete. Sentence (3) exemplifies the type of sentences that are not grammatically complete and, consequently, do not articulate all needed to express a complete proposition. The thought expressed must be completed by background items that are not articulated in the sentence, whatever object one looks for in this case. Sentence (4) is an instance of an utterance of a sentence where, besides articulating all that is required semantically speaking to express a concrete proposition, the proposition expressed shows fully articulated truth conditions, exceeding the scope of the intended proposition. Occasional utterances of this sentence would require appealing to some unarticulated constituents, the specific number and scope of those having fun as intended by the speaker, to provide the utterance's truth conditions.

7. It is worth mentioning that there is a wide variety of different and distinct pragmatic processes. For instance, examples (1)–(4) are cases of saturation, which "involves finding the intended content (or value) for a linguistically indicated variable or slot" (Carston 2009, 49). This is an obligatory communicative process for completing the sentence's truth conditions, and for this reason, Bach (1994) says that it can be considered a semantic process, which he calls "completion." Bach also distinguishes a second semantic process in that article: "Expansion." This process helps complete the truth conditions of sentences that are semantically complete but that literally taken must be considered false, for instance: "You are not going to die [from this cut in your finger]" and "The ham sandwich left without paying." This later semantic process is the equivalent to "free pragmatic enrichment," which includes many different phenomena: specification, semantic transfer, strengthening, loose talk, etc. These processes are considered "free because they involve pragmatic enrichment of the decoded linguistic meaning in the absence of any indication (overt or covert) within the linguistic form that is necessary" (Carston 2009, 49). The key here is that "unlike saturation cases, 'free' enrichments are optional, in that there could be contexts (somewhat unusual ones) in which they do not take place" (Carston 2009, 50). As Recanati (2004, 18) recalls, "While saturation is a bottom-up linguistically controlled pragmatic process, free enrichment is a top-down pragmatically controlled pragmatic process."

8. "A proposition P is a pragmatic presupposition of a speaker in a given context just in case the speaker assumes or believes that P, assumes or believes that his addressee assumes or believes that P, and assumes or believes that his addressee recognizes that he is making these assumptions, or has these beliefs" (Stalnaker 1974, 49). Realize that, in contrast with the notion of semantic presupposition, this notion of pragmatic presupposition is interested in highlighting what the speaker assumes or

knows when speaking but not what the words entail. What is relevant is that under normal circumstances, regular speakers would expect that the presupposition holds in the common ground (something similar to the above-mentioned background) when a particular sentence is uttered. I am expanding these ideas to connect them to the intuition that some instances of occasion sentences "are expressions that we have learned to associate with publicly observable concurrent circumstances" (Quine 1977, 178).

9. "The relation between common ground and speaker presupposition is this: A participant in a context presupposes that x if and only if she accepts that it is common ground that x, where 'accept' is the attitude that is iterated in the definition of common ground" (Stalnaker 2014, 4).

10. As Stalnaker (2014, 4) insists, this definition of common ground is more straightforward than what he previously defended, for instance, in Stalnaker (2002).

11. In formal terminology, for any worlds x and y, $x\text{R}fy$ iff $<f(x), x>\text{R}<f(y), y>$.

12. I suggest that the scope of this common ground extends to what Austin identified as the complete speech situation. It does not only apply to the proper identification of which drawer Nicole is speaking about but also that the train engine in question is a toy and not a real one, that this toy is the one Ausiàs got for his birthday, that the location refers to the speaker's and audience's shared location, at the moment the communicational interaction occurs, etc.

13. Notice the resemblance of my proposal with Goodman's (1977, 21): "Knowing cannot be exclusively . . . primarily a matter of determining what is true . . . often amounts . . . not to arrival at a proposition for declaration or defense, but to finding a fit." My approach argues that the content of an utterance can better be modeled as a propositional function: the content of a complex predicate which truth conditions are dependent upon some circumstances of evaluation established by the speech community in question. These circumstances are then set-theoretically individuated. Such content is true or false relative to (or in virtue of) its relevance within such speech community's point of view, or perspective, which will determine the utterance's conditions of satisfaction, or its being or not felicitous if you prefer.

14. Colomina-Almiñana (2017b) claims that this can be understood as a consequence of applying a rule. Nevertheless, this seems, at best, an understatement.

15. Of course, Stalnaker and Perry deny this conclusion. For Perry, besides that a sentence can have different contents depending on its different contextual utterances, the meaning of these utterances is not multiple. Somebody may even believe that Grice's parsimony principle favors a view along Perry's or Recanati's line. However, this is one of the flaws of their approaches and one of the motivations for proposing the Interactive Theory.

16. Strictly speaking, Martí's middle ground claims a third position between Recanati's nonmodular pragmatic view of the semantic components of grammar, or TCP, and Stanley and Szabó's (2000) defense of the necessity of tracing all truth-conditional effects of extralinguistic context through variables placed in the syntactic and logical level, the so-called Quantifier Domain Restriction, which is only one of the many accounts that fit in what has previously been identified under the TCS label. However, given Martí's insistence on finding variables at the logical/

syntactical level, besides their optionality, her position also qualifies as TCS, which also happens with Cappelen and Lepore's approach.

17. Martí borrows this Optionality Criterion from Recanati (2004, 101): "The Optionality Criterion: whenever a contextual ingredient of content is provided through a pragmatic process of the optional variety, we can imagine another possible context of utterance in which such ingredient is provided the utterance yet expresses a complete proposition." I agree with Zeman (2012, 619, footnote 1) that, besides Stanley's (2005) complaint, Recanati's criterion could be analyzed as a biconditional. Then the supposed wrong-directionality of the conditional Stanley identifies would vanish, which at the same time would make Martí's appropriation of the criterion for semantic reasons unnecessary.

18. In which way is this notion of salience dissimilar from the notion of common ground? As it should be obvious, two main differences can be pointed out. On the one hand, Recanati is in the same line proposed by Lewis regarding presupposition accommodation, given the fact that the presupposed sentence would be a consequence of the application of a rule in the linguistic game and not, as the notion of common ground supposes, a product of the rationality expected and exercised by speaker and audience under normal circumstances. On the other hand, the notion of salience accepts that the speaker and audience must always possess a certain level of awareness regarding the presupposed content. Given that the notion of common ground only assumes a certain level of agreement in attitudes, this vital cognitive requirement is not present, allowing for the possibility of being part of the context without noticing. This last weaker requirement would explain how speaking is an activity that people often perform without much effort.

19. According to Recanati (2013), mental files are the vehicles of singular thought (thoughts that are directly about individual objects and which content is a singular proposition), and they play the role of what Frege calls modes of presentation.

20. Remember that, according to Recanati, this is the case only for instances of saturation, but not for cases of free pragmatic enrichment, where the readings imply some metaphysical necessity.

21. As Martí (2006, 147) notes, this kind of metaphysical requirement is different from the metaphysical necessity advocated by Perry and Recanati for unarticulated constituents. Unlike her, Perry and Recanati argue that the place where it rains and the object eaten should always be available to the speaker and the addressee. Martí defends here a weaker, epistemically compromised requirement that, to a certain extent, is similar to the agreement in attitudes the Interactive Theory supports. However, since she will link such requirement to the optionality of a variable embedded in the sentence's logical form, only the Interactive Theory explains this agreement based on the externalist acceptance of maximally local contextual elements that are part of the common ground shared by the speaker and audience. Martí's position then endures the difficulties displayed by both TCS and TCP.

22. "In characterizing an episode or a state as that of *knowing*, we are not giving an empirical description of that episode or state; we are placing it in the logical space of reasons, of justifying and being able to justify what one says" (Sellars 1956, §36).

Chapter 5

Expanding the Interactive Theory

This chapter is theoretical. Nevertheless, it shows how many experiments and investigations provide strong empirical data to support the validity of both a sociocultural relativity thesis (SCRT) and a weak linguistic relativity thesis (WRT), as will be outlined in section 5.1. The previous chapter demonstrated how meaning and understanding among speaker and audience are built upon the interaction between conventions, the speaker's intentions, and audience's possible uptakes. WRT is legitimate only to the point that it recognizes physiological limitations on the possible cross-cultural differences in cognition and perception (limitations on the so-called cognates due to grammatical and conceptual obstacles). The goal of showcasing these results into the Interactive Theory is to demonstrate how the hypotheses inform theoretical and empirical studies about the crucial links between thought, language, and culture, which ground meaning.

Reviewing these studies can bolster claims about the connections between thought, language, and culture. The chapter, therefore, also examines any such claims with the rigorous evidence and hard scrutiny they deserve, which helps avoid the trap of exoticizing and othering foreign cultures based on scant evidence (Martin 1986, 421). These studies show that the hypotheses about a thought-language-culture influence are subject to empirical and theoretical investigation. Therefore, careful experimental work supports SCRT and WRT. Speakers' culture influences their language, and some particular aspects of language may influence concrete aspects of cognition.

Unfortunately, negating or misinterpreting evidence that supports linguistic relativity and a pluralistic perspectivism (and, hence, an interaction among conventions, the speaker's intentions, and audience's possible interpretations) based on ideological commitments to the universality of human experience and thought has been all too common. The current position of many scholars is to maintain that any strong link between thought, language, and culture is, in reality, either a persistent illusion (Pinker 1994) or that if such a link does exist, it is weak and easily overridden by universal factors (Chomsky 1957 and 1993). Nevertheless, it is fascinating how uncontroversial interlanguage and intercultural differences explain specific data. An obvious example is that different languages have different lexicons, subject to cultural needs. Anyone would admit that the reason some Amazonian Indigenous peoples lack terms for "carburetor" or "transistor" is best explained in terms of sociocultural, technological differences between such groups and societies with languages that have such terms. Similar reasoning tells us that a society lacking specific cultural practices (for instance, a particular religion) will also lack terms that refer to concepts connected with these practices, and so on, as section 3.4 mentions.

This is only a starting point. However, the evidence analyzed herein demonstrates that the thought-language-culture relationship goes beyond these assumptions. Recent data support a subtle reciprocal influence between thought, language, and culture. We can see the imprint of culture on language most clearly in its vocabulary, as section 5.1 shows, which is culturally influenced not only in the obvious way described above but also in unexpected ways beyond language itself (as Geertz 1984 anticipated). Other studies show that a language is not merely a repository of its speakers' cultures and views. Rather, language also expresses intentional social relations, providing particular forms of social behavior to represent speakers' interactions, as section 5.2 demonstrates. Thus, a language influences its speakers' understanding of the world to an extent (Hill and Mannheim 1992). Distinct languages' different lexical and grammatical patterns represent subtle patterns of social behavior and interaction (Sidnell and Enfield 2012).

Relatively recent research demonstrates that language shapes its speakers' metaphysical conception of colors (Berlin and Kay 1969), space (Levinson 1997 and 2003), measurement of time (Kockelman 2009; Kockelman and Bernstein 2012), qualia (Dennett 1988), natural kinds (Quine 1969), determinables (Charro and Colomina-Almiñana 2014; Colomina-Almiñana 2018), and perception in general (Goodman 1977; Silverstein 2006). Some scholars have pointed out other ontological themes in language affecting the link between social relations and semiotic processes about basic actions in linguistic interaction and its nonlinguistic consequences, such as the "structure of subjectivity" built around responses to assessment (Sidnell and Enfield 2012), verbal humor (Ferro-Luzzi 1986), poultry husbandry (Kockelman 2011a), and biosemiosis, technocognition, and sociogenesis (Kockelman 2011b).

These also extend to indexical relations between speech and its context of occurrence in taxonomies and partinomies in general (Kockelman 2005), perception of gender (Silverstein 1985), relations of power and hierarchy (Silverstein 2000; Romero 2012), relations of belonging and identity recognition (Silverstein 2003; Kockelman 2012), existential commitments (Kockelman 2010b), interdiscursivity (Silverstein 2005), "cultural" conceptualization (Silverstein 2004), metalinguistic awareness (Silverstein 1976; 1979; and 1981), and even the complete system of categories (Reding 1986; Kockelman 2006). Some scholars argue more tentatively that language also affects other areas of cognition (Sellars 1969; Kulvicki 2008; Gauker 2011). Sections 5.3 and 5.4 show strong evidence about the linguistic resources pushing toward choosing specific cognitive strategies over others upon confronting a new, vague, or unexpected task (Kay and Kempton 1984).

This chapter concludes that speakers and their speech communities create and re-create their languages so that they better reflect their changing thoughts, intentions, and needs, but that at the same time, this does not mean that languages constitute and limit thought (Brown 1958; Steinberg 2008, 52–54). Therefore, any approach to language that claims syntactical structures or logical forms underneath constrain the conditions where content is fixed necessarily fall short in foundational criteria. This does not mean that any language is merely a passive player in the dichotomy. Some aspects of language mold other aspects of thought, sometimes in unexpected ways, and language provides patterns to accomplish specific social actions adequately, since language encodes the myriad ways we do things with words.

5.1 EVALUATING THE SOCIOCULTURAL RELATIVITY HYPOTHESIS

A proposed interaction between thought, language, and culture has been a recurring topic of investigation in cognitive science, linguistics, anthropology, philosophy, and psychology. The most common version of this interaction is popularly attributed to linguists Edward Sapir and Benjamin Lee Whorf and is commonly known as "the Sapir-Whorf Hypothesis." Its most popular formulation is usually defined as follows:

> (SWH) One perceives and conceptualizes the world differently due to influence from her language's grammar and lexicon, which depend on her culture.

This hypothesis, also commonly called the linguistic relativity hypothesis, is provocative for studying interactions between language and culture because it argues that the way one thinks about the world depends on the language one speaks.

Nonetheless, despite its name, Sapir and Whorf never proposed a clear cognitive theory, which confused SWH claims. The term "Sapir-Whorf Hypothesis" was coined posthumously and lent to a loose collection of Sapir's and Whorf's views, without a clear consensus about what their actual views were. A clear understanding of their views remains elusive because

Sapir's and Whorf's views changed throughout their academic lives due to later misinterpretations of their work. An additional issue is that discussions of SWH tend to equate linguistic relativity with linguistic relativism and overlook an important distinction that was previously anticipated and will be further discussed here.

The main goal of this section is to alleviate confusion about SWH. There is no single proposition in Sapir's and Whorf's writings that corresponds to SWH as usually understood. SWH conflates at least three significantly different positions on the relationship between thought, language, and culture. Even though I am aware that further divisions of linguistic relativity have been made in other contexts (Swoyer 2010; Wolff and Holmes 2010), the importance of the distinctions bears on the fact that they broadly describe the full range of possible interactions between a language and the culture of its speakers. The sociocultural relativity hypothesis proposes that culture influences language, the weak relativity hypothesis proposes a mutual and reciprocal influence between language and culture, and the strong relativity hypothesis proposes that language controls the culture. I demonstrate that abandoning the last one is necessary. A valid account of the first and second thought further clarifies the interaction between any speech community and its speakers.

Due in part to the varied and easily misinterpreted views of Sapir and Whorf, popular treatments of the hypothesis regarding the relationship between thought, language, and culture tend to blur and distort different versions that can be outlined, intentionally or not. However, after examining their writings and pointing out where this confusion comes from, three different versions of the linguistic relativity hypothesis could be distinguished:

Sociocultural Relativity Thesis (SCRT):

A language acquires a particular grammar and lexicon from its speakers and reflects their culture and worldview.

The Weak Linguistic Relativity Thesis (WRT):

A speaker of a particular language perceives and conceptualizes the world differently due to her language's grammar and lexicon, which depend on its speakers' specific culture. Nevertheless, this concrete way of accessing the world also influences the language and the culture of the community that shares the language. This way of accessing the world is essentially bidirectional: how a community sees the world modifies the way they refer to it, and how they refer to the world influences their worldview.

The Strong Linguistic Relativity Thesis (SRT):

One's language's particular grammar and lexicon strictly determine how one perceives and conceptualizes the world.

Of course, these divisions could be further refined. Many make myriad subtler distinctions regarding these claims (Wolff and Holmes 2010). As Max Black states, "An enterprising PhD candidate would have no trouble in producing at least 108 versions of Whorfianism" (Black 1969, 30). The division outlined above is further confused when distinguishing WRT from SRT. SCRT is not usually addressed explicitly and often is simply assumed, though the effects tacitly endorsed tend to be fewer than those proven upon more careful analysis. Many refer to WRT as "linguistic relativity" and to SRT as "linguistic determinism," though others use the terminology basically as presented here (Shaul and Furbee 1998, 42–43). In my view, however, this three-way distinction accurately divides the various traditions of thought, with finer distinctions being debated among each division's advocates instead of between advocates of different views.

Which of these hypotheses did Sapir and Whorf advocate for? The answer depends on who and how presents it, though I believe that determining which version is the "real" hypothesis Sapir and Whorf defended is ultimately irrelevant, at least for the main purpose of this book.[1] What is important is that those committed to an innate, genetically endowed language acquisition device, such as Chomsky and his intellectual kin (for instance, Pinker 1994 and 2007), reject both WRT and SRT. Sometimes they confuse the two by conflating Sapir and Whorf's principle of linguistic relativity with linguistic relativism based on a misreading of many of their written passages (cf., for instance, Pinker 1994, 46–54; Pinker 2007, 134). Chomskyan analysis rejects linguistic relativity because it is broadly concerned with finding the biological, mental similarities that all humans share, allowing language acquisition and usage (Beletti and Rizzi 2002, 1; Chomksy 2002). As a result, studying the linguistic and cognitive variation implied by WRT is seen as orthogonal to "real" linguistic research, in which proper object should be determining the biological bases of linguistic competence (Chomsky 1979, 57).

The nativist argument against SRT is related to this, which asserts that language is a separate mental "organ" that interacts with but does not influence the rest of thought in exciting ways (Chomsky 1975, 34; Pinker 1994, chapter 10). As a result, a language's structure would allow expressing thoughts, but it would not influence them. In arguing against SRT, I agree with this position in that a particular language's structure does not constrain a speaker's possible thoughts. However, I disagree that studying linguistic variation is necessarily orthogonal to finding the biological bases of linguistic competence. Understanding language's roles in broader cognition and its realizations define the space of theories about the nature of linguistic cognition.

Therefore, the empirical studies this chapter presents demonstrate that there are exciting and vital conclusions to be drawn from the theoretical implications of empirical investigations in favor of WRT. The effects of language on thought are interesting, even if they are habitual and not absolute. Such studies help establish specific examples of the interactions between different aspects of the cultural-linguistic complex and inform further theoretical investigations.

Another set of scholars support WRT as the "true" (Sapir-and-Whorf-supported) version (Crystal 1987; Everett 2008 and 2012) and argue in favor of it. The issue with most presentations supporting WRT is that they tend to undersupport its more interesting claims, in some cases reducing it to a differently presented version of SCRT. For example, Pinker (2007, 129) recognizes the existence of WRT. Nevertheless, he dismisses it as a minor, dull phenomenon that suggests that a language can function as a mnemonic device (though one fails to grasp why such a phenomenon would be dull or uninteresting—different languages will help speakers remember different things due to the semantic differences they encode, which is interesting enough). I question this view about WRT since, in my view, it justifies the tradition of research that navigates between the two extremes of excessively fawning over the imagined inaccessible mystique of other cultures and denying that structural differences in languages may exist and have interesting effects on cognition.

To be clear at this point: the Interactive Theory supports SCRT, which is barely recognized or addressed as its hypothesis, even if it is tacitly supported. It also endorses WRT more robustly than most, as necessary to offer a perspectivist account. Nevertheless, it does not support SRT by any means. Alternatively, the Interactive Theory endorses appropriately constrained notions of linguistic relativity even though I will never refer to it by such a name, but there are no good reasons for supporting and defending linguistic relativism (as the following chapters demonstrate). The notions of linguistic relativity that are often dismissed as "uninformative" or "obviously true" forms of contextualism (the idea that meaning is relative and depends on the linguistic context of utterance) are important. Nevertheless, as I understand it, a proper theory of meaning (at least one that wants to explain how language functions) must base its theoretical positions on evidence to understand language and linguistic change in an empirical context. At the same time, empirical cases influence how we understand the theoretical positions outlined in this chapter beyond the apparent linguistic data.

One of the most easily noted and direct ways a language reflects the worldview and culture of its speakers is through its vocabulary. The overexploited presentation of this idea involves Boas's distinction between Inuit words for snow.² Boas lists four root morphemes that reference different kinds of snow in the Inuit language Inuktitut:

> Here we find one word, *aput*, expressing snow on the ground; another one, *qana*, falling snow; a third one, *piqsirpo q*, drifting snow; and a fourth one, *qimuqsus*, a snowdrift. (Boas 1911, 25–26)

Using Boas's data in support of linguistic relativity remains controversial. As we mentioned before, the prominent view takes Boas's paragraph above and Whorf's and others' later interpretation of it to attack the linguistic relativity thesis (for example, Pullum 1989). The controversy arises because of the agglutinative nature of Inuit languages, which predominantly construct words from a root attached to inflectional and derivational affixes and clitics (Krupnik and Müller-Wille 2010). Those opposed to the linguistic relativity thesis claim that the standard method of counting Inuit words for snow is thus an amateur mistake since the words are, in fact, variants of a single root (Pullum 1989, 277). According to them, Boas's intention was not to analyze the cultural and cognitive implications of the grammatical differences between different languages but to illustrate their different structures. Any who claim differently, they say, are doing lousy science and do not recognize Boas's proper cross-linguistic considerations. They point to Whorf (1950) as the origin of the misuse of Boas's data. According to them, Whorf provides:

> [A] curious sequence of distortions and inaccuracies, [and] offers both a case study in the creation of an oral tradition and an object lesson on the hazards of superficial scholarship. [. . .] Whorf's ideas were superficial or lacked insight [generating] the cautionary tale that serves to remind us of the intellectual protection to be found in the careful use of sources, the clear presentation of evidence, and, above all, the constant evaluation of our assumptions. (Martin 1986, 418 and 421)³

Nevertheless, as Cichocki and Kilarski have shown, those who misinterpret and trivialize Whorf's quotation of Boas "ironically [do so] by violating the standards of academic evidence and propriety, [they] themselves give" (Cichocki and Kilarski 2010, 369). They appeal to empirical research and proper investigation to avoid misuses and misinterpretations of data, but such empirical investigation proves the existence of a plurality of Inuit morphemes referring to snow. Woodbury (1991), for instance, identifies roughly fifteen lexemes in the Eskimo-Aleut language Yup'ik that identify different kinds of snow.⁴ As Silverstein claims, those who argue against a variety of Inuit *snow* lexemes "cite or allude to data the intended scholarly utility of which is opaque to them, or is simply reduced, over the time of cultural change, to slogans and epithets sometimes hurled at our predecessors and betters"

(Silverstein 1991, 29). The moral of the polemic about the Inuit words for snow is a warning about

> the double role assigned to English as both a compared language and the metalanguage of comparison, as a result of which misleadingly transparent native-speaker intuitions as to the English word "snow" are projected onto a language with a qualitatively different system of classifications. (Cichocki and Kilarski 2010, 371)[5]

Nevertheless, even upon admitting the existence of a variety of Inuit *snow* lexemes, one must be careful to avoid conclusions lacking sufficient evidence since the existence of different morphemes alone proves nothing. A typical and facile argument that accompanies such a presentation of the Inuit-words-for-snow data in support of the linguistic relativity thesis goes like this: In English, there is only one lexeme for snow (which is false). In a given Inuit language they have four (or more). Therefore, each of these four (or more) words must be conceptualized very differently from each other by a speaker of said language. For the English speaker, it is hard to see the differences between each snow that are so patent to the Inuit speaker, and for the Inuit speaker, it is not easy to see the underlying unity the English speaker effortlessly perceives. One is usually invited to marvel at the Inuits' privileged and hopelessly unattainable mastery in distinguishing different types of snow.

Nonetheless, this argument can be rejected. For example, the conclusion becomes suspect when we consider that English speakers invent such words without any problems upon finding themselves in need of specialized words to distinguish types of snow. Skiers have many more words for different kinds of snow than the typical English speaker, and these words do not even necessarily use the same snow lexical root. Employing an example from Boas, Shaul and Furbee (1998, 29) state: "English . . . also augments its two basic vocabulary distinctions (*snow* and *flake*) with a word stock which skiers cultivate in pursuit of their sport (*powder, corn, crud, bullet-proof, crust, death cookies, champaign powder, machine tilled, ball-bearings, sugar, corduroy*, etc.)."

Even in everyday English, there are many words for types of snow ("snow," "sleet," "slush," "blizzard," etc.). In contrast to what scholars imply, the fact that Inuit (and English) speakers have different lexemes that distinguish different types of snow is not what allows them to distinguish types of snow in the first place. It is much more reasonable to conclude that they find the need to describe different types of snow due to mainly geographical and partially cultural and practical reasons (just as English speakers do), and that is why they create or use different words. Their geography, culture, and thought affect their vocabulary, not vice versa.

One could be tempted to say that the difference is entirely geographically determined, but we should resist this interpretation because it simplifies the phenomenon. The fact that the members of the society employing the different morphemes encode the relevant distinctions leads to the different conceptualizations encoded in the morphemes, not their geographical location alone. The environment where a speech community lives becomes part of their culture before it becomes part of their language. We must remember that speakers often convey meanings, sometimes not intended. Words do not exist in a semantic vacuum but as part of a complete cultural context in which speakers provide their meanings in relation to other words and speakers' lives. If speakers did not control words, but words control speakers, one would expect English-speaking skiers to have found themselves utterly baffled upon trying to distinguish the different types of snow outlined above because they would not already have words to do so and would be unable to form conceptualizations necessary to distinguish them. It would be equally odd if a group of people did not form cultural attitudes and behaviors relating to where they live. Speakers create new words for things when necessary. They build new conceptualizations and verbalize them because their geographical and cultural environment offers them possibilities and needs.

To reiterate, the confusion between linguistic relativity and linguistic relativism motivates some to resist accepting a weakened linguistic relativity thesis. To say that we can conceptualize the same things differently does not imply that we must conceptualize the same things differently. It merely implies that we may. Nor is it sufficient to demonstrate a real difference in thought because sometimes additional extralinguistic factors are required. A very weak linguistic relativity principle operates here. Speakers could decide to make further lexical distinctions in case of necessity. Consequently, the old data about Inuit words for snow does provide partial evidence for a particular version of linguistic relativity: the above-mentioned SCRT.

The fact that cultures or subcultures distinguish different types of snow (or anything else) and create words to reflect this cultural impetus shows that cultural needs mold the lexicon.[6] I am not claiming that a lack of a lexically marked distinction in a particular semantic area means that it is impossible to make a mental distinction through contextual or cultural cues, nor that a distinction made in such a way may be unimportant. However, once a distinction is made in the lexicon, it will only survive if the speakers of a concrete speech community employ it, which means they must consciously or unconsciously pay attention to its creation and use conditions. This affects memory and attention and is precisely the influence of language on thought WRT and some interpretations of SRT propose. This is reminiscent of Slobin's (Slobin

1987 and 1996) notion of "thinking for speaking."[7] However, even linguists who do not strongly support SCRT admit that some lexical differences have to do with extant cultural differences between speaker communities, yet see this as an obvious fact, barely worth mentioning (Pullum 1989, 279). This is worth mentioning, though, because the influence of culture upon a language goes further. The Inuit-English example is merely the most obvious manifestation of it. The following examples will provide further evidence that the culture-language influence goes beyond marginality by taking an extended enchronic perspective, considering how sustained sociocultural practices drive linguistic development over time.

The term *enchronic analysis* was coined by Nicholas Enfield to refer to "the intersection of (a) a social causal/conditionality of related signs in sequences of social interaction and (b) a particular level of temporal granularity in a conditionally sequential view of language: conversational time" (Enfield 2009, 10). He contrasts this with diachronic analysis, which does not specify the "type of directness of causal/conditional relations" (Ibid.). However, I believe Enfield's part (a) of the enchronic analysis can be extended productively to analyses of the step-by-step processes at play in social interactions' influence on language within more extended time frames than conversations, which are usually treated diachronically (that is, without considering causality). The following example shows how this could be accomplished.

A standard criterion for evaluating the genetic relationship of two languages is the number of cognates they share. However, Comrie's (2000) study of the Haruai language (New Guinea) found that this criterion was insufficient to place it within a particular language family. Haruai shares approximately 29–37 percent of its vocabulary with languages of the Hagahai family, suggesting that Haruai was also a member of this family. Nevertheless, Haruai also shares 35 percent of its vocabulary with the Kobon language, suggesting it belongs to the same language family as Kobon. The results show that Hagahai and Kobon belong to different language families, meaning that Haruai could not be part of both simultaneously.

One common way of resolving such ambiguous cases is taking the words' meaning into account. What is called basic vocabulary consists of 100–200 words every culture/language tends to have (for instance, "sun," "head," "son," and so on). This is less likely to be replaced by loan words. Therefore, it tends to comprise true cognates, making such words reasonably reliable indicators of an actual shared genetic relationship where cognates appear (Crowley and Bowern 2010, 138). Another common strategy for distinguishing ambiguous cases involves determining the words' semantic domains. If a questionable set of apparent cognates belongs only to a single semantic domain (e.g., words relating to agriculture), they are most likely loan words and not actual cognates, which tend to run the gamut of semantic domains

(Comrie 2000, 73). In classifying Haruai, however, both of these common strategies proved unfruitful. Much of Haruai's basic vocabulary is shared with Hagahai and Kobon, and the questionable potential cognates from each language family fall into several distinct semantic domains (Comrie 2000, 84).

To determine the genetic status of Haruai, Comrie considers two factors. The first is the verbal morphology of the three languages, which exhibits several commonalities between Haruai and Hagahai and little to none between Haruai and Kobon. He concludes that these similarities alone are not enough to propose a genetic relationship between the former pair. Nonetheless, an explanation is missing for explicating the curiosities regarding apparent cognates. The explanation is provided, though, by a cultural practice of the Haruai: a specific sociolinguistic taboo. Haruai women are strongly discouraged from saying the names of their cross-cousins or their in-laws, which is complicated when considering that most proper names in Haruai consist of everyday words. This effectively means that when a Haruai's relative marries, Haruai women are often left unable to use words necessary for everyday communication. The extensive borrowing is therefore explained by relating it to cultural factors. The Haruai peoples migrated from their homeland, bringing themselves closer to the Kobon people than those they split off. Then, the taboo obliged them to borrow many essential words from Kobon to meet basic communicative needs without using prohibited words (Comrie 2000, 80).[8]

Consider how Lowland Q'eqchi' (the variety of Q'eqchi Maya spoken in the lowlands of the region of Alta Verapaz and Petén in north-central Guatemala) codifies power relations and interactions between individuals of different ethnic provenience (Romero 2012).[9] The different Q'eqchi' varieties provide salient and explicit alternations that mark speakers' specific ethnic, racial, and gender provenience. Q'eqchi' has dialectical stereotypes, or ethnic markers, to classify the grounded political and economic rivalry between the different villages that comprise the extension of its speakers, with additional indexical laminations to regulate the interaction between individuals with different statuses, political ideologies, or gender.

It is not enough to undertake a merely diachronic analysis in which language change is analyzed in isolation from causative and conditional factors. Instead, it is necessary to note how sustained sociocultural practices cause linguistic change over time. An extended enchronic perspective is required—an analysis that exposes historical time frames while stressing the role of social practices in linguistic development. For both sociolinguistics and historical linguistics, suitably extended enchronic perspective bolsters SCRT's conclusions while showing that its explanatory power is not restricted to cases of seeing an expanded semantic domain in culturally significant areas, even if this is its most commonly noted effect.

5.2 EVALUATING THE WEAK LINGUISTIC RELATIVITY THESIS

This chapter has demonstrated how a language serves as a cultural index of a speech community by exposing how communities change their languages over time to match their thoughts and cultural values and serve their cultural needs. Extending this conclusion, one can infer that these thoughts and values change before the language reflects them. A speech community may change its thought patterns without relying on linguistic resources, retroactively creating the linguistic resources to express themselves after developing new concepts. New ideologies driving linguistic changes are evident in the sciences. For instance, the fact that electricity and magnetism had different names did not hinder Maxwell when he recognized the unity of the two through his studies (Greene 2003, 23), nor does it prevent the modern physicist from understanding that these are two ways of perceiving the properties of a single underlying force. Moreover, much of science studies things lacking names, which are then explained theoretically and may be labeled appropriately (Rovelli 2020). If we can think in such new ways, some may argue that perhaps the possible effects of language on thought are not very interesting since they do not seem to prevent us from doing anything we may wish to do or thinking anything we may wish.

However, this conclusion is merely evidence against the strong linguistic relativity thesis (SRT). According to different criteria, one must evaluate WRT since, as Whorf noted, language may affect habitual thought even if it does not limit thought potential. As said before, rejecting WRT while arguing against SRT is common, but that does not mean that WRT should be so summarily dismissed (because only SRT implies linguistic determinism). Culture and language may exist in a mutually sustaining equilibrium, with the ability to influence one another but neither claiming absolute control.

Research on color perception by Kay and Kempton (1984) determined possible habitual perceptual differences relating to color between English speakers and Tarahumara speakers (a Uto-Aztecan language spoken in Chihuahua's Cañón del Cobre, Mexico). Tarahumara lacks separate words for "green" and "blue." Instead, a single term covering both: *siyóname*.[10] Kay and Kempton presented their participants with three color chips that varied between different shades and combinations of blue and green and asked them to identify which was the "most different."

The key to the experiment lies in the fact that in some cases, one of the "green" chips had a wavelength closer to that of the "blue" chip than to that of the other "green" chip, making it objectively closer in color to the "blue" chip than to the other "green" chip. However, English speakers tended to identify "most different" as whichever chip had a color corresponding to a different word, even if that chip was more similar to the color of a chip with a different word for its color. They suggest that "the presence of the *blue-green* lexical boundary [caused] speakers of English to exaggerate the subjective distances of colors close to this boundary" (Kay and Kempton 1984, 72). In contrast, the Tarahumara speakers chose the "most different" color with a wavelength more different from each other than those. That is to say, they accomplished the task *objectively*, according to the measurable wavelength of the colors, not according to any lexically codified semantic border between them, since Tarahumara codifies no such border.

This explanation may tempt some to conclude that a language makes its speakers unable to see the difference between specific colors during its acquisition, defending some sort of incommensurability or holophrastic indeterminacy (Quine 1960 and 1969). However, this conclusion is mistaken. English speakers might perceive specific colors differently because their language changes how their brains process specific inputs. The assumption is that they are incapable, unless they know a language such as Tarahumara, of seeing an example of "green" as more similar to "blue" than to another shade of "green," due to some sort of mental postprocessing that English imposes. Tarahumara speakers would lack this postprocessing since they lack the linguistic motivation conditioning it, explaining the experiment's results.

If we accept this reasoning, perhaps we could extend this view to other cultures. Different languages and cultures codify color differently. For instance, some languages use only two color terms, one referring to dark colors and the other referring to light colors (Deutscher 2010, 61; Berlin and Kay 1969, 22–25). Languages add further terms to these generally one-by-one in a reasonably specific universal order until we see very robust and specialized color codification systems (Berlin and Kay 1969, §2.3). Perhaps the reason for this apparent lack of detail in some linguistic color systems is that the systems in question impose physiological limits on the vision of each new generation of speakers.

Nonetheless, although these differences have been noted for centuries, all nonlinguistic tests have affirmed that every human being, regardless of which language they speak, is perfectly capable of distinguishing all colors with the same high degree of precision. For example, in the nineteenth century, one of the many things that interested those exploring the globe was testing foreigners' vision. The results of color-blindness tests always showed that although a group of people might lack a technical term for a specific color, all of them were still able to see the difference between it and other similar colors. For instance,

> No tribe was found that failed to see the differences between the colors. Virchow and the gentlemen of the Berlin Anthropological Society administered a Holmgren color test to the Nubians and asked them to pick from a pile of wools those matching in color to a master wool. None of the Nubians failed to pick the right colors. . . . No tribe, be they ever so rude, was found to be blind to these distinctions. . . . [They] simply thought it was ridiculous that there should be different names for these two shades of the same color. (Deutscher 2010, 62)

Kay and Kempton's (1984) study corroborates that all people can perceive colors equally well. Both English and Tarahumara speakers distinguished the colors objectively when linguistic factors were controlled. They hypothesized that English speakers, rather than having "green" or "blue" color categories psycho-linguistically imposed on them, used the linguistic resources at their disposal to accomplish the task, particularly in interpreting the vague instructions of "deciding which of the three chips is the most different." Kay and Kempton called this problem-solving technique *the name strategy*:

> It's hard to decide here which one looks the most different. Are there any other kinds of clues I might use? Aha! A and B are both called green while C is called blue. That solves my problem; I'll pick C as most different. (Kay and Kempton 1984, 72)

Of course, the Tarahumara speakers could not employ this strategy since different names for the colors do not exist in the language, so they were forced to reason extralinguistically to complete the task, unlike English speakers. Generalizing, we can claim that one way a language may influence habitual thought is by offering its speakers different recurring strategies when confronting a situation where such strategies could be helpful, like when no other strategy for reasoning is apparent or other strategies are less accessible. This is one way in which a language does affect our patterns of thought: it allows us specific modes of reasoning, based on lexically codified semantic distinctions, that speakers of languages lacking these distinctions do not have, at least until they modify their language to include distinct names for such things. Understanding modes of reasoning should interest the anthropologist who studies their cultural variation, the linguist who studies how and why people use them, and the philosopher who studies how language's semantics could potentially affect them, but often it does not.

How languages codify space is perhaps the most striking example of reasoning method that a language affords its speakers. Linguistically, organizing space usually occurs in one of these two instances: egocentrically and geocentrically. The former is most commonly used in English and other Western languages. Speakers refer to the position of an object in ways that relate to the speaker's perspective on the position of a linguistically or contextually fixed reference point, whether it is *in front of, behind, to the right of,* or *to the left of* it. Geocentric systems refer to objects in relation to their position relative to some salient aspect of the environment. Different geocentric systems are found in the Tzeltal language (eastern Chiapas, Mexico). This language uses the directional terms *up-slope, down-slope,* and *cross-slope,* even when the relevant mountain slope is not in direct view. The Pirahã language (Maici River, north-western Brazilian Amazon region) uses coordinates that refer to the river near its speakers' villages (Pinker 2007, 141; Everett 2008, 215–217).[11] The upshot is that when an English speaker moves around a tree, an object goes from being *in front of* it to *behind* it, and when a Tzeltal speaker does the same, the object remains in the same *up-slope* or *down-slope* position. In other languages, one may refer to an object's position using the cardinal directions *north, south, east,* and *west,* like the Australian aboriginal language Guugu Yimithirr.

Levinson (1997 and 2003) investigates Guugu Yimithirr language's possible effects on spatial reasoning and perception relative to English speakers. First, Levinson set up a table with three objects in a straight line across it and asked participants to memorize the order of the objects. Then, experimenters asked them to put the three objects in "the same order" on a table in another room. From an egocentric perspective, this room looked the same but was flipped 180 degrees on a geographic axis. The results revealed another example of the name strategy in how speakers treated the ambiguity inherent in the phrase "the same order": was the same order relative to the speaker's subjective point of view or relative to the geographic orientation of the room? Participants organized the three objects exactly how their languages would treat them. English speakers organized them egocentrically so that the situation would appear the same in the speaker's field of vision. That is, so that they would use the same words to describe the objects on the first and second tables. Guugu Yimithirr speakers organized them relative to the cardinal directions so that the objects were in the same positions from a geocentric perspective, so that, once again, speakers would describe the positions of the objects the same way.

In this case, though, the name strategy operated on a subtler level, since these results depend not on the semantics of a couple of words, but rather depend on how an entire spatial deictic system categorizes space: individual-centered for English speakers versus the communal point of view of Guugu Yimithirr. Regardless of what some have said about the universal primacy of egocentric coordinate systems, participants organized objects in the second room according to how their language would classify them as "the same" or "different," not according to any innate classification scheme. Interestingly, these results are that the task required no linguistic reasoning for completion. Speakers internalized their language's codification of space, basing their nonlinguistic conceptual representation on its spatial deictic and value system. This experiment demonstrates that Guugu Yimithirr speakers and English speakers remember the "same reality" according to different representational spatial schemes. If a person walks into a room flipped 180 degrees geographically without moving anything inside, an English speaker would say that it is laid out the same as before. In contrast, the Guugu Yimithirr speaker would disagree, saying that the room was organized in precisely the opposite way. Therefore, speakers orient themselves and their memories according to the spatial deictic system of their language, whether consciously or unconsciously.

Pinker has objected to this analysis, arguing that it may be the physical environment, not the linguistic environment, leading to a particular type of coordinate system and its concomitant spatial reasoning processes (Pinker 2007, 148), a geographic rather than linguistic determinism. Nevertheless, different peoples live in similar environments that use different coordinate and value systems. Furthermore, even children as young as two years old more or less consistently use the coordinate system of their language, mastering it at around the age of seven (Deutscher 2010, 191). It is unlikely that the child herself has interacted with the geographic environment enough to necessitate developing a coordinate system on such a basis or that the language she speaks plays no important role in pushing her toward the geographic system.

This does not mean that language determines the set of coordinate systems one can learn and use, only that it affects the system that speakers *tend* to learn and ordinarily employ. For instance, many Guugu Yimithirr speakers learned English as adults and use the egocentric system well, to the point of warning a translator of one of their traditional tales to change the address "west of the Cooktown airport" to "to the right as you drive to the airport," since he believed that English speakers would not understand something so opposed to English's egocentric system (Deutscher 2010, 171). The fact that this speaker had indeed learned the egocentric system and that the anthropologists studying Guugu Yimithirr were able to learn their language shows us that the existence of one particular coordinate system in our language does not prevent us from learning a different one.

This example shows that even though some linguistic relativity operates behind speakers' coordinate systems, linguistic determinism should not be confused with this perspectivism. In English, one sees the two different systems used at once, each serving a different discursive function, with the use of the cardinal directions typically restricted to giving directions and referring to long distances from a bird's-eye view. One would be hard-pressed to find an

English speaker casually telling another: "There is an ant to the north of your east foot," which a Guugu Yimithirr speaker would find entirely unremarkable. Language affects how we habitually codify spatial relationships, which we consider a critical cognitive effect, although it is not an absolute effect.

All previous examples show different instances of what Whorf called language habituates. They display formal properties that condition some language uses and the meanings of some expressions until the speaker internalizes them. These examples show that internalization occurs most clearly in habitual reasoning and categorical conceptualizations. However, this does not mean that speakers cannot change how they reason about and conceptualize various aspects of the world.

5.3 ADDITIONAL DATA AND DIRECTIONS FOR FURTHER RESEARCH

So far, this chapter has argued for three different but related conclusions. First, the single hypothesis called the Sapir-Whorf Hypothesis is a conflation of at least three different positions on the relationship among thought, language, and culture. As a result, it often fails to distinguish between linguistic relativity and linguistic determinism. Second, it advocated adopting an extended enchronic view when interpreting certain linguistic phenomena that support SCRT, especially in Indigenous languages, since this considers how cultural processes influence language development. Finally, it has shown how languages are employed to reason about the world, which may influence speakers' conceptualization, supporting WRT and perspectivism. Because SCRT holds, SRT and linguistic determinism must be rejected since cultures and thought change before languages do. This implies that language cannot constrain either. Here additional data supporting the second two points are presented. First, determinables explain how language reflects and may influence categorization, and second, ethnic slurs appropriation further expands on the value of the extended enchronic view.

Johnson (1921) presented the notion of "determinable" in the context of the traditional logical division of a class into disjointed subclasses. In classical logic, this division must be based on some principle of *fundamentum divisionis*, the principle that a genus is divided into species. Johnson proposes that *fundamentum divisionis* are determinables. Johnson defines determinable as follows: "I propose to call such terms as color and shape determinables in relations to such terms as red and circular, which will be called determinates" (Johnson 1921, 174). A determinable concept can be further specified if necessary, and further specification endows determinate values.

Johnson's definition is linguistic, referring only to "terms." However, from an ontological viewpoint, determinables should be analyzed as abstract linguistic terms and as qualities, properties, or dimensions of things. The exact nature of these terms and determinables more generally is controversial. Johnson prefers determinables as abstract names that stand for adjectives. As does Prior, who stated that "'red' is the proper name of an individual universal, if we may speak so; while 'color' is the name of the class of universals to which this individual one belongs" (Prior 1948, 8). For others, "color" (a determinable term) may be nothing more than an abstract general term, whereas "red" (a determinate term) is a concrete general term (Quine 1970). (See also Charro and Colomina 2014; Colomina-Almiñana 2012 and 2018; Hautamäki 1986 and 2020; Rovelli 2021).

Therefore, one could argue that determinables are functors that associate entities to their values, which can be schematically presented as follows: "the X_1 of X_2." For example, the phrase "the color of the fence" refers to the determinable color of one particular fence. How a particular language represents these aspects or features of entities depends on the specific cognitive system speakers codify in the language, which depends on cultural standards of relevance and pertinence. Determinables are related to the situations where speakers live and act, and, in each context, speakers will select a helpful set of determinables when available. When a helpful set of determinables is unavailable, people construct new concepts to talk about their situations, consequently creating and re-creating new vocabulary and grammatical structures to express these new conceptual constructs as necessary.

A determinable's relationship to its determinate is that of a class to its members. These members may be subclasses that have members of their own. That is, a determinate may be a determinable as well. The structure of a determinable encodes a particular taxonomy, which may or may not be hierarchical. Different languages differ in how they encode these taxonomies. Let us return to the example of color terms in Tarahumara compared to color terms in English. In English, "green" and "blue" are separate determinates of the determinable "color," but in Tarahumara both are encoded by a single determinate, *siyóname*. As Kay and Kempton (1984) explain, this reflects that English speakers and Tarahumara speakers habitually categorize the colors picked out by these terms differently based on their linguistic labels. Perhaps a more salient example for English speakers is "pink." In English, "pink" is a basic color term; that is, it is a determinate of "color" but not a determinate of "red." Some languages do not have a basic color term for colors described in English "pink," instead of referring to these colors as a particular kind of their basic color term for redlike colors[12] (see Berlin and Kay 1969, §2.3 for a broad survey of different languages' color systems). The color "pink" in English is represented as a particular determinate of the redlike color in other languages. A similar phenomenon occurs in Russian, which has two unrelated terms for what English speakers would refer to as different shades of blue, *siniy* and *goluboy*. These terms are descriptively as different as "pink" and "red" are for English speakers (Winawer et al. 2007).[13]

As said before, it has been found that all humans can perceptually distinguish colors equally well. Nevertheless, this does not necessarily mean that all humans ontologically categorize colors in the same way. Colors vary continuously along a spectrum, and yet they are represented hierarchically in languages, with specific colors being subcategories of other colors (i.e., "crimson" is a kind of "red," at least to English speakers). The fact that these hierarchical relationships vary cross-linguistically suggests that how speakers mentally organize colors does it. Of course, the next question to ask is whether a particular language helps its speakers conceptualize and categorize colors this way, or whether speakers conceptualize and categorize colors differently due to the cultural status of the colors and then encode these categories in their language. The first case produces a WRT effect, and the second case produces an SCRT effect. The most likely answer is that both effects occur to some extent. The existence of a particular word in a language likely causes speakers to reify the category it picks out (Boroditsky and Prinz 2008, 110–111). However, the category picked out must be nonlinguistically relevant, or else there is no reason to refer to it, and the word will eventually drop out of the language as it is employed. An extended enchronic analysis applies to this process since speakers re-create their language to reflect how they categorize "green" and "blue" relative to *siyóname*, "pink" relative to "red," and *siniy* relative to *goluboy* as the cultural and mental status of the color changes for them.

A related process deals with how speakers challenge and modify the meanings of words over time through social processes. There is probably no better example than undertaking the beautiful art of cursing and insulting. Moreover, the target's appropriation of such pejorative words is probably an excellent example of how prolific and inventive our thought and natural languages are. Here, the chapter picks some caveats from how we do bad things with words, particularly slurring words. By employing such words, people intentionally or unintentionally insult and derogate a particular individual, the target, and by extension all those individuals that share specific properties, which the slurring word highlights in a negative way. There are myriad examples demonstrating how people develop words to express their disdain for a specific individual or group. People constantly find new social differences to mock and disparage people, typically disrespectfully focusing on their shared characteristics. Though, the creation and use of slurs are driven by sociohistorical linguistic processes—the exact kind of processes amenable to an extended enchronic analysis.

We know that people can offend by using certain words in a particular way. Think about the N-word. For a long time, racists have used it to refer to those of African descent in the United States, and one cannot think of a single-use that is not offensive and derogatory. The euphemism "N-word" comes apparently from its use in court by African American lawyers in the 1990s, who refused to employ the full-spelled word due to its potential for offense and denigration. Nonetheless, we can identify a related phenomenon that involves using the same slur but cannot be associated with any contempt or derogation: "appropriation." Appropriation is the use of a pejorative or a racial epithet (such as the N-word) not to derogate the target but rather to express some kind of camaraderie, solidarity within, or belonging to a group to which the target supposedly belongs. Of course, there is no way to use such words without getting in trouble. Consider, for example, how Richard Prior, Chris Rock, and Dave Chappelle (all African-American comedians) have employed the N-word in their routines. Alternatively, Cardi B. uses a lexically similar term in Twitter to evolve the force of the racial epithet to signal her political commitment and consciousness as an Afro-Latinx woman. They, of course, do not use the N-word to derogate certain people because of their race. They are mocking specific individuals because of their social class or simply referring to African Americans. Although some individuals could still be offended by its use even if appropriated. However, for some reason, there seems to be a tacit agreement between some members of the targeted group that some individuals can employ the word without necessarily expressing contempt, and even specific uses are nonderogatory. For instance, consider the following scenario:

[S]omeone drives by a group standing on a corner and yells out:

(1) You N-word and S-word (to refer to Hispanics) don't belong here!

Imagine that everyone in this group is African-American, and that one of them attempts to clear up the confusion created by (1),

(2) I think you three must be the N-word, and the rest of us are the S-word. (Anderson and Lepore 2013, 353)

Since the speaker may not intend to derogate, it is tempting to say that the speaker is not performing anything in using those words. Nonetheless, it is a common mistake to think that performatives, as we must define slurring words, depend on only the speaker's intention. The derogatory force of the pejorative does not derive from the speaker's intention alone, but the social conventions surrounding its use are of high importance.[14] The fact that the speaker does not intend to offend or derogate does not mean that the speaker did not do so at all for two reasons.

The first reason is that there is some inaccuracy in the previous analogy between the N-word and the S-word, which becomes apparent upon taking an extended enchronic analysis. We have to remember the origins of these words. The N-word originated in chattel slavery to derogatorily refer to African Americans. In contrast, the S-word originated on the northeast coast of the United States in the early twentieth century, mainly employed inside the Army, to derogatorily refer to Puerto Ricans regardless of race, specifically after the 1917 passing of the Jones Act to grant US citizenship to Puerto Ricans to forcing them to enlist as soldiers in WWI. We cannot simply say that both terms are equally derogatory and offensive. The former is undoubtedly more derogatory and offensive than the latter due to the different social and historical circumstances in which each term arose. Understanding how the origins of such terms contribute to the conventions of their use is necessary to understand why they are not equally offensive.

The second reason derives from the first. The illocutionary force of performatives mainly depends on the entire situation and context in which they are employed, viz., the conventions surrounding their use, which in part derive from their origins. In our previous example, one could say that the speaker had no intention of derogating the target (perhaps because she was placed in a scenario where she was using appropriated words). However, this does not mean that the slurs (both the N-word and the S-word) do not have the potential to derogate, even when a speaker targeted by the word uses it to refer to other individuals within the same ethnic group. In other words, the social conventions embedded in the speakers' uses of language, or even an idiom, which depend on more than just a particular speaker's intention in uttering the word in particular circumstances, always could potentially drive to a perlocutionary act that causes such harm.

What these speech acts of derogation accomplish is not the inferential or semantic pattern that reflects a negative attitude toward the targets of such words but a conventional understanding of such terms that encodes some particular speakers' bigoted, diminishing worldview. However, it is also clear that speakers can resist and change these conventions. Formerly offensive words can become unremarkable as conventions shift, and formerly inoffensive words can become highly charged in the same way (see Pinker's discussion of the "euphemism treadmill" in Pinker 2007, 319–320). In the case of appropriation, we see ways speakers intentionally re-create linguistic conventions to reflect their views better. These changes are best explained as extended enchronic processes since they are examples of how speakers create and re-create their linguistic conventions over extended periods of time to express their changing values and attitudes.

5.4 CONCLUSION

Contemporary research about the relationship between thought, language, and culture provide a new perspective on the linguistic relativity hypothesis, which buttresses the Interactive Theory for explaining meaning. Advocating for linguistic relativity without specifying its limits is unhelpful because there are limits. It is not good to speculate on potentially different worldviews without testing the truth of our claims regarding their possible effects. This can lead to an undesirable principle of linguistic determinism that ends in the incommensurability of different languages and the inability to determine meanings. As Lucy (1996, 153) reminds us, there is an unfortunate lack of hard evidence in the area of linguistic relativity, but this is slowly being remedied. Theoretical developments in linguistic relativity should and do motivate further empirical discoveries and have attempted to show in part how this process works by explaining how the extended enchronic analysis presented can be applied to some empirical studies and further applied to the analysis of determinables and slurring words.

Nothing can be achieved by discussing the relation between thought, language, and culture without the ability to appeal to specific, quantifiable, and (re-)testable data to demonstrate its truth or untruth. Without such data, one risks converting this area of study into a mere repository of trivialities, hastily leaving aside the critical contributions to understanding the complicated interactions between thought, language, and culture. However, no one can approach this topic without a proper theoretical framework to guide the studies. In doing so, one may prematurely dismiss claims that later turn out to be supported by evidence, ignore possible future research directions, or misinterpret results that support linguistic relativity and perspectivism. Thankfully, philosophical accounts of language have provided these theoretical frameworks about meaning, and although some shortcomings are still present, they provide a path toward foundational analysis.

The historical and analytical development proposed by the Interactive Theory regarding meaning determination formulates an alternative foundational theory by successfully combining conventions, the speaker's intentions, and the audience's possible uptakes, as chapter 4 demonstrates. Further comprehension of the origins of the claims for linguistic relativity that led to modern misinterpretations allowed outlining three different formulations of the linguistic relativity hypothesis, which capture the key differences between some of these different interpretations, as seen in section 5.1. Using these as a basis, this chapter has documented how thought, language, and culture interact in meaningful and interesting ways, and it has demonstrated how culture and thought might be shaped by language. This is crucial to understand the interrelation between a speech community and its speakers, between language and conventions. Specific evidence from theoretical and empirical studies from several fields supports the view while setting limits on interaction, contributing to further refinements. Thought, language, and culture are interdependent, mutually influencing each other in a cyclic process. Any one of these may be prioritized when necessary. This view is consistent with Whorf's position that culture and language are inseparable aspects of a single cultural-linguistic system and inconsistent with SRT and linguistic determinism. Only analyses and explanations that consider both language's and culture's roles in their respective cultural-linguistic complexes can adequately account for specific socially driven processes of linguistic change and the effects of languages on their speakers' habitual thought and conceptualizations. It is also, more importantly, in agreement with Austin when he said:

> Our common stock of words embodies all the distinctions men have found worth drawing, and the connections they have found worth marketing, in the lifetimes of many generations; these surely are likely to be more numerous, more sound, since they have stood up to the long test of the survival of the fittest, and more subtle, at least in all ordinary and reasonably practical matters, than any that you or I are likely to think up in our armchairs on an afternoon—the most favored alternative method. (Austin 1956, 182)

NOTES

1. This does not mean that I do not take it seriously. That is the purpose behind Colomina-Almiñana (Forthcoming).

2. As a reminder, only to point out that Boas initially used the pejorative term "Eskimo," which must be avoided in favor of the more accurate term "Inuit." However, it should be noted that his term includes some languages that the modern term "Inuit" does not. "Eskimo" languages include the Inuit language Inuktitut, spoken in Baffin Island (and described by Boas) as well as Kalaallisut (or West Greenlandic) and Nunavik, but also Yup'ik and Iñupiak (Boas 1894; Fortescue 1984; Schneider 1985; Sturm 2009a and 2009b).

3. Not all anti-relativistic accounts are so disrespectful. For instance, Bertalanffy (1955) takes Whorf seriously and accepts and recognizes the value of the linguistic evidence of his arguments, even though Bertalanffy rejects the notion of relativity and states the possibility of the existence of an objective knowledge behind every language expressed in terms of "a process of progressive de-anthropomorphization of our world picture" (Bertalanffy 1955, 262). Another example is Black (1959).

4. Others give between seven (Steckley 2008) and even up to 123 different lexemes for snow (Halpern 2006). However, the exact number is not relevant to my broader point, which relies on interpreting how the semantics of lexemes relate to speakers' cultures and conceptualizations.

5. It is necessary to keep in mind the relationship between English, as a dominant "killer" language, with the subordinated Indigenous languages and the power relations such relation has historically endorsed (cf. Ricoeur 1993).

6. However, as Wierzbicka (1997, 10–12) claims, even if the number of Inuit words for "snow" was just an empirical misrepresentation of the actual number of terms for referring to it, this fact does not invalidate the relativistic conception of the language-culture relation.

7. "There is a process of 'thinking for speaking' in which cognition plays a dynamic role within the framework of linguistic expression" (Slobin 2003, 158).

8. There are also many similarities between Comrie's Haruai study and Irvine and Gal's (2000) study of Hlonipha and click consonants in Zulu, which shows how this analysis can be applied to a language's phonetic and phonological developments in addition to their lexical development.

9. Something similar can be said about cases when gender differences in peer-group structures can affect the use of bilingual repertoire, even when there are no apparent sex differences in second language acquisition (Woolard 1997), or in cases when an overt/covert distinction in the acquisition of plural marking in Yucatec languages is established (Lucy 1992 and 1996). Other examples refer to some attitudinal explanations toward the use of certain honorifics in languages such as Japanese and Korean, and even some varieties of Spanish (see, for instance, Colomina-Almiñana 2017a).

10. This assimilation is due to Tarahumara mythology and, more specifically, to the cosmological explanation of the origin of the Cañón del Cobre and their people. Again, the influence of culture on language is present in Tarahumara.

11. We can also compare this with the representation of time. Western languages usually represent time as a sequence, such as one proceeding from a time "being two days ago," to "being one day ago," to "being the present-day," to "being one day in the future," to "being two days in the future," and so forth, where the "present" serves as a tense-establishing reference point to which other terms are contrasted. In contrast, some non-Western languages tend to represent time as a tenseless ordination of time slots. This system employs a two-place relation: "two days later than X," "one day later than X," "simultaneous with X," "one day earlier than X," and "two days earlier than X." (McTaggart 1908, for instance, exploited this intuitive distinction to claim the unreality of time). Other languages, including some Australian Aboriginal languages (e.g., Martuthunira, Jiwarli, and Wajarri), show a gradually complex codification of time (Stirling and Dench 2012). Wintu uses different suffixes to codify the future concerning subjective and objective points of view (Lee 1938). Chapter 6 delves into issues regarding the semantics of temporal sentences.

Nevertheless, many psychological studies present data advocating for these and other so-called "Whorf effects," or Whorfianisms (language habituates). See, for instance, the treatment of perception of space and time in Boroditsky (2001 and 2011). As she says, "People who conceptualize space differently also conceptualize time differently, suggesting that people co-opt representations of the physical world in order to mentally represent more abstract or intangible entities" (Boroditsky 2011, 333). Boroditsky's work also analyzes how certain color words affect color discrimination (Borodistsky 2006), or how the comparison of similar objects develops knowledge (Borodistky 2006), among other phenomena. Studies in modern quantum physics seem to corroborate these findings (Rovelli 2018).

12. Typically, "red" is used instead of the more complicated expression "redlike color" in discussions of color hierarchies in languages, presumably since it is easier to understand. Nevertheless, this usage presupposes that color categories are the same cross-linguistically, which *prima facie* are not. A "redlike color" as described here encompasses colors that span the range of colors encoded by the English words "red" and "pink" (among others), whereas "red" does not include colors described as "pink" (though the exact extensions of such terms may vary from language to language).

13. Austin (1939, 49) said: "But surely, speaking carefully, we do not sense 'red' and 'blue' any more than 'resemblance' (or 'qualities' any more than 'relations'): we sense something of which we might say, if we wished to talk about it, that 'this is red.'"

14. As seen in section 3.4, his idea is related to Austin's speech acts theory and his seminal three-partition among locutionary, illocutionary, and perlocutionary acts and the types of uptakes that belong to the illocutionary act. I am working on a manuscript defending what I call Perlocutionarism: slurring words and other so-called "thick" concepts are perlocutionary acts that always cause harm and discrimination because they produce changes in attitudes and have the potential to modify behaviors. In my modest opinion, using slurs supposes participating in a *categorical mistake* shared by the bigots (the "categorical mistake" of believing or acting as if some individuals could be described or referred to by such pejorative term). We need the capability to refuse recognition of such derogatory force (blocking the harming illocutionary for) by not recognizing such an act as valid.

Chapter 6

Application 1: Tensed Sentences

Previous chapters highlight the existence of a contextualist position that argues in favor of truth value shifting sentences. As we saw, this relativist account explains that a good amount of the sentences in our language are undetermined because they express subjective judgment. They propose a truth-theoretical semantics where a sentence truth value is the function of parameters constrained by a context of use and a context of evaluation or assessment. This also applies to tensed sentences. The presence of a tensed verb makes the content expressed by the sentence ambiguous. Therefore, temporal sentences have shifting truth value depending on when they are uttered and when they are assessed.

Although capable of fine-graining certain circumstances of assessment that resist other proposals, this account cannot explain some basic facticity regarding time. For instance, elements involved in such assessment are embedded in the evaluation context. Therefore, the truth of any sentence is relativized to the evaluation context. However, it does not necessarily respond to the context of use since the evaluation dimension of the latter is something other than truth.

Consider the quintessential example, offered by future contingent sentences such as:

(1) There will be a sea battle tomorrow.

In order to properly account for the truth of (1), some believe that one needs to relativize the truth of any utterance to a context of assessment (the judge's parameter, a subjective standard to contrast with the sentence's content), and sentence-truth to both a context of utterance (which includes the time of an utterance) and the context of assessment (MacFarlane 2003). However, as Brogaard (2008) and many others have pointed out, assessment circumstances have objective features that cannot change under any intensional operator, which invalidates the relativist's expectations. Furthermore, such features depend upon some objective normative conditions that indicate whether such a sentence is successful, but not necessarily true or false since these conditions have to do with the proper employment of the sentence in question. In other words, the fact that the content of such a sentence is determined does not only depend upon the ontological status under which time is considered but necessarily depends on the set of rules that will entertain such content.

This chapter offers an alternative interpretation of tensed sentences based on the Interactive Theory. This approach is the opposite of analyses provided by contextualist and relativist accounts. The Interactive Theory explains the same data from a perspectivist approach while defending pluralism regarding propositions, at least when talking about temporal sentences. The idea behind this claim is twofold. First, based on Austinian more than Strawsonian ideas, the statements made by the use of sentences, and not sentences themselves, are what can be either true or false. Second, the truth value of any statement cannot change because it is determined by the conditions of constraining established by the speech community that both speaker and audience belong (or the linguistic exchange takes place) and the audience's possible uptakes of such statements. The difference between any contextualist and relativist solution and what I propose here is that my account considers how only from a particular normative perspective can one approach any statement's truth. Such a perspective always includes objective temporal coordinates beyond speaker and audience and is embedded in the communicational common ground. Therefore, to properly approach the propositions any statement displays, one first has to center the speaker's perspective (in communal and conventional terms, as demonstrated in chapter 5) and, then, account for the conditions that will turn it into a successful act.

The chapter is organized as follows. The three first sections critically overview classical theories about temporal sentences that precede current debates about contextualism and relativism. These sections analyze their flaws and highlight their strengths. Section 6.4 offers many caveats employing the alternate account based on the Interactive Theory. My approach demonstrates that a temporal point of view dominates over all subordinate clauses, which determines any temporal operator employed. This temporal point of view is beyond both speaker and audience and is embedded in the shared common ground since it is established and part of the speech community. Therefore, any evaluation context would always be subordinated to such a temporal perspective and whichever accompanying truth-conditional determination.

6.1 PRESENTISM AND TENSED SENTENCES

Arthur Prior developed one classical approach to tensed sentences in the 1950s and 1960s. Prior advocates for a presentist theory that considers time a logical construction from tensed propositions. According to Prior's account, a sentence such as

(2) I am eating my breakfast

in an instance such that

(3) It was the case that I am eating my breakfast

is nothing other than a propositional variable p which may have different truth value at different times depending on which time such a variable refers (Prior 1957, 8; 1967, 14–16; 1968, 8). For Prior, all sentences are evaluated relative to the present time, and all sentences can only be true or false relative to some time or other. However, the explicit mention of time occurs only at the level of the metalanguage and never in the object language.[1]

Prior states:

> For in English sentences, the point of view of the speaker dominates even subordinate clauses. When an English speaker, for example, wants to say on Tuesday that someone complained on Monday of a sickness that he had that day, the correct form of words will be "He said he was sick," although the man was in fact complaining not of a then-past but a then-present sickness, and his own words would have been "I am sick." (Prior 1967, 14)

It is clear that, in natural language, tenses are devices one can employ to refer to time without explicitly mentioning any time in particular. Prior's theory is the perfect example of displaying semantic referential mechanisms for indexical expressions about time. For Prior then, English is an object language in which tense operators are constructed as analogs of sentential modal operators in the metalanguage.[2]

However, despite the advantages that Prior's theory has, it does not explain sentences making explicit reference to a time, since such sentences cannot be true or false relative to any time at all, but they must be true or false in reference to such a determined moment in time. In order to prevent this system from failing, Kamp amended Prior's theory to include a *now* operator 'N' (in a Montagovian semantics) to rescue the idea of propositions with contextually variable truth value. According to Kamp (1972), any sentence referring to the present moment will be true if and only if it is true at the present moment, relativizing in a two-step semantics that sentence's truth value to the contextuality of the present moment.[3] However, Kamp's system has the same problems as Prior's since the time variability still permits some sentences to shift truth value depending upon the concrete time to which the variable refers.

A further attempt to amend Prior's system includes the individual attitudes of the speaker in the determination of the sentence's truth value. In this fashion, Needham (1976) introduces another 'now' operator, an explicit indicator of the present tense, since he states it is necessary to introduce an operator in tensed contexts where we quantify items other than moments (see also Needham 1975). In this renewed system, "now" picks out a definite time just as a date does. According to this system, then, a sentence such as

(4) Someday, all those who took part in the plot will be brought to justice

translates as

(5) $N^\alpha\ {}^\alpha F^\beta \forall x({}^\alpha P^\eta \varphi x \supset {}^\beta \psi x)$

In other words, the speaker's point of view dominates all subordinate contexts. The division of time into past, present, and future depends on the concrete individual speaker's point of view at the time of the utterance of any sentence, which will remain the same in all subordinate contexts where the speaker is involved. Hence, although the past tense in the antecedent of (4) occurs within the scope of a future tense operator, it takes us to an earlier moment than the present rather than to some moment earlier than the future.

This is, of course, in direct opposition to Prior's view, where it is possible to iterate tense operators generating structures like "the future past," "the past future present," and so forth. However, Needham argues, it is not possible to iterate expressions that indicate pastness, presentness, and futurity since it does not seem possible "to formulate complex tense structures without also taking account of the serial order of time explicitly" (Needham 1976, 316). Needham sides with Reichenbach (1958) when considering that the time-reference points preclude iteration: "Any formula containing one or more occurrences of the 'now-operator' not taking the whole sentence as their scope, and binding one or more distinct variables, is logically equivalent to a formula (which appropriate change of variables to avoid clashes) in which the operator does have the greatest possible scope" (Needham 1976, 317).

Needham's main idea is that any sentence's tense is a date (or behaves as a date does) determined by the moment when a speaker utters a sentence and links it to a concrete time. Therefore, any sentence must be understood as an occasion sentence anchored to the concrete time the speaker utters it. One problem with this position is understanding the claim in terms of eternal sentences: is any occasion sentence understood as a type-sentence, or should one understand an occasion sentence as a token sentence? To me, Needham's approach is mistaken if sentences are understood in invariant terms as embedded within the speaker's point of view, for this means that the same sentence settles its truth conditions relative to the speaker even before any use. In other words, if the speaker's point of view determines the time of reference for any utterance, then it is not possible to say that such determination occurs independently of the individual point of view's bearer. If this is the case, Needham means the occasional concrete use of a sentence by a specific speaker at a specific time. Therefore, Needham speaks about utterance-truth and not sentence-truth. Under this standard, though, Needham does not provide better conditions than Prior and Kamp when they stated that a sentence could only be assessed relative to the time of utterance since a sentence's truth value will still shift depending upon who utters that sentence and when. The difference between Needham and Prior-Kamp is how they treat the assessment.

Think of the following example:

(6) I am thirsty (now).

According to Prior, this sentence type has a different truth value depending on when one utters it. For Needham, this is wrong because the correct way to interpret (6) is by referring to a time variable embedding the concrete date of the utterance to a speaker on a specific occasion—the present moment in this case. The key for Needham is then to understand (6) as a tenseless sentence, and the concrete occasions of utterance have a tense/date. Needham compares this with the moment when one writes a letter. If one writes now in a letter, "It is raining," this means that it is raining when she is writing the letter (also, at the place the letter writer is located). When receiving the letter, that person will learn that it was raining when the writer wrote the letter, which binds to the sentence.[4]

A priori, this appears sound. However, it is still problematic. The reason is that "now" refers to the moment of speaking (or writing), no matter how deeply embedded a sentence is independent of the speaker/writer. Since the time is different on any two occasions, one cannot employ the same sentence (6) as part of another sentence employed at a later time to report the same state of affairs that would have been reported when (6) could have been used to make a true statement. Furthermore, the same holds for the case of the letter, for there is an objective temporal perspective independent of any speaker and content that dominates any speaker's point of view. In other words, if the time of a sentence is determined by the speaker's temporal position when uttering it, then it is not easy to link such occurrences beyond that concrete speaker and that particular moment.

6.2 CONTEXTUALISM, KAPLANIAN CHARACTER, AND TENSED SENTENCES

Kaplan, Lewis, and others pursue a different approach to the previous problem. They developed a two-dimensional semantic analysis based on possible worlds to correctly represent the different ways in which the determination of the proper truth value of the sentences in natural language depends upon the concrete context of utterance.

Kaplan (1989) proposed a two-step derivation about meaning. This view establishes that the determination of the truth conditions of any sentence depends upon what he called their *character* (a function that relates a context to a content) and their *content* (as a function from world-time pairs to truth values).[5] According to this framework, the semantically fundamental two-dimensional relation is that of sentence s being true at context c at index i, where a context is a concrete location that centers the sentence (this is, the time, the place, and the possible world that the concrete sentence is talking about, or centered world) and an index is the n-tuple set of features of this particular context (for instance, a concrete speaker and a concrete audience). In all particular contexts c, we can find the concrete index i for this particular context, or i_c, where the mentioned index provides the correct coordinates, demonstrating appropriate features that define c. In formal terms, sentence s is true at context c if and only if s is true at context c at index i_c (Lewis 1980).[6]

However, this account does not explain the evident truth of some instances involving explicit indexical temporal terms. Think, for instance, about the following sentence:

(8) I am here now.

Following Kaplan's two-dimensional semantics, the previous sentence would be true if and only if the speaker is in the place of utterance at the moment of uttering the sentence, which implies that such a sentence must be analytically true (Predelli 2011) since virtually the sentence would be true whenever uttered. However, the same logic should apply to its negation,

(2) I am not here now.

In Kaplan's framework, (9) would be true only if the speaker is in the place of utterance when uttering it, which leads to a contradiction. Hence, (9) must always be false, which violates the basic intuitions we have regarding such a sentence, like for example when one writes (9) on a sticky note and leaves it attached to her office door, or when one listens to a recorded message left on somebody's answering machine or voice mail.

The preferred solution to this problem, as stated by Predelli (1998), is that sentences in recorded messages and written notes are to be evaluated concerning the intended context of interpretation, which need not coincide with the context of utterance. In example (8), although the context of utterance determines who is the speaker and where and when the utterance takes place, one should interpret it as being intentionally uttered (recorded or written) for a posterior moment (the moment of listening or reading it) and not as embedded in the concrete time of utterance when recorded or written. Furthermore, there is no requirement for the speaker to be anywhere near the utterance's location at the time of uttering it, but only that the speaker has some expectation that her utterance will be assessed via the original time when the utterance took place.[7]

Despite its apparent soundness, this solution is still incomplete. Even though one relocates the time of utterance to the moment in the future when the sentence is heard or read, this cannot be the sole product of an intentional move by the speaker, since it is not up to the speaker to determine what is the past, the present, and the future. One has the intuition that these moments are independent of the speaker and even the audience and that their existence should depend upon, or at least have something to do with, semantic reference. (In fact, this case is similar to this other. Consider somebody that believes the name "Aristotle" [as occurs in a sentence like "Aristotle is Greek"] only designates Aristotle when he was alive. This confuses between designation and denotation, since although, indeed, nobody could now designate to Aristotle in the present time, the name "Aristotle" still denotes Aristotle.)

6.3 RELATIVISM, TENSED SENTENCES, AND SHIFTING TRUTH VALUE

Following Kaplan's two-dimensional framework, some relativists have argued that certain sentences, including temporal sentences, even though referring to the same content across contexts, shift their truth value not only according to where and when a sentence is uttered but also to who utters it. Some sentences have changing truth value according to individual subjective judgments. These authors introduce a new judge-index to evaluate such sentences. The value of this new parameter is provided by the derivation of truth value from content but never by the derivation of content from character (Lasersohn 2005, 643). Truth value for the different judgments is relative to the pragmatic context established from the world-time-judge triple. Therefore, a sentence can be true for one speaker relative to w at t but false for another speaker relative to the same *w* at the same *t*. Every time a speaker utters a sentence, it is evaluated according to the particular pragmatic context in which such utterance is made. This is clear for the so-called faultless disagreements, as shown in chapter 7.

MacFarlane's (2003) analysis of future contingents accounts for the truth of sentences, including tense, such as (1). According to him, one must relativize utterance-truth to a context of assessment (the judge's parameter pointed out before) and sentence-truth to both a context of utterance (in a Kaplanian fashion, which will center the speaker, the time, and place in which the sentence is uttered) and the previous context of assessment. In this case, when one asserts (1), the truth value of the specific sentence token is embedded in the context of evaluation for the instance the sentence is uttered. However, the truth of the sentence type is relative to a double-indexing, accounting for the time the sentence is uttered and the standards of evaluation at hand when uttered. MacFarlane (2009) calls this approach non-indexical contextualism to distinguish it from Kaplan's indexical contextualism.

In this account, the propositional content expressed by a sentence would be the same in every possible judgment scenario. However, such a sentence would take different truth values in any of the different judgment scenarios under scrutiny. For MacFarlane, the truth value of a temporal sentence depends on the judge's perspective of who utters it, which relativizes a sentence's truth-value besides accepting the same sentence's content. As shown, when evaluating truth-utterance as relative, MacFarlane (2005) suggests going beyond a two-dimensional framework for correctly discerning the truth value of sentences, including temporal linguistic items such as tenses. Because a sentence *s* at a context *c* at an index i_c could be true from a particular judgment but false from another, these judgments are thought to share similar contexts but represent different locations depending on where a concrete sentence is valued. The result is then a relativistic position that values the same sentence *s* in the centered context *c* defined by i_c depending on the judgment where it is applied. Consequently, sentences' truth values depend again upon an individual speaker's point of view that dominates any possible context.

However, this position is highly problematic. Suppose one considers, as MacFarlane does, that the same sentence can have different truth value depending on how different speakers utter it under different judge's parameters. In that case, we have to accept that either the sentences are contradictory (since they apply different truth values to the same state of affairs) or refer to a different state of affairs. MacFarlane, though, is explicit about how the sentence's content is the same for all the occasions when the sentence is uttered. However, the speaker's judgment represents different locations depending on where a concrete sentence is valued. The conclusion is then that, under MacFarlane's framework, two occasions of the same sentence cannot have a shifting truth value since the different truth value for such sentences refers to different scenarios.

The key to understanding why is provided by Goodman (1977), who asserts that conflicting true sentences must correspond to different versions of the world, and such true sentences then express different truths about those different versions. Think, for instance, about the two sentences below (the example is from Goodman 1977, 112):

(10) The kings of Sparta had two votes.
(11) The kings of Sparta had only one vote.

According to Goodman, the previous sentences, if they describe the same world, must be contradictory. However, Goodman claims those sentences do not describe the same world but are part of different versions of the world. They are different descriptions of how the world might be. To reiterate, Goodman claims that the previous sentences refer to different versions of the world:

(10') According to Herodotus, the kings of Sparta had two votes.
(11') According to Thucydides, the kings of Sparta had only one vote.

Since both sentences express different truths, it is tempting to claim that one must be at fault and the other speaks truthfully. Goodman further specifies that this is wrong since none of the sentences say anything regarding Sparta and the world itself, but actually about what both Herodotus and Thucydides, respectively, said about Sparta. If this is true, then both sentences are about two different worlds. If one wants, both sentences may even state straightforward, plain truths about a specific world, but with the inconvenience that that world cannot be the same for both sentences. According to Goodman, we can have a genuine contradiction between contrary sentences, but since there is no other way to solve such a conflict, one must accept that these sentences refer to different interpretations of the world.

6.4 TEMPORAL PERSPECTIVE AND TRUTH IN THE INTERACTIVE THEORY

In the previous sections, I have seed doubts regarding whether there is such a thing as a truth value shifting sentence, including linguistic items such as tense and temporal adverbs. The main reason is due to data from supposed contrary sentences regarding the same state of affairs. As seen, if they are not contradictory, they cannot be about the same state of affairs. Furthermore, no account that appeals to a speaker's point of view would successfully explain the apparent phenomenon of the existence of a sentence with variable truth value. Any such approach would only consider subjective relativist engagement with sentence content, making any sentence's truth entirely judge-dependent. As the chapter has shown, these accounts side with the mistaken idea that semantics guides our ontology, which is at odds with the fact that true sentences state what is the case.

However, there is still a strong intuition that some sentences of our natural language have different truth value depending on the moment that one utters them. Think, for instance, of whales. One can now indeed assert

(12) Whales are mammals.

However, there was a time when one could assert without fault that

(13) Whales are not mammals.

If this is, in fact, correct, the question now is: who is then at fault? One is inclined to say that, on the one hand, there are two different meanings of the word *whale*, one in which whales are mammals and another in which they are fish instead. If this is the case, the difference between both meanings is merely verbal, to rely only on the use of the two different concepts of the word *whale*. Nonetheless, the dispute between the two meanings goes beyond mere discrepancy in language usage. The difference is substantive and not merely verbal. This appeals to the normative status of what counts as *being a whale*. It depends on some intrinsic characteristics in conventional more than semantic terms that distinguish a whale from something else is, for instance, fish. It depends upon what the speech community considers to be a whale.

On the other hand, suppose that the meaning of the word *whale* is the same for ancients and moderns. If this is the case, we have to agree that the ancient was wrong when considering whales are fish and not mammals since it is now scientifically proven that whales are mammals. However, given that many defining characteristics of things are opaque to speakers, it may be the case that the ancient was unaware of what makes whales different from fish and be mistaken when considering as fish what is a mammal. Hence, what a priori appeared a false assertion would merely be an error, which is corrected by pointing out the proper characteristics that allow classifying whales as mammals and not as fish.[8] In other words, both sentences belong to different temporal perspectives. Each temporal perspective establishes different truth conditions for testing the different statements and assertions that one can make from within it and which dominates any further context.

The same holds for sentences such as (1). When one utters "There will be a sea battle tomorrow," she makes a statement considering the different open possibilities that could determine the sentence's truth value in the future when the state of affairs in question would have occurred. It would not be until the concrete temporal perspective settles that one can be aware of the conditions that apply and, then, be capable of determining the truth or falsehood of such sentence. Therefore, when one says that whales are fish and not mammals or that there will be a sea battle tomorrow, such a statement must contrast with the truth conditions established by the temporal perspective dominating the structural conditions that one inhabits. Those determine whether whales belong to fish or mammals and whether there is a sea battle. In other words, there is a set of criteria and conditions beyond both speaker and audience established by the speech community that determines the truth conditions constraining any statement and speech act made within such a perspective and which refer to the concrete state of affairs. These would be something similar to what Massimi (2018) calls standards of performance adequacy.[9] These standards of performance adequacy are normative pragmatic and conventional tests that any sentence should pass to be satisfactory. They determine whether a sentence is true or false.

The modification or negotiation of such criteria, the changing and reshaping of such standards, explains the apparent variability of some sentence's truth value. As shown, some sentences may be contrary but not contradictory since they refer to different conditions regarding the same state of affairs: those established by the two different temporal perspectives to which the two sentences respectively belong. Therefore, there is no real change in sentence truth value, but simply two different statements since modifying the standards of performance accuracy open new truth conditions that create new statements and acts that a speaker could perform. The state of affairs represented in language (the proposition) does not change. Our point of view is updated. This reflects using the two different sentences on different occasions to refer to the same state of affairs. It is intuitive that a theory about temporal reference leaves room for obtaining a relation between two propositions just in case one reports the same state of affairs as the other but from a different point of view. This is what temporal perspectives provide and is, after all, a general feature of tenses and temporal adverbs.

NOTES

1. Given Prior's analysis of past and future tensed sentences as Pp and Fp respectively, and where Pp is true at t iff is true at t', for some t' earlier than t, and Fp is true at t iff is true at t', for some t' later than t.

2. Prior's redundant theory of the present tense understands the proposition "It is now the case that p" as the very same proposition that p. Hence, Prior considers that the present tense is the understood tense of any tensed proposition, so there is no need for any other operator for *now*. The reason behind this is Prior's metaphysical theory of time: Presentism. According to Prior, only the present time exists, and both past and future are constructs from the present moment, being the former fixed (because it has already occurred) and the latter open (since it is still to come).

3. In formal terms, Nφ is true at t iff φ is true at t_n.

4. There is a debate inside the contextualist tradition based on the seminal work by David Kaplan devoted to analyzing this kind of example from a two-dimensional semantics framework. However, this tradition has problems explaining precisely this kind of example regarding recorded notes. Section 6.2 delves into further details.

5. To me, Mott's (1973) semantic analysis of Prior's 'T' operator could be understood as a failed precedent of Kaplan's theory. Mott's reinterpretation is as follow:

(7) T$m\varphi$ is true at t iff φ is true at the time designated by m.

Since the time at which T$m\varphi$ is evaluated on the left hand of the equivalence is irrelevant to the right hand, Mott (1973, 79) concludes that if T$m\varphi$ is true at any time, it must be true at all times. However, this is incorrect since every proposition seems to be evaluated precisely at one time, including those sentences in which time is explicit.

6. Besides that Lewis's and Kaplan's theories are based on possible worlds, they are different. Kaplan's analysis accepts possible worlds as epistemological/logical possibilities (like Kripke does), whereas Lewis considers them material possibilities. Both options present their caveats and challenges, but this chapter shall only focus on Kaplan's approach as applied to tensed sentences.

7. In an important sense, Predelli's solution to the paradoxical appearance of recorded messages resembles Needham's solution to truth-variability of occasion sentences. Predelli appeals to an intentional movement from the speaker that recenters the context from the context of utterance to the context of interpretation, whereas Needham prefers reducing any context to that determined by the individual speaker's point of view. In the end, as Plumer (1988) states, perhaps this distinction is already captured by the differences existing between the phenomenon of the speaker's reference as opposed to semantic reference.

8. It is worth mentioning that this discussion assumes a historical approach about names instead of the currently more accepted Barcanian-Kripkean causal approach.

9. Rosenberg (2002) introduces standards of performance adequacy to defend a perspectival theory of epistemic justification. Massimi believes that such performance adequacy "must be met by scientific claims for them to be retained across scientific perspectives, i. e., for their ongoing performance to be judged as adequate by practitioners of different scientific perspectives" (Massimi 2018, 354).

Chapter 7

Application 2: Disagreements

Some scholars have argued that the linguistic meaning is sufficient to determine truth conditions, as defended by the Traditional View. If this is the case, every natural language sentence carries one proposition independently of the context of utterance. Then, truth-utterance is invariant context to context, and the truth value of any sentence can be reduced to its semantics. Every time two speakers utter conflicting sentences about the same situation, one and only one of them is talking truthfully, and the other one is at fault. Otherwise, if both expressed propositions were true, the two sentences must be about different situations, not contradictory. Nevertheless, everyday conversation is full of situations where two different speakers make contradictory utterances about the same issue and, nevertheless, neither of them is at fault. Think only about cases where two speakers disagree about the spiciness of the chili they are eating or about the boringness of the movie they have just watched. These situations are usually called *faultless disagreements*.

As we saw in the previous chapters, it is assumed that a literalist account of meaning like those depicted above is too constrictive. It is a normal finding among the current literature that semantics alone cannot determine the content of the sentences of our language and that it requires, even though only minimally, some contextual elements to center such content. As seen in chapters 2 and 3, these contextualist positions about meaning flourish after Montague (1970) and Kaplan (1989) and mainly acknowledge the existence of a minimal number of context-sensitive terms. As seen in the previous chapter, some scholars have gone even further and held a relativist position regarding some philosophically and linguistically relevant cases, including future contingents (MacFarlane 2003), predicates of taste (Egan 2010; Lasersohn 2005; 2009; and 2011; Stephenson 2007), evaluative predicates in general (Lasersohn 2008), epistemic modals (Egan et al. 2005; Egan 2007), knowledge attributions (MacFarlane 2005; Kölbel 2009), and adverbs and adjectives of comment (Liu 2009). This relativist position rejects that the truth conditions of at least some utterances are absolute and require other factors (external to the sentence and its linguistic content) to establish the adequate truth value of a particular utterance of a sentence in a concrete context.[1] They usually appeal to a *judge parameter* to illustrate that this situation involves embedded subjective meaning. Situations of faultless disagreement include sentences that are not truth-evaluable until the speaker and audience coincide in *the attitude* that the situation reports.

I accept the intuitive fact of faultless disagreement cases. This chapter applies the Interactive Theory developed in chapters 4 and 5 to cases of disagreement. As spelled out there, this theory advocates for a combinatorial explanation of the meaning expressed in any linguistic exchange that takes into account three elements: the speaker's intentions, the audience's potential interpretations, and the conventions established by the speech community where such exchange takes place. This chapter, therefore, defends a response to the complexity of faultless disagreement scenarios based on what chapter 5 introduced as the speaker's point of view. Unlike relativist approaches, this position understands disagreements as expressing the speaker's communal perspective about a particular issue without unilaterally constraining the truth conditions of the sentences in our natural language. The Interactive Theory argues that instances of faultless disagreement are not a matter of opinion but fact and, besides the appeal to the speaker's intentions, they cannot rely on any subjective framing of the situation.

The chapter is organized as follows. Section 7.1 defines faultless disagreement, using predicates of taste as the paradigm. Sections 7.2 and 7.3 survey some purely semanticist and relativist solutions, respectively. The former reduces any instance of disagreement to nonsubstantive or philosophically irrelevant cases because, they argue, any sentence's truth conditions are determined semantically. Therefore, when disagreement occurs, one side must be necessarily at fault, otherwise there is no disagreement. Relativists insist that these situations of genuine disagreement occur, and I concur. They, however, appeal to a judge parameter to solve the faultless disagreement cases, a parameter that constrains the truth conditions of the sentence uttered not only within the context of utterance but also within the assessment context. Therefore, the individual judge's conception of the world determines the truth conditions of any sentence in a concrete scenario. Every time two speakers disagree about any matter, one must suppose that it is the judge's conception of the world they are talking about. The problem is that this view changes in every situation and from speaker to speaker. Hence, when two speakers disagree, they are not talking about the same issue but about how the particular matter solipsistically appears to each of them (their individual opinion).

Even though I consider that faultless disagreement is an integral part of our ordinary language, the relativist solution is highly counterintuitive. Suppose it were the case that when two speakers disagree, one must appeal to an additional individual judge parameter to center the sentence's truth conditions or linguistic exchange in question. In that case, it could not be real cases of disagreement but only cases of mismatch (where speakers are talking about different worlds, their own) or cases of incomprehension (where they communicate no information at all because their points of view are so different that they can never overlap).

Section 7.4 rejects the relativist distinction between matters of fact and matters of opinion in cases of faultless disagreement and distinguishes between a weak and a strong sense of disagreement. It provides the Interactive Theory's solution based on a communal speaker's point of view to cases of faultless disagreement. Unlike semanticist and contextualist solutions, this chapter proposes that one cannot defend the standard view (a shared context, if preferred) that contrasts every possible expressive sentence. The sentences involved in cases of faultless disagreement are truth-evaluable only according to the perspective that the speaker manages to center, that is true, as the relativist suggests. Nonetheless, this perspective must somehow be related to a community standard rather than individual judgments. Therefore, the speaker's point of view, as presented in the previous chapter, plays a crucial role in establishing the perspective according to how a speaker must evaluate any sentence. This is the only way that the speaker has to express her access to the reality, the only way she can share her view of the world with her audience. Nevertheless, this viewpoint cannot be subjective-dependent but dependent upon the conditions externally established by the speech community.

To summarize, the chapter demonstrates that faultless disagreements are substantive because they exhibit some doxastic disagreement, something that some contextualists and semanticists often negate. These situations are not instances where we find embedded propositions with shifting truth value depending on who utters them. As the Interactive Theory proves, accurate analysis of these cases supposes, on the one hand, negating the existence of subjectivity in favor of the acceptance of some normativity that constrains the speaker's intention and, on the other hand, accepting a plurality of perspectives about the world embedded in our ordinary ways of speaking.

7.1 PREDICATES OF TASTE AND FAULTLESS DISAGREEMENTS

Faultless disagreements are cases where two different speakers utter opposite sentences about the same object, event, or situation, but neither is at fault. We can say that they disagree about the same issue, but we cannot say that this disagreement is at fault because the speakers are not contradicting each other.

There is no contradiction.² Paradigmatic instances of faultless disagreement are situations that involve predicates of taste.³

In a predicate of taste, a speaker expresses her view about some nonobjective matter. When I talk about nonobjective matters, I mean situations where a speaker is talking about her internal feelings, sensations, perceptions, and so on (*what it is like* for her to perceive something, or it is the expression of her own opinion about some concrete situation). In other words, a predicate of taste expresses a particular view about a concrete issue depending on who utters it in a concrete situation. This approach foregrounds the existence of subjective meaning. In sum, the meanings of predicates of taste are dynamic and fluctuate with the speaker, which indicates the presence of shifting truth value. They are always interpreted from an autocentric perspective (the individual judge's perspective) in which there is no adverbial quantifier *taking scope over* the predicate (Percus 2000; Sauerland and Schenner 2009, 200–201).

In recent debates about this topic, two different general examples clarify what predicates of taste are. On the one hand, we find those who define predicates of taste as a kind of interpersonal variation in the assignment of truth value to the same object. Two different speakers can predicate different properties about the same issue without contradiction. Hence, predicates of personal taste function as scalar adjectives or adjectives that express degrees regarding the object in question. On the other hand, some define predicates of personal taste as verbs expressing concrete subjective opinions about objects or events. Thus, two different speakers can disagree about the same matter without fault because they will express their subjective perceptions and opinions about it.

These are all cases of embedded sentences with apparently shifting truth value. These cases include predicates of taste as instances of faultless disagreement. They challenge the standard literalist account of truth. As previously seen, literalism claims that the truth value remains invariant between different contexts of use or utterances since what a sentence means is what it literally says (its semantic content). Accordingly, when two speakers disagree about the same issue, one of them has made a mistake (or is at fault), and the other is right (or is speaking the truth). They are contradictory because they express conflicting meanings about the same propositional content.

Nevertheless, situations involving predicates of taste show that like relativist approaches maintain, when two speakers disagree on some matter, it is possible that neither of them has made a mistake or one is at fault (Kölbel 2004, 53). According to the standard relativist view about such cases, when two speakers utter conflicting sentences that include predicates with the adjectives "spicy," "fun," "delicious," or "tasty," they express the speaker's sensibilities about them. In cases where nonobjective matters are involved, two different speakers can utter conflicting sentences about the same issue, but both can ascribe it to different truth-properties simultaneously. Though the two speakers disagree, we have no significant intuition of contradiction between the two assertions because the speakers talk about their own subjective personal taste (Cappelen and Hawthorne 2009, 109).

To exemplify this differentiation between objective and nonobjective matters, consider the following situations in which the speakers disagree about different issues.

(1) Nicole: Does this cake contain wheat flour?
James: Yes, this cake contains wheat flour.
Domino: No, this cake does not contain wheat flour. It is made for celiac.
James: Oh, sorry. I did not know that. I have made a mistake.
(2) Grandma: How tall is Ausiàs?
Juan: Ausiàs is fifty-one inches tall.
Nicole: No. Ausiàs is fifty-three inches tall. The doctor said so during his annual medical revision yesterday.
Juan: Oh, ok. I was wrong.
(3) Nicole: Is this roller coaster the biggest in the state?
James: Yes, this roller coaster is the biggest in the state.
Domino: No. This roller coaster is not the biggest in the state. According to the *State History Book* published this year, this other is the biggest.
James: Sorry, I am at fault.
(4) Nicole: How is this cake?
James: This cake is delicious.
Domino: No. This cake is not delicious.
James:?Oh, sorry. I guess I was wrong.
(5) Grandma: Is Ausiàs tall?
Juan: No. Ausiàs is not tall.
Nicole: Ausiàs is tall.
Juan:?I made a mistake.
(6) Nicole: How is this roller coaster?
James: This roller coaster is fun.
Domino: No. This roller coaster is not fun.
James:?Sorry, I am at fault.

On the one hand, cases such as (1)–(3) assert objective, measurable facts (metaphysical modalities, if preferred, since the propositions asserted only affirm the verifiable state of affairs). The predicates in these cases are used objectively. They only inform about objective facts. Any time two speakers disagree about this kind of issue, we can appeal to some external standard (or truthmaker) to verify the adequate truth conditions of the sentences. Hence, both speakers are in contradiction if they disagree, and consequently, one of them must necessarily be at fault. On the other hand, in cases such as (4)–(6), where we find two speakers that seem to express conflicting predicates (or epistemic modalities), it is typically accepted that neither of them is at fault. Both speakers disagree about nonexternally measurable matters. They express their subjective personal interpretation or opinion about a tangible thing. The sentences express how these particular objects appear to each individual's subjective standards. Thus, the contradiction between them is only apparent since both speakers can speak their truth simultaneously. The proof is that unlike cases (1)–(3), where one of the speakers admits their point is at fault, in cases (4)–(6), such a retraction of the original statement is not that clear. Cases (4)–(6) demonstrate that when two speakers are talking about matters of opinion, each speaker can talk truthfully even though they are in disagreement with each other. In this sense, each sentence allows for different interpretations. This idiosyncrasy is demonstrated in its semantics.[4]

Semantics for (1)–(3):

(7) ||does the cake contain wheat flour|| = {wheat flour(cake), ~wheat flour(cake)}
(8) ||is Ausiàs tall|| = {tall(Ausiàs), ~tall(Ausiàs)}
(9) ||is the roller coaster the biggest|| = {biggest(roller coaster), ~biggest(roller coaster)}

Semantics for (4)–(6):

(10) ||Is the cake delicious|| = {delicious(l,Domino)&delicious(l,James),delicious(l,Domino)&~delicious(l,James),~delicious(l,Domino)&delicious(l,James), ~delicious(l,Domino)&~delicious(l,James)}
(11) ||is Ausiàs tall|| = {tall(b,Juan)&tall(b,Nicole),tall(b,Juan)&~tall(b,Nicole), ~tall(b,Juan)&tall(b,Nicole),~tall(b,Juan)&~tall(b,Nicole)}
(12) ||is the roller coaster fun|| = {fun(rc,James)&fun(rc,Domino),fun(rc,James)& ~fun(rc,Domino),~fun(rc,James)&fun(rc,Domino),~fun(rc,James)&~fun(rc,Domino)}

Thus, when speakers talk about objective matters, matters of fact, a metaphysical modality says how the world is, which overcomes any knowledge that a concrete speaker possesses or the concrete attitude she may have toward it. Metaphysical modality is nondescriptive and can change across contexts but not across speakers. Examples (1)–(3), in which two speakers assert or state how (they think) the world is, really express contradiction because only one of them can have a true belief (or can speak truthfully) when we contrast their utterances with the way that the world is. These examples are cases of real semantic disagreement since they are not faultless: one of the speakers has made a mistake and is at fault.

Scenarios (4)–(6) are cases of epistemic modality. In these cases, speakers express their own opinion about how things in the world are. When the speakers utter conflicting sentences, neither of them can be mistaken or at fault because they only express how the world might be (some kind of possibilities, how things are for them). They express how things are according to their perspective. In these cases, we have confirmed cases of faultless disagreement.

Examples (1)–(3) are situations where two speakers disagree about an objective metaphysical content. These examples seem to be governed by the following principle:

> (ITC) Invariantist Truth-Conditionalism: In interpersonal situations where there is a speaker A, a speaker B, and a content p, such that A asserts that p and B asserts that non-p, it will always be the case that one of them has made a mistake, or is at fault.

Nevertheless, in situations such as (4)–(6), when speakers utter their sentences, they express different subjective opinions about the same issue, and, despite all, neither of them is at fault. When both speakers utter their sentences, they express their concrete views about the same issue. This kind of situation suggests the existence of the following principle:

> (NITC) Non-Invariantist Truth-Conditionalism: In interpersonal situations where there is a speaker A, a speaker B, and a content p, such that A asserts that p and B asserts that non-p, neither A nor B has made a mistake or is at fault.

If (ITC) is correct, then, in any situation where two speakers disagree, one of them is at fault. Therefore, (NITC) is false and cases of faultless disagreement are impossible. Nevertheless, if (NITC) is correct, there are situations where two speakers disagree, but neither of them is at fault. Therefore, (ITC) is false and cases of faultless disagreement are possible when speakers entertain matters of opinion.

Some scholars argue that (ITC) is the only available claim about truth, even when speakers address matters of opinion. They defend a monism regarding propositions: one and only one possible content is always present in every possible sentence of our natural languages, and that proposition cannot change. Since this view assumes that the truth conditions of natural language sentences are absolute, a semantic constraint is always present in any linguistic exchange. When two speakers utter conflicting predicates, either there is always a contradiction, one is at fault, or they are talking about different matters, and there is no disagreement. However, this kind of situation where two speakers express different opinions about the same issue happens all the time in our ordinary lives. We can always disagree about the most delicious flavor of ice cream, about the beauty of this city, or even about the appropriateness of Joe's behavior. People always propose some subjective content in these cases. They prioritize their own opinion regarding such matters. However, does this imply that subjective content is nonabsolute, like (NITC) claims?

7.2 PREVIOUS ANALYSIS AND CONTEMPORARY RELATIVIST APPROACHES

The relativist's claim that faultless disagreement exists when we talk about predicates of taste is motivated by the development of the framework initially advocated by Kaplan, Lewis, and others about a two-dimensional analysis in order to correctly represent how sentence truth value depends on utterance context, as seen in section 6.2.

Following this two-dimensional framework and based on the insights offered in MacFarlane (2003), Lasersohn (2005) argues that predicates of taste, even though they refer to the same content across contexts, shift their truth value according to who utters them because they are not speaking about matters of fact (objective truth conditions) but about matters of opinion (subjective truth conditions). In other words, the truth value of any sentence involving predicates of taste changes or is relativized, according to the speaker's subjective opinion. Then, they introduce a new judge-index, or parameter, to evaluate the sentence. The value of this new judge parameter is a derivation of truth value from content, but never by the derivation of content from character (Lasersohn 2005, 643). Therefore, the truth value for different perspectives is relative to the pragmatic context but not the logical context established from the world-time-judge triple. Every time that a speaker utters a predicate of taste, it must be evaluated according to the concrete, pragmatic context from which it is made. A sentence can be true for one speaker relative to w at t but false for another speaker relative to the same w at same t because each sentence's truth value must be assessed from the standard proposed by the subjective-centered world established with that judge parameter.

Think again about some of our previous examples involving cases of faultless disagreement. In semantic terms, we can say that the possible answers to the previous question formulated by scenarios such as that offered in (4) is something like the following:

(13) $||\text{delicious}||^{c;w,t,j} = [\lambda x_e.x \text{ tastes delicious for } j \text{ in } w \text{ at } t]$

After further developing the initial approach started by Lasersohn, Stephenson (2007) claims that predicates of taste are two-place predicates, in which PRO is taken as the second argument substituting the judge.[5] In her words, a sentence such (13) translates as

(14) $\|PROj\|^{c;w,t,j} = j$

resulting in at least the following three distinct interpretations:

(15) a. $\|$The cake tastes delicious $PRO_j\|^{c;w,t,j}$ = true if and only if the cake tastes delicious for j in w at t
b. $\|$The cake tastes delicious $PRO_{Nicole}\|^{c;w,t,j}$ = true if and only if the cake tastes delicious to Nicole in w at t
c. $\|$The cake tastes delicious to Nicole$\|^{c;w,t,j}$ = true if and only if the cake tastes delicious to Nicole in w at t

The essential difference between both approaches is that Lasersohn treats the operator "delicious for" as a modifier of the adjective "delicious," while Stephenson considers it as an argument of it (Stephenson 2007, 520). According to Stephenson, only the first interpretation is judge dependent and, therefore, truly responds to a judge parameter like the one a relativistic interpretation requires. The other two interpretations depend on either a linguistic context (15.b) or a pragmatic context (15.c), and neither of them provides the adequate value of the judge's argument for the sentence. Lasersohn's truth-theoretical semantics then fails to provide evidence for the subjectivity of predicates of personal taste and, hence, for truth value shifting depending on the speaker and the context of utterance. According to this view, sentences with predicates of taste are judge dependent only if they take PRO_j as an argument: when they include some subjective content in the account (Stephenson 2007, 500). The question is, now, whether this is possible at all.

When evaluating truth-utterance as relative, relativists claim the need to go beyond the two-dimensional framework established by Kaplan and other contextualists for correctly discerning the truth value of sentences, including predicates of taste and other matters of opinion. The reason is that it seems intuitive that a sentence s at a context c at an index i_c can be true for a particular speaker but false for another. This claim has a problem, though, since the speakers share the same context. If they represent different locations (or slots) of such context depending on where what they say is evaluated, we have a radical relativism that assesses differently the same sentence s in the centered context c defined by i_c depending on the speaker that utters it (cf. López de Sa 2009, 3–5. See also Richard 2004; Stojanovic 2007, 699–703; von Fintel and Gillies 2008; and Francén 2010).

If we pay close attention to the two-dimensionalist program, the truth value of any sentence, including indexicals and demonstratives (and matters of opinion) can be contextually variable. Its truth value shifts depending on the context of utterance. Nevertheless, when the truth value is determined in a concrete context, it cannot change. In other words, no semantics can facilitate what Kaplan (1989, Section VIII) dubbed *monsters*. Therefore, any position that claims, like the relativists mentioned above, that a sentence's truth value can change within a context is necessarily doomed.

Remember that, according to the two-dimensional framework, the concrete act of uttering a specific sentence determines just one unique context (the context of utterance), and in turn, this context determines just one unique possible world (the centered world, or the world which this utterance talks about). Hence, this analysis accepts that a concrete utterance determines one and only one unique context. Therefore, any time two speakers utter conflicting sentences, one of them has made a mistake (or is at fault) because they evaluate their sentences according to the same semantic truth conditions stipulated by *the* context. This situation, by definition, negates the existence of faultless disagreement. However, again, these cases seem to abound in ordinary life. We all know of situations where a speaker has asserted the opposite view than somebody else regarding a particular matter or affirmed a sentence with conflicting content about such and such, and nonetheless, both speakers are speaking the truth. It would be counterintuitive to say these sentences collide in a semantic contradiction. The point is, why?

7.3 CONTEXTUALIST APPROACHES

According to contextualist improvements of the Kaplanian program, there are two modes compatible with the two-dimensional approach, which construct a semantics for predicates of taste (see, for instance, Iacona 2008, 291–293). The first takes a relevant-experiencer argument. This argument refers to an individual sufficiently informed of the context (or *salient*) to center the speaker's world. Under this speaker-indexical option,[6] the experiencer is just the speaker in any situation, and the expressed view is just that of the speaker. An unarticulated constituent, which necessarily refers to the experiencer, always operates in these cases.[7]

Thought this way, sentences including disagreement regarding any matter of opinion cannot be interpreted otherwise than contradicting one another, as contextualists say. Suppose scenario (4) again:

(4) Nicole: How is this cake?
James: This cake is delicious.

Domino: No. This cake is not delicious.

If we interpret the sentences in (4) under the speaker-indexical position, we must understand (4) as saying something as

(17) Nicole: How is the cake?
James: It is delicious to me.
Domino:?No, it is not delicious to you.

Thus, it seems that (4) and (17) are cases of disagreement that behave differently. In (4), Domino's claim is motivated because she (the speaker) does not find the cake delicious. This supposes some subjective disagreement with James's claim. In (17), Domino's claim argues that James is not speaking sincerely or does not think that the cake is delicious, is confused about his thoughts, and so forth. Nevertheless, this is counterintuitive because James said that the cake is delicious to him. In (4), Domino says that the cake is not delicious to her. On the contrary, in (17), Domino says that the cake is not delicious to James because the implicit experiencer-indexical becomes objective in the subjective situation.

This interpretation is problematic, however. If we treat (4) as (17), it seems that we are always involved in semantic contradiction when facing situations with sentences including predicates of personal taste. This position is extremely close to the classical Kaplanian framework, which is not a priori an issue. The position claims that the experiencer standard establishes the truth conditions of the sentence in question because the indexical operates at the context level. Also, it determines for once and always its truth value, which will not change within the same context or the same experiencer-indexical. Therefore, once more, situations of faultless disagreement appear impossible. Nevertheless, it is still intuitively true that James and Domino have disagreed about the cake without either of them being at fault.[8]

There is a more complex account that cannot be treated just as having a contextually subjective-salient argument but including generic pronouns. This second contextualist mode appeals to the standard of taste endorsed or promoted by the speaker. Someone can give a non-subjective-dependent interpretation of a predicate "x is p." In this case, the claim describes the actual features that characterize as p the concrete x, independently of subjective interpretations. If two speakers utter conflicting sentences about x (for instance, a specific wine), we can say that they disagree because they utter sentences about different properties of x, but they are really in contradiction with one another. If this interpretation is correct, cases of disagreement are possible, but they are always in contradiction, and consequently, someone will always be at fault. Then, faultless disagreement is impossible because they will always be involved in semantic contradiction in such cases.[9] How to explain, then, the intuitive existence of cases of faultless disagreement if it is impossible to avoid contradiction in terms?

There is a communalist moderate-relativist response in contemporary contextualist literature that does not appeal to speaker-indexicals. This view claims a pragmatic rather than semantic account to the content of at least some of our utterances. DeRose (2004) defends a *single scoreboard contextualism* regarding our knowledge attributions.[10] This contextualist response asserts that when two speakers utter conflicting sentences, they are not indexed under a subjective standard of taste but rather under a shared standard that underlies the entire situation.

Recanati (2008, 59–61) claims that the speakers talk for the community in this kind of situation. There is a *community standard* with which the conflicting sentences juxtapose for him. Hence, when a speaker utters a sentence as "This cake is delicious" and another speaker disagrees, like in situation (4), they express something intuitively stronger than some speaker-indexical sentences such as:

(18) James: This cake is delicious according to my standard.
Domino: According to my standard, this cake is not delicious.

When the speakers utter the sentences, they mean something like:

(19) James: This cake is delicious.
Domino: This cake is not delicious, according to the community-shared standard.

In these cases, therefore, some flexibility is introduced to the community from whose standard we evaluate the semantic content to accept that one of them has a different taste. This fact foments cases where two speakers can disagree on a matter. However, such disagreement cannot be faultless. In cases of disagreement, the community standards settle the situation, and one speaker must always be at fault.[11]

Similarly, López de Sa (2008, 304) advocates for the *presupposition of commonality* to predicates of taste. Since contextualism explains the difference between two speakers uttering conflicting sentences in terms of truth conditions and establishes the nonexistence of faultlessness, he appeals to pragmatic elements to defend that the subjective meaning expressed in our utterances is, in fact, conventional meaning with equivalence in semantic content. This approach is based on common ground in certain situations with presuppositions. In this view, the conversation is based upon a common ground identified as a context set. This set includes the worlds in which all participants in the communicational exchange believe. In situations with faultless disagreement such as (4)–(6), first, a speaker makes an assertion. Second, she presupposes only the worlds where the sentence is true (or negates the contexts in which the sentence is false). And then, the rest of the speakers accept or do not accept this presupposition. In other words, speakers adjust the content of their sentences according to this common ground. Hence, on the one hand, both speakers are in disagreement because they presuppose at the very same time that their respective standards are about (or are applied to) the same state of affairs. On the other hand, this disagreement is not faultless because both utterances are in pragmatic conflict, but they are semantic contradictions. These situations are pragmatically permissible but semantically punishable. Thus, cases of faultless disagreement do not exist if we think this way because semantic contradiction is always involved. Nevertheless, again, cases of disagreement fulfill our ordinary language, and they appear faultless. How can we avoid the semantic contradiction in these cases?

7.4 THE INTERACTIVE THEORY: DEFENDING THE COMMUNAL SPEAKER'S POINT OF VIEW

So far, the chapter has shown that the main problem when addressing opposing sentences about matters of opinion is that they risk semantic contradiction. Even under a context-sensitive framework, it seems that the content of any sentence will be determined once the utterance context is centered, and therefore the sentence's truth value cannot change. Any other sentence negating the original uttered sentence will be not only in conflict but also in contradiction with its truth, and, hence, the one who utters it will be at fault.

Some suggest that in cases of disagreement, as (4)–(6), speakers talk from a speaker or perceiver subjective parameter while others appeal to a generic standard. The main problem with these accounts is that addressing conflicting sentences about matters of opinion will always involve semantic contradiction (Lasersohn 2005, 654–655). Nevertheless, these cases happen all the time in ordinary life, and we do not have an intuition of contradiction about them in our ordinary linguistic exchanges. Therefore, these cases are perfectly adequate in our daily discourses, and they always express the speaker's view about the situation she is talking about.[12]

This section argues in favor of an approach that considers predicates of taste from an experiencer argument different from the approach developed by individualized indexical contextualism and that, at the same time, takes seriously the idea of a communal standard provided by the utterance context. As Stephenson (2010) advocates, we can understand this argument overtly, as individualized indexical contextualism does. Nevertheless, as we saw, this interpretation is problematic. This section reinterprets the argument by linking the speaker's intention to the conventions constraining the linguistic situation. The argument is, then, covertly supplied by what in previous chapters I call the speaker's point of view, since the speaker consistently re-creates the values and perceptions of the speech community to which she belongs, and that is at the grounds of the Interactive Theory.

It is assumed that the world objectively has properties that can be further fine-grained into other properties. A particular point of view inherits this characteristic because it is an ontologically primitive entity of the physical world. In this way, a point of view structures the world through attributes of objects of the real world. Thus, properties are characteristics of objects in the physical world, and, in this sense, they exist independently of points of view, even though only from the point of view one has access to reality. In other words, a property would not exist if the characteristic from which it stems were not present in the object in the first place. Nevertheless, at the same time, the point of view creates such property in accessing the particular object. In this sense, the world's properties that the relevant point of view can access serve as a model of the physical world, a particular logical form if preferred.

When a subject adopts a concrete point of view and behaves accordingly, she will express the properties accessed from the concrete adopted point of view. This is the speaker's point of view, as introduced in chapters 4 and 5. She expresses how the properties of things are from this concrete point of view, how they appear, without the necessity to describe them. Hence, in a situation such as

(4) Nicole: How is this cake?
James: This cake is delicious.
Domino: This cake is not delicious.

when James utters

(20) This cake is delicious

what he says, seen from the concrete adopted point of view where she is placed, is that the cake in question is delicious or has the property of being delicious. When Domino claims a conflicting sentence such as

(21) This cake is not delicious

referring to the same cake that James, one can say that even though both sentences seem to be in contradiction to each other, Domino is simply saying that, from the point of view she adopts, the cake she is talking about is not delicious or does not have the property of being delicious. Unlike other approaches to truth conditions, what we have here is not a real case of semantic contradiction because it is not the case that the sentences uttered by James and Domino are mutually exclusive. After all, they talk about the same proposition. Indeed, they are in epistemological opposition, and they work as complementary opposite descriptions of the same matter. Since they are not incompatible propositions but mutually dependent and complement each other, one is allowed to have situations like (4) where two different speakers claim conflicting propositions about the same matter at the same time. Real disagreement without fault is therefore possible.

Interpreted this way, cases of faultless disagreement should be understood as dialectical contradictions. Traditionally, dialectical contradictions have not been considered contradictions at all.[13] They are more often understood as epistemological antinomies, as considering a particular subject from opposite points of view. If my approach is correct, an object can be considered distinctly from different viewpoints.

Consider scenario (4) again. From Domino's point of view, the cake she is talking about is not delicious. We can understand what she means by negating that this particular object identified as a cake is delicious. From the point of view adopted by James, it makes perfect sense to predicate the same object, the particular cake they are talking about, as having the property of being delicious. Intuitively, we see how the same cake can have both properties because both properties complement each other. If, as I propose, we follow the argument based on the concept of the speaker's point of view, the paradoxical character of apparent conflict that some situations of disagreement face (including predicates of taste) disappear.[14] This kind of case asserts the complementary perspectives of different speakers expressing different ways of accessing the world from different points of view without fault.

As strongly suggested by our ordinary language, situations of disagreement about questions like, for instance, taste are habitual. As interpreted from the speaker's point of view, these disagreements are faultless. To appeal to some communal-standard parameter is, in my view, unnecessary if we pay proper attention to the speaker's point of view introduced herein. If we accept the shared parameter, we assume that every time someone utters a sentence about her taste, she always expresses everyone's view, which is a very strong supposition. If we accept this fact, we have to conclude that faultless disagreement is impossible because it is necessary to assert that every time someone utters a conflicting sentence like in scenario (4), she speaks from within a shared perspective that everyone has to accept, which will determine the truth value of any sentence one can utter. In other words, this kind of communal principle concludes that everyone who utters a sentence of the same type as (4) subscribes to the same shared-standard community view about the particular matter the sentence refers to. One has to accept utterance too as necessarily true by semantic standards. Hence, whenever someone utters a conflicting utterance like that included in scenario (4), she conflicts with the shared-standard community view, and her utterance is necessarily at fault.

Unlike the communal view that accepts the implicit presence of generic pronouns, this chapter has demonstrated that there is a speaker-centered account that, even though defending that when someone utters a conflicting sentence like that included in scenario (4), expresses objective properties of objects while allowing the sentence having different truth value. Therefore, when someone else utters a conflicting sentence, we can say that she objectively expresses her taste as well but does not negate and, hence, does not contradict the personal taste of the other speaker about that particular matter. The question now is how to maintain the reality of faultless disagreements.

This chapter has argued that if someone advocates for a particular use (a subjective one) that expresses personal inclination toward a particular thing x, the idea that when two speakers utter their personal view about such specific x vindicates disagreement. If someone uses subjectively "x is p," it seems adequate to conclude that she expresses some particular properties that characterize it as p from her point of view. In addition, when someone else uses subjectively "x is non-p," she expresses some particular properties that characterize it as non-p from her point of view. Hence, if this is correct and they are talking about the same matter, the possibility of disagreement is plausible, even though they express distinctly objective properties of the same matter. As seen, the reason is that both speakers are not simply giving their personal opinion about the matter, but are expressing how things are for everyone that shares the same point of view.

Therefore, if we conserve the central claim of subjective uses (that when someone subjectively uses "x is p," she is expressing what it is like to see x from her point of view), it is plausible to assert that any time a speaker utters a sentence of the type "x is p" and another speaker utters some conflicting sentence of the type "x is non-p," both speak truthfully.[15] These statements are not necessarily in conflict. They are complementary rather than excluding. If my view is correct, as some cases of our ordinary language intuitively affirm, one can conclude that the disagreement is faultless, at least in the type of cases described when two speakers disagree about some issues.

NOTES

1. This characterization identifies extremely opposed positions. Nonetheless, an ample variety of accounts can be characterized as essentialist, even though they will

accept a context-sensitivity of the truth conditions of a sentence, like, for example, Kaplan (1989). These accept that, even though a different truth value can be assigned to the same sentence in different contexts, once the context is centered, the truth conditions for that sentence would remain invariantly determined. Similarly, some relativist positions do not reject that truth-utterance is absolute since once a sentence has been uttered, the context of utterance supplies the relevant parameter concerning how the utterance must be evaluated. Thus, the truth of the utterance is absolute. For this reason, this last position is usually characterized as non-indexical contextualism, even though it defends a "moderate" relativism (see, for instance, Kölbel 2004, 2009; MacFarlane 2014).

2. Although there are recent accounts of disagreement that conceive it as not necessarily involving propositions and thus a fortiori neither contradictory propositions (see, for instance, Huvenes 2012; Marques 2014; López de Sa 2008, 2009), there is nevertheless a still widespread notion of disagreement that at least involves minimally contradictory proposition-like contents. Since this last notion of disagreement is the one employed by some relativists when raising the challenge for contextualists as not being able to account for the disagreement part of faultless disagreement, if one wants to be accurate, one has to characterize disagreement as including these entities. Thus, one can say that, when proposition-like contents are involved, both speakers can be in contradiction to each other without, nonetheless, either of them being at fault.

3. Many authors also include in this category refinement of taste statements, aesthetic and moral judgments, tensed sentences (including future contingents, as seen in chapter 6), scalar adjectives, epistemic modals, and even instances of derogation such as sentences including slurring words. They establish a well-defined distinction, as it will be analyzed later, between matters of fact and matters of opinion. This is a strong claim, and I agree with Lasersohn that perhaps it is better to place all the above cases in "a middle ground between fully subjective matters of opinion and fully objective matters of fact" (Lasersohn 2017, 214). Lasersohn's position is still unsatisfactory, but this is a caveat that the Interactive Theory would later entertain. The idea of a middle ground between subjective and objective matters is based on a meliorist account of subjective perspectives, recognizing that sometimes one subjective perspective can be objectively better than others if it is closer to reality. This view, of course, also carries some problems that will not be discussed here.

4. This chapter employs inquisitive semantics because it better characterizes both informative and expressive content.

5. Stephenson (2007) understands PRO as the subject of the lower clause, which is directly identified with the core of the centered world the speakers are talking about.

6. This first way is called Individualized Indexical Contextualism (IIC) by Baker (2012) to signal its contrasts with the Common Indexical Contextualism defended by Kaplan (1989). According to him, "The semantic content of aesthetics judgments like 'Dubrovnik is beautiful' contains a hidden indexical parameter which picks out the speaker's standard. An utterance of 'Dubrovnik is beautiful' by S expresses that Dubrovnik is beautiful according to S's standard of use" (Baker 2012, 109). See also Baker (2014). The second strategy is analyzed later.

7. When I talk about unarticulated constituents, I refer directly to the nonlinguistic elements external to the sentence that refer to its context of utterance and that, nonetheless, are required to complete the semantic content, or proposition, the sentence expresses in such a context. Chapter 4 presents and discusses them. For the use of unarticulated constituents directly applied to cases of predicates of taste, see Zeman (2012). The Interactive Theory employs them differently to solve the conundrum of faultless disagreements, though, as shown in section 7.4.

8. One could object that situations like (17) are perfectly sound. James could be confused or under the influence, and Domino could be in a better epistemic position than he is to know his preferences. This is usually the case in a good number of medical decisions in which the patient does not show the proper control over their cognitive capabilities to consent to a treatment or procedure, for instance. Perhaps the best movement here is not the appeal to the intuition of disagreements but appealing to normal circumstances, since denying the relevant intuition in the case at hand has been the contention of some contextualists to dissolve the intuition of disagreement. See, for example, Glanzberg (2007), López de Sa (2008), and Stojanovic (2007).

9. Different versions of this criticism are also available in Stojanovic (2007) and López de Sa (2008; 2009). As mentioned before, some relativist positions also deny the subjective-dependency of truth-utterance since the context of utterance would supply the relevant parameter for which the utterance will be evaluated. Nevertheless, since non-indexical contextualism (remember, the way MacFarlane dubs his relativistic position) agrees with the contextualism described later in the existence of some standard that applies to the comparison between disagreement predication, the criticism offered here also applies to it.

10. In a previous paper, he also talked about a community of knowers regarding epistemic modals that is relatively free but required to include the speaker (DeRose 1991).

11. My interpretation of Recanati's communalist contextualism may seem overlooked since Recanati postulates another source of disagreement other than the flexibility as to what counts as a community. For these more complicated cases, what makes people disagree is how each speaker thinks the future community standards will be developed. Since "[t]he disagreement ultimately bears upon what the community standards should be . . . then it is, arguably, faultless, but even in that case the disagreement is over the complete content" (Recanati 2008, 61). Nevertheless, it is still the disagreement about the conventional meaning (the *lekton*) but not the Austinian meaning that will determine the disagreement and, consequently, the contradiction. By pointing out the first kind of cases, my purpose was to emphasize that Recanati, and by extension other nonindexical contextualisms, are only invested in claiming all disagreements as contradictory, independently of whether propositions or proposition-like contents are involved or not.

12. In a similar fashion to Hume (1751, 56–57) when complaining about those that confuse the language of self-love with the language of morals, Emerson said: "Most men have bound their eyes with one or another handkerchief and attached themselves to some of these communities of opinion. This conformity makes them not false in a few particulars, authors of a few lies, but false in all particulars. Their truth is not

Application 2: Disagreements

quite true" (Emerson 1841, 1036). James Cox realized that my argument could easily be associated with this anticonformist, skeptical spirit.

13. In a classical approach, Antti Hautamäki claims: "Dialectical contradictions are not logical contradictions because in them the opposite concepts are connected with a subject in different respects" (Hautamäki 1983b, 222). In other words, since these contradictions are associated with how the speaker approaches and expresses reality, they have just an epistemological rather than an ontological nature. Then, opposite does not mean incompatible in these cases. They are the two sides of the same coin.

14. The main reason to consider that the contradiction disappears is provided by Hautamäki (1983a, 195–196). As he says, the logic of viewpoints can express dialectical contradictions because two formulas, P and Q, are confronted at the same time to the same model $\Re$ according to

a) $\Re \therefore P \to RQ \land \Re \therefore P \to RP$ (completeness)

more than

b) $\Re \therefore \sim(P\&Q)$ (exclusiveness).

As he points out, if we have $\Re \therefore P$, then $\Re \therefore \sim Q$ follows. If we have $\Re \therefore Q$, then $\Re \therefore \sim P$ follows. Nevertheless, in the case of dialectical contradictions, if we have, for instance, V (P, w, i) = 1, there is a point of view i' such that $<w, i>S<w, i'>$ and V (Q, w, i') = 1. In this case, P and Q can be true at w but, of course, from the different points of view i and i'.

15. Only from this position does it make sense for a speaker to change her mind or retract what she said. That individual is not contradicting herself but changing her point of view. This way, there is no semantic contradiction or true value shifting. She is only adopting a different viewpoint. In the same fashion, progress in someone's perceptions is only possible from a speaker's point of view like the one outlined herein, and the same applies to a more robust thesis like meliorism, which claims that even though different points of view can co-occur, not all are equally valid. As seen in Section 6.4, conceptual engineering can perfectly be constructed this way as well without incurring in semantic contradiction.

Chapter 8

Application 3: Presupposition Projection

Among the variety of acts that speakers perform, probably the most relevant is the act of asserting. An assertion is the linguistic act of claiming or stating something. The speaker is not simply saying it but committing to the truth of what asserts. Thus, utterances of "The atomic weight of uranium is 238," "The grass is green," or "There are two beers in the fridge" are assertions, or so is assumed because the speaker compromises with the audience regarding "what is said." The speaker is not simply describing a state of affairs but committing to the fact that some features of the world (relevant for the speaker, at least) are true (and so the speaker believes). Thus, an assertion is an act that relates speakers to propositions and is, therefore, the quintessential example of propositional content (Pagin 2007). For this reason, many authors consider knowledge the norm of assertion.

Nevertheless, because an assertion is an open, explicit, and direct action with propositional content, it contrasts with other acts that indirectly convey propositions. Often speakers presuppose many things when talking. The presupposed content in these cases is information that the speaker takes for granted but influences what the speaker may decide to say and how the audience should interpret that. Therefore, presuppositions are sentences that predispose the speaker and audience to conduct themselves in specific ways.

Nevertheless, presuppositions carry some problems. As Morgan (1969) says, it is difficult to explain the relationship between the presuppositions of complex sentences and the presuppositions within their sentential components. In other words, given the nature of propositions, it is difficult to provide specific compositional norms that explain how the truth value of a complex sentence is a function of the truth value of its component clauses in complex sentences. A preferred solution to the problem is distinguishing between semantic and pragmatic presuppositions. A semantic presupposition works almost as a logical entailment. When something is semantically presupposed in a sentence, such presupposed content is present in one of its component clauses, which triggers the presupposition at the sentence level. Pragmatic presupposition is different. Sometimes, the content presupposed in a sentence has nothing to do with its meaning. Therefore, one cannot appeal to any operator to explain how the presupposed content is embedded. In these cases, the presupposition *projects*. A successful theory to explain how employs the notion of common ground (Stalnaker 1970, 1973, and 1974). Since speakers have similar interests in conversation, one must take for granted that speakers and audience share some information and beliefs that allow *accommodating* the presupposed contents in a sentence from the presuppositions of its components (Lewis 1979, 340).

Kripke (2009) introduces a new way to analyze some presuppositional acts included in compound sentences in purely semantic terms. Against the abovementioned pragmatic conception of presupposition, Kripke thinks that many presuppositional elements are anaphoric to previous discourse, which will explain the difficulty of finding triggers for some presupposed contents. On his account, therefore, Kripke refines the so-called *projection problem for presupposition*: in some complex sentences whose clauses bear particular presupposition, this does not necessarily project. Furthermore, sometimes we presuppose some new information not present in any sentence's clauses. According to Kripke, then, literature on presupposition and the projection problem ignores an anaphoric element that must be taken into account to clear up what is going on with presupposed propositional content.

This chapter analyzes presupposition projection and provides a solution from the Interactive Theory. Specifically, it introduces and challenges classic semantic responses to presupposition and confronts Kripke's reconstruction and solution of the problem. As the chapter demonstrates, one should prefer the solution proposed by the notions of common ground and accommodation, since this is a more natural way to understand language as a consequence of intentional and conventional actions with a specific recognized purpose and direction without necessarily linking it to the mental life of speakers.

8.1 CLASSIC APPROACHES TO PRESUPPOSITION

As stated above, there is a distinction between types of speech acts. On the one hand, there are direct and explicit ways of communicating propositional content, such as assertion. On the other hand, there are indirect acts. These are characterized for communicating information not necessarily explicitly contained in language. Sometimes, this content is implicit and somehow linked to the meaning of the uttered sentence. Other times, the implicit content is not related to such meaning but somehow embedded in the conversation as a whole. This demonstrates that, sometimes, one needs to attend to the many ways communication can happen and not only to the semantic mechanisms found in language.

There are differences between indirect speech acts, implicatures, and presuppositions inside this second group. Usually, indirect speech acts are characterized as the utterances that try to obtain a requirement from a primary speech act and whose success depends on the success of this prior action (Bach and Harnich 1979, 70).

The success of an implicature, especially a conversational implicature, does not depend on the success of any type of primary act. On the contrary, an implicature succeeds if the audience entertains what is going on within a sentence beyond what is said. This is, an implicature's success depends upon the audience's ability to make sense of an apparent odd sentence's literal meaning by grasping the speaker's communicational intentions (Grice 1975; 1989). As it is well known, and chapter 2 mentioned, much of this success depends on violating some communicational maxims and the assumption that speakers are rational agents with cooperative purposes.

A presupposition is some implicit information embedded in a sentence that a speaker utters consciously or unconsciously while she asserts something. Frege gives a classic example. The sentence

(1) Kepler died in misery

cannot be true without assuming that the singular term "Kepler" has a reference. Therefore, Kepler's existence is a presupposed content embedded within (1). Nevertheless, Frege argues that a speaker asserting (1) cannot say that "Kepler" has a reference and presupposes his existence. The reason why is that if someone would assert its negation,

(2) Kepler did not die in misery,

the speaker then would be asserting that "Kepler" has no reference, and hence presupposing that Kepler does not exist (or he is a nonexistent object, as Meinong would say), which is contradictory. For Frege, whether the proper name "Kepler" has or does not have a reference, then, cannot be part of its meaning (Frege 1892, 191). Therefore, in Frege's account, the paradigmatic case is a sentence that seems to imply a referential presupposition. For him, all presupposition implies a referential binding (since names are often descriptions in disguise), which is why the presupposition fails when a sentence lacks reference. As we know, and chapter 1 argues, this is on the grounds of Frege's distinction between sense and reference, which he employs in his response to the problem.

In contrast with this Fregean picture of presupposition that supposes a gap in the truth value of sentences with "empty names," Russell advocates for a new theory that explains cases of definite descriptions as quantifying expressions, as seen in chapter 1. In this view, there is no gap in true value since a quantifier will always fulfill the description (basically, because Russell considers it absurd to speak about nonexistent entities). Strawson says that in a presuppositional sentence, we have two strains. On the one hand, there is a Fregean strain bound to reference, and, on the other hand, in sentences such as (2) nothing is said because the presupposition fails (Strawson 1950). All because it is incoherent to claim that sentences presuppose something since there are speakers who presuppose content by employing certain locutions.

On Stalnaker's pragmatic account to presupposition, propositions that do not straightforward respond to a semantic operator are projected. They presuppose content in a conversation as part of a common ground shared by speakers. When an assertion is made and accepted in conversation, its content is added to the common ground, and the truth of the proposition in question will be presupposed in later stages. Stalnaker uses a possible worlds framework and characterizes the common ground as a set of possible worlds: the worlds where all that is presupposed is true, or context set. What is presupposed at a given stage affects the interpretation of new utterances made in conversation (Stalnaker 1973; 1974). In this sense, there is no presupposition unless the speaker and audience share background assumptions that proper beliefs hold. The audience must accept the conditions of the speaker's assertion (Karttunen 1974; Heim 1983).

Nevertheless, there are cases in which this rule does not follow. For instance, somebody introduces a presupposition into the conversational context through an assertion that intuitively presupposes the truth of another proposition. The presupposition cannot fail, so it must modify the common ground somehow. This is the so-called *accommodation principle* (Stalnaker 1974; 1978; Lewis 1979). This new content adjusts the set context so that any prior content in the common ground will be updated to fit the new content accordingly. As previous chapters mentioned, this set context will not necessarily be consciously present in the speaker's mental life. Most times, speakers only need to behave as if that content were true. Therefore, instead of admitting an active set of beliefs in everybody's heads, this position claims an externalist account that explains the speaker's behavior in dispositional terms.

Another typical feature of presupposition is that it can survive when sentences are lodged under a denial or are the antecedent of a conditional sentence. This interpretation generates the *cumulative thesis*, the idea that if a concrete clause has a presupposition, it carries to the complex sentence. According to this thesis, truth functions have a cumulative property absent in other indirect discourse. In this sense, indirect discourse is a plug, a sentence that does not inherit the presupposition of its clauses (Karttunen and Peters 1979).

It is easy now to see how the projection problem raises. Semantic accounts to linguistic content based on the Traditional View presented in chapter 1 claim that propositional content is always present in an invariant form. Therefore, if some additional presupposed content is present in a sentence, that content is embedded within the linguistic content of a sentence (the sentence's truth conditions and meaning) and, therefore, must be identified in their component clauses. If that is not possible, no such thing as presupposed content exists. Since, if it were true that a sentence's clauses carry some additional presupposed content, that would also be a function of the sentence as a whole.

As seen before, one preferred solution is to defend that some presuppositions project from their clauses but are not necessarily embedded by any presuppositional operators triggered when a sentence is uttered. This is particularly important, as mentioned above, when there is some presupposition somehow unrelated to the meaning of the primary sentence. In these cases, many semanticists have said, pragmatic approaches cannot adequately respond (they mean from a purely linguistic and truth-conditional standpoint) to how some presuppositions embed in some sentences. An early response is Langendoen and Savin (1971), who offer a linguistic account of several complex presuppositional sentences under generative semantics with lexical insertion rules. Heim (1992) offers a sophisticated solution to the projection problem based on context change semantics, which includes the caveat that information can get updated in response to complex sentences (Stalnaker) while generalizing suitable assumptions about the lexical semantics of attitude predicates. Of particular importance is a recent view by Kripke (2009). According to Kripke, some presupposed content, specifically when embedded in complex sentences, are better explained if we take into account that some of its clauses (especially some modifiers such as the adverbs "too" or "instead") have anaphoric properties and, hence, trigger some prior conversational content that is now presupposed in the new uttered sentence. The following section introduces the notion of anaphora and its importance in discussing presupposition projection.

8.2. CLASSIC APPROACHES TO ANAPHORA

Anaphora is the phenomenon whereby the interpretation of the occurrence of one expression is dependent on the interpretation of the occurrence of another, or whereby the occurrence of an expression has its referent supplied by the occurrence of some other expression in the same or another sentence

(King 2004). Thus, anaphora refers to the interpretative dependences among expressions (Neale 2006, 355).

Some anaphoric pronouns refer to expressions that inherit their referents from other referring expressions. In this sense, one can think of several unproblematic examples of anaphoric relation: demonstrative pronouns are used to refer to things, personal pronouns are used to refer to persons, possessive and reflexive pronouns are used to refer to property relations, and so on. In these cases, the anaphoric pronouns achieve their references from a previous referring expression as a part of the conversational discourse. The semantics of anaphoric pronouns is simple: the anaphoric pronoun's reference is the reference of its antecedent.[1]

Still, one can think of cases of anaphoric pronouns that cannot be understood as having their references fixed by their antecedents or as variables bound by their quantifier antecedent. King (2004) analyzes three paradigmatic cases. First, there are cases in which an anaphoric pronoun has an antecedent in another sentence, but such antecedent seems to be not a name but a quantifier. This is the so-called *discourse anaphora*. In a sentence such as

(3) Few professors came to the party. They had a good time

a quantifier treatment would imply wrong truth conditions (Evans 1977) because if we treat "they" as a quantifier, the sentence obtained is

(3') Few professors: x (x came to the party and x had a good time).

Nevertheless, (3) entails that few professors attended the party, but (3') is still true if many professors attended the party. In this sense, construing the pronouns in these examples as variables bound by the quantified description upon which they appear to be anaphoric yields vague and ambiguous results. It is possible to think of an utterance of (3) in which the speaker does not claim that only the professors that came to the party had a good time. This claim is still consistent with the idea that other professors did not come to the party. Nonetheless, this would not be possible under the interpretation offered by (3').

The second problematic case that King presents as an example of anaphora that cannot be understood as a referring expression or a bound variable is, in fact, a particular case of discourse anaphora. It is the so-called *Geach's discourse*. These cases appeal to pronouns that apparently cannot be a referring term because their alleged reference does not exist. These cases include sentences containing psychological verbs, identified as examples of intentional identity. As Geach (1967) argues, there are anaphoric links between indefinite terms and pronouns across sentential boundaries and propositional attitude contexts where the actual existence of an individual for the indefinite term is not presupposed.

The so-called *donkey anaphora* is the third case in which an anaphoric pronoun cannot be understood as a referring expression or a bound variable. It has two versions, one involving conditional clauses and another with relative clauses.

Think of the following sentences:

(4) If Sarah owns a donkey, she beats it.
(5) Every woman who owns a donkey beats it.

Neither sentence refers to a specific donkey. Therefore, the pronoun "it" cannot refer to any specific donkey either. Moreover, even though it could, it would be required for (4) that Sarah beats every donkey that she owns to obtain a straightforward anaphorical reading. In (4), quantifiers cannot scope out of relative clauses, and so again, the pronoun is not within the scope of its quantifier antecedent. Therefore, it is not bound by it. In (5), all independent evidence suggests that a quantifier cannot take wide scope over a conditional or binding variable to its consequent. This suggests that "a donkey" there cannot bind the pronoun in the consequent either.

Now it is time to analyze the most important approaches to these problems. In the early 1960s, generative linguistics explored the idea that anaphoric pronouns were the superficial manifestations of fuller noun phrases. Speakers construct compound anaphoric terms through pronominalization and reflexivization transformations. This solution carries a problem because pronominalization does not explain all anaphoric pronouns. For instance, it does not explain cases where anaphora refers to quantifiers or cases where cross co-reference includes two anaphoric pronouns. In these cases, the anaphoric pronouns on quantified phrases do not work as a repetition of their antecedents or an ambiguous pronoun as an antecedent (Bach 1970).

In the 1970s, it was generally accepted that at least some anaphoric pronouns were present at the deep structure rather than derived by a pronominalization transformation. In this sense, the idea that anaphoric relations were marked in syntax was itself called into question (cf. especially Evans 1977 and 1980). Think of a sentence with an anaphoric pronoun in which nothing in the grammar precludes it from co-referentiality. A solution employing conditions of co-reference would only work in symmetric relations. Nevertheless, anaphoric relations are asymmetric. A solution employing *de facto* co-reference (or intensional co-reference) needs to be complemented with some referential dependence between the mentioned terms (*de jure* co-reference).

Kamp (1981) and Heim (1982) independently formulated a theory (the Discourse Representation Theory, or DRT) about anaphora that claims that indefinite noun sentences are essentially predicates with free variables rather than existential quantifiers. On DRT, the above indefinite sentences introduce a new variable, and an anaphoric pronoun on an indefinite is interpreted as the same variable as introduced by its indefinite antecedent. Therefore, this theory builds into the assignment of truth conditions default existential quantification over free variables. In cases where an indefinite noun appears to have the force of an existential quantifier, this is not because it is an existential quantifier but the default existential quantification of a free variable.

DRT is problematic. Think about

(6) A man broke into Sarah's apartment. Scott believes that he came in the window.

(6) attributes a general belief to Scott. However, DRT does not get this reading. Under the default existential quantification of a free variable reading, (6) acts as a wide scope existential quantifier over the entire discourse. Thus, (6) is read as "There exists an x such that x is a man and x broke into Sarah's apartment, and Scott believes that x came in the window." This approach attributes a belief to Scott and links the truth value of the complex sentence (6) to the fact that Scott's belief is true. Nevertheless, (6) truth value is independent of such requirement since the sentence can be true even though x did not come in the window, or Scott believes it.

In response to this difficulty, King (1987 and 1991) develops an alternative theory of anaphora: the Context Dependent Quantifier approach, or CDQ. On this approach, there is an analogy between the semantics of discourse anaphora and the semantics of "instantial terms." An instantial term is a singular term introduced in applications of existential instantiations and eliminated in applications of universal generalization. These terms are quantifier-like expressions of generality, where the precise nature of such a generality is determined by features of the natural language argument or derivation of a system of natural deduction in which the instantial term occurs. Thus, CDQ emphasizes that instantial terms and discourse anaphora are both expressions of generality, and the sort of generality they express depends on features of their linguistic contexts. Therefore, instantial terms and anaphoric pronouns express quantification, and their type is partly a function of the linguistic environment in which they are embedded.

Davies (1981) and Neale (1990) argue that anaphoric pronouns, in some sense, work like definite descriptions. According to this view, the anaphoric pronouns *go proxy for* definite descriptions understood as quantifiers along roughly Russellian lines. Thus, in a sentence such as

(7) John bought a donkey. Harry vaccinated it

the pronoun "it" goes proxy for the definite description "the donkey that John bought."

We can also find other accounts on anaphoric pronouns, such as the Dynamic Logic approach, which holds that certain features of a discourse affect the interpretation of sentences in the discourse, which preserves the dynamic element of DRT. For this account, what an anaphoric sentence means is how adding a sentence to a discourse changes the information available to a listener of the discourse (Groenendijk and Stokhof 1991).

Section 8.4 employs the Interactive Theory to propose an alternate response to the presupposition problem. Before that, though, with all the information this chapter has offered so far regarding presupposition and anaphora, the following section critically analyzes Kripke's lexico-semantic account to presupposition and the projection problem.

8.3 KRIPKE'S ACCOUNT ON PRESUPPOSITION AS ANAPHORA

According to Kripke (2009), any Fregean approach to presupposition is wrong because it only reveals the referential character of presupposition seen in section 8.1. The alternative explanation is the standard Russellian response to the projection problem: the Karttunen and Peters' algorithm to the presupposition of conditionals,

$$Ap \ \& \ (Ax \to Bp)$$

for cases of complex sentences that include presuppositions, such as

(8) If Herb comes to the party, the boss will come, *too*.

According to such a view, sentences that appear as an antecedent of complex conditional assertions can assert the implication of such assertion and its presupposition.[2] Thus, this algorithm presupposes both the presupposition of A and the claim that if the assertive content of A is true, then the presupposed content of B is also true.

According to the algorithm, in sentences like (8), the presupposition in the consequent is "someone other than the boss will come," and the complete presupposition is "if Herb comes, some other than the boss will come." Nevertheless, Kripke claims that this explanation is problematic because, if one agrees with the standard algorithm, the presupposition in the consequent is then that "Herb is not the boss," and this can be understood only as "If Herb comes, then there exists an x not equal to the boss such that x comes to the party" (where *x* is Herb). The claim that presupposition in a clause must also be the presupposition of the whole complex sentence does not hold and, therefore, the projection solution for presupposition must be rejected.

To see why, Kripke asks to consider a sentence such as

(9) If Herb and his wife both come to the party, the boss will come, *too*.

According to the algorithm, the presupposition in the consequent in (9) is "someone other than the boss will come," and the presupposition of the complete sentence is "if Herb and his wife both come to the party, some other than the boss will come." According to Kripke, on cumulative approaches such as that offered by the standard algorithm, the presupposition in the consequent is that "neither Herb nor his wife *is* the boss," and the complete presupposition in sentence (9) is "if Herb and his wife come to the party, then there exists an *x* not equal to the boss such that *x* comes to the party" (where *x* is both Herb and his wife). Nevertheless, Kripke says, this conclusion is trivial since that single individual represented by *x* cannot be both Herb and his wife at the same time since no extra information is required to demonstrate that Herb and his wife are two distinct persons and are not the single individual the boss is. Therefore, there is no implied or presupposed content regarding whether Herb and his wife are or not the boss. The proposition previously said to be presupposed by an utterance of (9) is not presupposed. In addition, Kripke says, if the simple suggestion is that the presupposition is "He [the boss] is an extra person," this presupposition is not in addition to but replaces the existential presupposition given by the algorithm. In other words, it is not only the case that the previously presupposed content is not presupposed, but it is the case that there is a new presupposition that has not been previously recognized.[3]

For Kripke, the presupposition is triggered by a lexical element containing an anaphoric function in this type of sentence: *too* in this case. In sentences (8) and (9), speakers presuppose some parallel information contained either in another clause or in the previous discourse. If that element is a singular term, like in (8), the presupposed content cannot be co-referential with the other elements in the parallel clauses or other bits of information in the active discourse. According to Kripke, then, it is necessary a new theory, parallel to that of pronominal anaphora (see especially Kripke 2009, section 2.B.), that specifies the types of anaphora that would explain all possible presupposition in these complex sentences and, at the same time, how these new types of presuppositional anaphora relate to more familiar types of anaphora, including ordinary anaphoric pronouns. Kripke does not provide this new countertheory but introduces some examples that, first, question the standard algorithm view of presupposition in conditional sentences and, second, can illustrate future conclusions.[4]

8.4 PROBLEMS IN KRIPKE'S ACCOUNT ON PRESUPPOSITION AS ANAPHORA

Besides Kripke's innovative way of presenting presupposition as triggered by lexical elements, his account is problematic because it still holds a semantic solution. For Kripke, if a presupposition appears in a complex sentence, it must be because it is a presupposition of one of its clauses, which is why its true value contributes to the meaning of the whole sentence. If this is not the case, either the presupposition at the sentence level is apparent and no presupposition occurs at the clause level, or there is a lexical item (such as *too*) with an anaphoric function that will contribute to the sentence's meaning even though the presupposed content is sometimes new information. In other words, by treating this anaphorical relation in purely semantic terms, Kripke suggests that a sentence's invariant logical form is always underlying all truth-conditional effects. According to Kripke, the anaphoric effects of lexical terms such as "too" would only reveal operators in the logical form of utterances, a conclusion that some counterexamples question.

Consider the following sentence:

(12) If Clark Kent comes to the party, Superman will come, *too*. (in the context of a party in the *Daily Planet* redaction where Clark Kent shall receive the Pulitzer prize)

According to the Russellian standard algorithm, the consequent presupposes that "someone other than Superman will come," and the presupposition of the whole sentence is "if Clark Kent comes to the party, some other than Superman shall come." For Kripke, this cumulative view considers that the consequent presupposes that "Clark Kent is not Superman," and the presupposition in the whole sentence is "if Clark Kent comes to the party, then there exists an x not equal to Superman such that x comes to the party" (where x is Clark Kent). However, we know that Clark Kent is Superman. Therefore, this interpretation of the presupposition is bizarre. This is why Kripke says that, in cases of singular terms in presupposition, the terms cannot be co-referential. If one were acquainted with the background context, then the speaker would know that Superman and Clark Kent are co-referential terms and, therefore, no presupposition arises.

Nevertheless, this solution is unsuccessful where the speaker does not have such epistemic access. Suppose Lois Lane utters (12). According to her, the complete presupposition in (12) is that "someone else than Superman shall come," since she does not know that "Superman" and "Clark Kent" are co-referential. In cases where the speaker knows such co-referentiality, the utterance is bizarre. However, it is not in Lois Lane's case. After all, she does not know that "Clark Kent" and "Superman" are one and the same person and, therefore, the presupposition is perfectly acceptable in her case. If this is correct, the presupposition of "too" cannot be anaphoric in this case, at least not in Kripke's terms, since it does not appeal to any previous content that is now presupposed. In (12), "too" does not presuppose previous discursive elements, but contextual requirements: the epistemic access to the crucial information that "Clark Kent" and "Superman" are co-referential.

Nevertheless, since Kripke explicitly rejects a Fregean position in explaining presupposition, this possibility is not available for him. I doubt that Kripke will ever accept that the presupposition in these cases would depend on the speaker's and audience's epistemic accessibility to some contents. Because Lois Lane does not know that "Superman" is co-referential with "Clark Kent," she can presuppose that "someone else than Superman shall come." It is then necessary to consider contextual elements and mental processes for this conclusion to hold. It requires the speaker's intention of referring to his belief that two different persons shall come to the same place at a specific time. In other words, the success of the presupposition in (12) depends on the Fregean assumption that different descriptions can describe the same object, can be co-referential.

Someone could reply that this interpretation rescues a new version of Geach's intentional identity (Geach 1967). When speakers assert an utterance where the presupposed content appeals to intensional contexts, the existence of opaque meaning is assumed. By accepting Kripke's account, these cases can be easily solved because the anaphoric element in "too" refers to the same antecedent (the person that is Superman and Clark Kent at the same time), and there is no straightforward way of treating both halves in (12) as ambiguous, since "too" in the second half bounds to the antecedent, and opacity prevents such syntactical liaison. Therefore, for Kripke, (12) is always a nonintensional context.

This analysis is not correct, however. Geach considers a sentence with anaphora and psychological verbs. This complex sentence contains propositional attitude verbs and an indefinite description in the first simple sentence that serves as the precedent of the anaphorical pronoun present in the second simple sentence:

(13) Hob believes that a witch has blighted Bob's mare, and Nob believes she killed Cob's sow.

Application 3: Presupposition Projection

According to Kripke, (13) presupposes, first, that witches exist and, second, that it exists as a particular entity (one concrete but unknown witch) to which Hob's and Nob's beliefs refer, something like

(13′) $(Ex)(x$ is a witch and [Hob believes that x blighted Bob's mare] and [Nob believes x killed Cob's sow])

This reading is problematic. The interpretation only works if the indefinite description "a witch" is read as an existential quantifier and the anaphoric pronoun "she" functions as a variable bound to such quantifier. Nevertheless, if this were the case, the obtained reading is a cumulative response similar to the one provided by the standard algorithm against which Kripke proposes his alternative.

King (1993, 74) provides a modified interpretation:

(13″) Nob believes $[(Ex)(x$ is a witch who blighted Bob's mare and x killed Cob's sow)]

According to this reading, the presupposition only says that the same entity ("*the* witch") that provoked Bob's mare disease also killed Cob's sow, independently of whether such a witch is the same that Hob and Nob believe is behind each event because this solution does not require the existence of any concrete individual who fits the indefinite description.

I think that Kripke would agree with this interpretation for a number of reasons. First, it would allow the presupposition in the second simple sentence to be anaphoric since "she" would refer to previous information in discourse. Second, the above-mentioned presupposition contained in a part of a complex sentence is the presupposition contained in the compound sentence, triggered by a purely lexical term and independent of any attitudinal context. The problem, in my view, is that this theory is still cumulative, precisely what Kripke wants to avoid.

A more significant issue, I think, is that such interpretation rejects any relevant role of the speaker's intention in meaning-determination. In this concrete case, the differentiation between the attributive and the referential uses of descriptions depicted by Donnellan (see chapter 1) disappears (see also Kripke 1977). According to Geach, (13) includes an indefinite description "a witch" and an anaphoric personal pronoun "she," which replaces the description in the second simple sentence. However, according to his reading, (13) does not presuppose the existence of either the above-mentioned witch (since this supposes a semantic existential reading) or a particular entity that Hob and Nob must have in mind (since this supposes a second quantificational interpretation) nor projects the presupposition in the second simple sentence to the complex sentence. Keeping in mind Donnellan's distinction, the speaker is employing the indefinite description referentially, since Hob and Nob use "a witch" to refer to the reason behind Bob's mare disease and Cob's sow killing, whichever this reason might be, independently of whether the reason of each event is the same, and independent of whether Hob's and Nob's beliefs refer to the same entity. In Kaplanian terms, Hob's and Nob's beliefs would share the same character, but they could differ in his content, and the reading above would still be feasible.

If my view is correct, then when we assert sentences with presuppositions (more clearly when the sentences include psychological or attitude verbs), attention to the speaker's intention is required to properly analyze how presupposition projects and how the sentence's meaning is determined. When someone asserts a presuppositional sentence, what she is talking about could be determined by her knowledge or her propositional attitudes. To properly entertain this content, the audience must sometimes be aware of the particular epistemic point of view from where the speaker is speaking. In cases such as (13) where the difference between the referential and attributive uses of a definition is crucial, whether the audience is able of entertaining which use is the one the speaker performs in her utterance is determinative for grasping the proper presupposition in the sentence since it is crucial for the presupposition to be able to project from the clause to the whole. Briefly, keeping in mind the *speaker's point of view* is necessary for presupposition projection and accommodation. Therefore, when Lois Lane utters (12), she adopts the point of view of anybody who does not know that Clark Kent is Superman (that "Clark Kent" and "Superman" are co-referential) as contraposed but complementing the viewpoint of anybody who does.

Furthermore, in my view, many nonintensional contexts are apparent and really include contexts within propositional attitudes. Thus, when Lois Lane utters (12), she says something like "I [Lois Lane] believe that . . . " transforming it into an intensional scenario. Besides the lexical element present that allows to point out anaphoric content, what is needed for adequately entertaining the presupposition is to grasp the epistemic context in which Lois Lane is unaware that "Clark Kent" and "Superman" are co-referential terms. In other words, besides requiring for the speaker to adopt the conventionality of properly communicating what she means by saying what she says, the audience should also make an effort to wear the speaker's shoes by grasping (or at least being aware) that she might lack some crucial information. Sometimes we are lucky enough that both speaker's and audience's points of view align, but sometimes this is not the case. This is why I believe in, and this book presents and defends, an alternative theory in metasemantics that appeals to the active interaction between conventions, the speaker's intentions, and the audience's possible uptakes to properly entertain the meaning of the sentences of our natural language.

NOTES

1. If the reference were a clause that is yet to appear in discourse, the anaphoric properties still hold, but the phenomenon is called *cataphora*.

2. This approach is Russellian because it is grounded on the Russellian caveat that in the case of a conditional sentence where the presupposition of the consequent is asserted in the antecedent, the participants do not need to assume that the presupposition is true. As Russell (1905, 484) says: "The king in *The Tempest* might say, 'If Ferdinand is not drowned, Ferdinand is my only son' . . . But the above statement would nevertheless have remained true if Ferdinand had been in fact drowned." Kripke thinks this example is artificial, but it enables reasonable mathematical examples (cf. Kripke 2005, 1018–1019).

3. Kripke gives other examples:

(10) Sam is having dinner in New York tonight, *too*.

According to Kripke, to interpret it as "someone other than Sam is having dinner in New York tonight" would be bizarre.

(11) If John walked on the beach last night, then it was Betty Smith who walked on the beach last night.

According to Kripke, an interpretation as "if John walked on the beach last night, then someone walked on the beach last night" is also bizarre.

4. I once heard Scott Soames argue that, besides the richness of Kripke's claims, the true contribution of Kripke's view about presupposition as anaphora is that his appealing to lexical mechanisms supposes the formulation of new presuppositional requirements that allow far-reaching consequences for the notion of conversational contexts incorporating shared common ground information that utterances are used to update. Supposedly, Soames has a paper about this, which I have not been able to find.

Conclusion

This book presented and developed a novel approach to metasemantics based on what I call the Interactive Theory. This theory argues that the meaning of any linguistic item is its cognitive content. Nonetheless, what I consider the cognitive content of words and sentences depends upon three different but interconnected elements: the speaker's intentions when making a statement, the audience's possible interpretations of "what is said," and the conventions that allow both phenomena to occur in very specific and maximally local circumstances. This theory does not seem different from any other accounts that take seriously the context of use or any pragmatic theory that considers Gricean ideas. Nevertheless, my theory is different for a number of reasons.

First, it is the only theory to my knowledge that successfully combines the speaker's intentions, the audience's possible uptakes, and conventions to explain the meaning of our natural language. Second, the meaning that a given audience would entertain is always different and determined by the conditions established by such a community, not only the context and the circumstances. Any statement that a speaker can make in any of the over seven thousand natural languages (and their dialects) spoken on Earth is sanctioned differently by the speech community to which the speaker belongs (or the linguist exchange occurs). In other words, each speech community constrains "what is said" and how one can say it. Third, given the fact that the speaker always wants something concrete out of their utterance, determining the content of such a statement obliges us to pay attention to what that might be, mostly when the interpretation of "what is said" does not match any of the expected outcomes. Given that we respond to reasons, we must include the speaker's intentions when choosing what is said and the audience's potential interpretations in our analysis of language and meaning as part of a collective rational endeavor.

The Interactive Theory then explains how and why each sentence of our language gets associated a cognitive content and, as a corollary, why that content can change its truth value within the same context, contradicting the semanticist's claim against the existence of such possibility in any natural language. As a secondary goal, it argues for a pluralism regarding propositions grounded in the idea that different speech communities impose different conditions to determine their languages' content and meaning. This perspectivism provides a crucial advantage over the relativist's proposal. Since the content of any statement depends on the objective conditions offered by the speech community under what the book dubbed the speaker's point of view, no content is subjectively relative to the speaker's assessment conditions, and the determination of meaning depends on the norms established by the speech communities in maximally local contexts.

The book proposes a hybrid theory that accounts for our intuitive view about what contents our audience entertains in ordinary conversation and a pluralistic approach to the criteria that individuate linguistic content. More specifically, it more accurately accounts for the relationship between language and reality, the type of knowledge speakers possess when they know a language, and the mechanisms that explicate its acquisition and production. My approach, therefore, answers questions regarding the nature and understanding of language, its origin and structure, and, more importantly, how our natural, ordinary languages work.

Against contextualist theoretical frameworks, the Interactive Theory proposes a pragmatic account that complements compositionality. It also completes empirical research that relies on syntactically savvy individuals by societally explaining the context-shifting sensitivity of language, something that is intuitively true to any competent speaker of any language. Without the Interactive Theory, the former is psychologically void since speakers have no relevance in what they say and what language means. Reduction to syntax assumes that speakers can automatically talk without being necessarily aware of (the knowledge of) their language, which raises well-known flaws. Something is missing. A semantic frame is required to establish a simple way to fix "what is said" by a particular speaker in a concrete occasion. We need to explain how the syntactical structures and elements of any language also capture such sensitivity. However, it is also evident that neither meaning grows in a tree nor syntax is independent of the speakers of a language. We build meaning, and we are those who arbitrarily determine what each structure and term of a language represents.

The Interactive Theory defends that a reductive approach to language undermines the scope of semantics and leaves unexplained many of its foundational aspirations. The meaning of our words and sentences is not, and cannot be, only dependent upon any content words possess by themselves, but is grounded in their societal usage, their utterance in a given context, the intentions speakers have when uttering such words and sentences, and its possible uptakes by the audience. If this is the case, we must abandon the illusory endeavor of finding a unitary theory of language and focus our attention on the analysis of ordinary speech instances.

Conclusion 157

This book also challenges the traditional view of meaning, which dominates the current literature. As seen, literalists argue that each sentence of our language carries and displays only one proposition (its content) in a context because truth conditions constrain truth value. Contextualists arrive at similar conclusions employing some context-sensitive elements. In contrast, the Interactive Theory argues for a pluralism regarding the propositions one can associate with the sentences of our languages. This pluralism is grounded in how speech communities build conventions that constrain utterance success, the speaker's intentions when selecting a particular sentence, and the audience's potential interpretations of such an utterance. Separately these views are not particularly new, and others have also defended them in the past.

Nevertheless, combined, they explain the determination of any concrete proposition and reshape any sentence's scope and, hence, the generation of new propositional content. What is novel, then, is twofold: first, the Interactive Theory combines conventions, the speaker's intentions, and audience's potential uptakes, and second, the way I defend it by assuming a multifunctional theory of language based on empirical data. The Interactive Theory argues that meaning determination requires constant interaction among speech communities, speakers, and audiences. Language itself is not established by the speaker or the audience in isolation, nor appears by itself, but through interaction with the speech community to which they belong. The speech community determines what the speaker says by saying what she says and the speech act she performs when uttering it. The speech community also constrains how any act can be interpreted by the audience (both constitute a convention), determining what the speaker must say, how, when, to whom, and so forth, to display specific content. It is an institutionalized behavior.

Moreover, the speaker must decide which of all the possible behaviors a specific society or community makes available she would employ to accomplish her intentions: to be successful in her communication, to successfully promise, etc. To summarize, the Interactive Theory defends that the speaker's intentional display of specific content when making a statement and the proper institutionalized act performed by such statement altogether with the audience that adequately recognizes and interprets the speaker's intentions when making it determine the proposition within, the linguistic content everybody could entertain. After all, as Austin said, only when one considers "the total speech act in the total speech situation" the true meaning of statements is revealed (1962, 37). Therefore, the interaction between a speech community's conventions, the speaker's intentions, and the audience's possible uptakes constitute all propositions that the shared natural language can express.

The Interactive Theory then claims that language was not created in a vacuum. Language is a human artifact and, as such, evolved to respond to human needs and demands. As humans, we reason, have dispositions, perform inferences, act in various ways, and are sensitive and cognitively aware of others and the world surrounding us. Our language must display all of these facts, and any serious analysis that pretends to be complete must, therefore, address and explain them.

Bibliography

Anderson, Luvell. 2017. "Hermeneutical Impasses." *Philosophical Topics* 45 (2): 1–20.
Anderson, Luvell, and Ernest Lepore. 2013. "What Did You Call Me? Slurs as Prohibited Words." *Analytic Philosophy* 54 (3): 350–363.
Austin, John L. 1939. "Are There A Priori Concepts?" In *Philosophical Papers* (third edition), edited by John Urmson and G. J. Warnok, 32–54. Oxford: Oxford University Press, 1979.
———. 1956. "A Plea for Excuses." In *Philosophical Papers* (third edition), edited by John Urmson and G. J. Warnok, 175–205. Oxford: Oxford University Press, 1979.
———. 1962. *How to Do Things with Words*. Oxford: Clarendon.
Bach, Enoch. 1970. "Pronominalization." *Linguistic Inquiry* 1 (1): 121–122.
Bach, Kent. 1994. "Conversational Impliciture." *Mind & Language* 9 (2): 124–162.
———. 1999. "The Myth of Conventional Implicature." *Linguistics & Philosophy* 22 (2): 327–366.
———. 2006. "The Excluded Middle: Semantic Minimalism without Minimal Propositions." *Philosophy and Phenomenological Research* 73 (2): 435–442.
———. 2007. "François Recanati, *Literal Meaning*." *Philosophy and Phenomenological Research* 75 (2): 487–492.
———. 2013. "The Lure of Linguistification." In *What Is Said and What Is Not*, edited by Carlo Penco and Filippo Domaneschi, 1–11. Stanford, CA: CSLI Publications.
Bach, Kent, and R. M. Harnich. 1979. *Linguistic Communication and Speech Acts*. Cambridge, MA: MIT Press.
Baker, Carl. 2012. "Indexical Contextualism and the Challenges from Disagreement." *Philosophical Studies* 157 (1): 107–123.
———. 2014. "The Role of Disagreement in Semantic Theory." *Australasian Journal of Philosophy* 92 (1): 37–54.
Barcan Marcus, Ruth. 1962. "Modalities and Intensional Languages," *Synthese* 14 (2/3): 132–143.
Barwise, Jon, and John Perry. 1999. *Situations and Attitudes*. Palo Alto, CA: CSLI Publications.

Belletti, Adriana, and Luigi Rizzi. 2002. "Editors' Introduction: Some Concepts and Issues in Linguistic Theory." In Noam Chomsky's *On Nature and Language*, edited by Adriana Belleti and Luigi Rizzi, 1–44. Cambridge: Cambridge University Press.

Berlin, Brent, and Paul Kay. 1969. *Basic Color Terms: Their Universality and Evolution*. Berkeley: University of California Press.

Bertalanffy, Ludwig von. 1955. "An Essay on the Relativity of Categories." *Philosophy of Science* 22 (2): 243–263.

Bezuidenhout, Anne. 2001. "Radical Pragmatics." In *Topics in Contemporary Philosophy: Meaning and Truth*, edited by Michael O'Rourke, Daniel Schier, and John Campbell. New York: Seven Bridges Press.

___. 2006. "The Coherence of Contextualism." *Mind & Language* 21 (1): 1–10.

Bianchi, Claudia. 2004. *The Pragmatics/Semantics Distinction*. Palo Alto, CA: CSLI Publications.

Black, Max. 1959. "Linguistic Relativity: The Views of Benjamin Lee Whorf." *The Philosophical Review* 68 (2): 228–238.

___. 1969. "Some Thoughts with Whorfianism." In *Language and Philosophy*, edited by Sandy Hook, 30–35. New York: New York University Press.

Blanco Salgueiro, Antonio. 2021. "Uptake." *Theoria* 36 (1): 63–79.

Boas, Franz. 1894. "Classification of the Languages of the North Pacific Coast." *Memoirs of the International Congress of Anthropology*, 339–346. Chicago: Schulte.

___. 1911. "Introduction." In *Handbook of American Indian Languages, Part I*, edited by Franz Boas, 1–83. Washington, DC: Government Printing Office.

Borg, Emma. 2004. *Minimal Semantics*. Oxford: Oxford University Press.

___. 2012. *Pursuing Meaning*. Oxford: Oxford University Press.

Boroditsky, Lera. 2001. "Does Language Shape Thought?: Mandarin and English Speakers' Conception of Time." *Cognitive Psychology* 43 (1): 1–22.

___. 2006. "Comparison and the Development of Knowledge." *Cognition* 102 (1): 118–128.

___. 2011. "How Languages Construct Time." In *Space, Time, and Number in the Brain: Searching for the Foundations of Mathematical Thought*, edited by Stanislas Dehaene and Elizabeth M. Brannon. London: Elsevier.

Boroditzky, Lera, and Jesse Prinz. 2008. "What Thoughts Are Made Of." In *Embodied Grounding: Social, Cognitive, Affective, and Neuroscientific Approaches*, edited by Gün R. Semin and Eliot R. Smith. Cambridge: Cambridge University Press.

Brandom, Robert. 1983. "Asserting." *Noûs* 17 (4): 637–650.

___. 1998. *Making It Explicit*. Cambridge, MA: Harvard University Press.

Brogaard, Berit. 2008. "In Defense of a Perspectival Semantics for 'Know.'" *Australasian Journal of Philosophy* 86 (3): 439–459.

Brown, Roger W. 1958. *Words and Things*. Glencoe, IL: Free Press.

Camp, Elizabeth. 2005. "Critical Study of Josef Stern's *Metaphor in Context*." *Noûs* 39 (4): 715–731.

___. 2006a. "Contextualism, Metaphor, and What Is Said." *Mind & Language* 21 (3): 280–309.

___. 2006b. "Metaphor and That Certain 'je ne sais quoi.'" *Philosophical Studies* 129 (1): 1–25.

___. 2007. "Prudent Semantics Meets Wanton Speech Acts Pluralism." In *Context-Sensitivity and Semantic Minimalism*, edited by Gerhard Preyer and Georg Peter, 194–213. Oxford: Oxford University Press.

___. 2008. "Showing, Telling, and Seeing: Metaphor, Fiction, and Thought Experiments." *Midwest Studies in Philosophy* 33 (1): 107–130.

___. 2009. "Two Varieties of Literary Imagination: Imagination, Metaphor, Fiction, and Thought Experiments." *Midwest Studies in Philosophy* 33 (1): 107–130.

___. 2012. "Sarcasm, Pretense, and the Semantics/Pragmatics Distinction." *Noûs* 46 (4): 487–634.

___. 2013a. "Metaphor and Varieties of Meaning." In *A Companion to Donald Davidson*, edited by Ernest Lepore and Kirk Ludwig, 361–378. London: Wiley-Blackwell.

___. 2013b. "Slurring Perspectives." *Analytic Philosophy* 54 (3): 330–349.

___. 2015. "Metaphors in Literature." In *The Routledge Companion to Philosophy of Literature*, edited by Noël Carroll and John Gibson, 334–346. London: Routledge.

___. 2016a. "Convention's Revenge: Davidson, Derangement, and Dormativity." *Inquiry* 59 (1): 113–138.

___. 2016b. "Metaphor in the Mind: The Cognition of Metaphor." *Philosophy Compass* 1 (2): 154–170.

___. 2017a. "Pragmatic Force in Semantic Context: Robert Stalnaker's *Context*." *Philosophical Studies* 174 (6): 1617–1627.

___. 2017b. "Why Metaphors Make Good Insults: Perspectives, Presupposition, and Pragmatics." *Philosophical Studies* 174 (1): 47–64.

___. 2018a. "Insinuation, Common Ground, and the Conversational Record." In *New Work on Speech Acts*, edited by Daniel Harris, Daniel Fogal, and Matt Moss, 40–66. Oxford: Oxford University Press.

___. 2018b. "A Dual Act Analysis of Slurs." In *Bad Words*, edited by David Sosa, 29–59. Oxford: Oxford University Press.

___. 2020. "Imaginative Frames for Scientific Inquiry: Metaphors, Telling Facts, and Just-So-Stories." In *The Scientific Imagination*, edited by Arnon Levy and Peter Godfrey-Smith, 304–336. Oxford: Oxford University Press.

Camp, Elizabeth, and John Hawthorne. 2008. "Sarcasm 'like': A Case Study in the Interface of Syntax and Semantics." *Philosophical Perpectives* 22 (1): 1–21.

Cappelen, Herman, and John Hawthorne. 2009. *Relativism and Monadic Truth*. Oxford: Oxford University Press.

Cappelen, Herman, and Ernest Lepore. 1997. "On Alleged Connection between Indirect Speech-Acts and the Theory of Meaning." *Mind & Language* 12 (1): 278–296.

___. 2005. *Insensitive Semantics*. Oxford: Blackwell.

___. 2006a. "Précis of *Insensitive Semantics*." *Philosophy and Phenomenological Research* 73 (2): 425–434.

___. 2006b. "Replies." *Philosophy and Phenomenological Research* 73 (2): 469–492.

———. 2007. "The Myth of Unarticulated Constituents." In *Situating Semantics. Essays on the Philosophy of John Perry*, edited by Michael O'Rourke and C. Washington, 199–214. Cambridge, MA: MIT Press.

Carnap, Rudolf. 1937. *The Logical Syntax of Language*. London: Routledge.

Carroll, J. B. 1956. *Language, Thought, and Reality: Selected Writings of Benjamin Lee Whorf*. Cambridge, MA: MIT Press.

Carston, Robyn, 1988. "Implicature, Explicature, and Truth-Theoretic Semantics." In *Mental Representations: The Interface between Language and Reality*, edited by Richard Kempson, 155–181. Cambridge: Cambridge University Press.

———. 2002. *Thoughts and Utterances*. Oxford: Blackwell.

———. 2004a. "Relevance Theory and the Saying/Implicating Distinction." In *Handbook of Pragmatics*, edited by Laurence Horn and G. Ward, 633–656. Oxford: Blackwell.

———. 2004b. "Truth-Conditional Content and Conversational Implicature." In *The Semantics/Pragmatics Distinction*, edited by Claudia Bianchi, 65–100. Stanford: CSLI Publications.

———. 2009. "The Explicit/Implicit Distinction in Pragmatics and the Limits of Explicit Communication." *International Review of Pragmatics* 1 (1): 35–62.

Charro, Fernando, and Juan J. Colomina-Almiñana. 2014. "Points of View beyond Models: Towards a Formal Approach of Points of View as Access to the World." *Foundations of Science* 18 (2): 137–151.

Chomsky, Noam. 1957. *Syntactic Structures*. London: Mouton.

———. 1975. "Reflections on Language." In *On Language*. New York: The New Press, 2007.

———. 1979. "Language and Responsibility." In *On Language*. New York: The New Press, 2007.

———. 1993. *Language and Thought*. Wakefield, RI: Moyer Bell.

———. 2002. *On Nature and Language*. Cambridge: Cambridge University Press.

Cichocki, Piotr, and Marcin Kilarski. 2010. "On 'Eskimo Words for Snow': The Life Cycle of a Linguistic Misconception." *Historiographia Linguistica* 37 (3): 341–377.

Collins, John. 2007. "Syntax, More or Less." *Mind* 116 (464): 805–850.

Colomina-Almiñana, Juan J. 2012. "The Feasibility of Determinables and Its Relation to Scientific Image." In *Proceedings of the VII Conference of the Spanish Society for Logic, Methodology, and Philosophy of Science*, edited by Concha M. Vidal, José Luis Falguera, J. M. Sagüillo, Víctor M. Verdejo, and M. Pereira-Fariña, 382–388. Santiago de Compostela: Universidade de Santiago de Compostela Press.

———. 2014. "Insults, Slurs, and Other Pejoratives: A State of Art." *Cuadernos Salmantinos de Filosofía* 41 (1): 61–83.

———. 2017a. *Contemporary Advances in Theoretical and Applied Spanish Linguistic Variation*. Columbus: Ohio State University Press.

———. 2017b. "Scope and Partitivity of Plural Indefinite Noun Phrases in Spanish." *Pragmatics & Society* 8 (1): 109–130.

———. 2018. *Formal Approach to the Metaphysics of Perspectives*. Heidelberg: Springer.

___. Forthcoming. "A Defense of a Weak Linguistic Relativist Thesis." Manuscript under review.
Comrie, Bernard. 2000. "Language Contact, Lexical Borrowing, and Semantic Fields." *Studies in Slavic and General Linguistics* 28 (1): 73–86.
Crowley, Terry, and Claire Bowern. 2010. *An Introduction to Historical Linguistics*. Oxford: Oxford University Press.
Crystal, David. 1987. "Language and Thought." In *The Cambridge Encyclopedia of Language*, edited by David Crystal, 14–15. Cambridge: Cambridge University Press.
Davidson, Donald. 1978. "What Metaphors Mean." *Critical Inquiry* 5 (1): 31–47.
___. 1986. "A Nice Derangement of Epithets." In *Truth and Interpretation: Perspectives in the Philosophy of Donald Davidson*, edited by Ernest Lepore, 433–446. London: Blackwell.
Davies, Martin. 1981. *Meaning, Quantification and Necessity*. London: Routledge.
Dennett, Daniel. 1988. "Quining Qualia." In *Consciousness in Modern Science*, edited by A. Marcel and E. Bisiach. Oxford: Oxford University Press.
DeRose, Keith. 1991. "Epistemic Possibilities." *The Philosophical Review* 100 (3): 581–605.
___. 2004. "Single Scoreboard Semantics." *Philosophical Studies* 119 (1): 1–21.
Deutscher, Guy. 2010. *Through the Language Glass: Why the World Looks Different in Other Languages*. New York: Metropolitan Books.
Donnellan, Keith. 1966. "Reference and Definite Descriptions." *The Philosophical Review* 75 (3): 281–304. https://doi.org/10.2307/2183143.
Egan, Andy. 2007. "Epistemic Modals, Relativism and Assertion." *Philosophical Studies* 133 (1): 1–22.
___. 2010. "Disputing about Taste." In *Disagreement*, edited by Richard Feldman and T. Warfield, 247–286. Oxford: Oxford University Press.
Egan, Andy, John Hawthorne, and Brian Weatherson. 2005. "Epistemic Modals in Context." In *Contextualism in Philosophy. Knowledge, Meaning and Truth*, edited by G. Preyer and G. Peter, 131–170. Oxford: Oxford University Press.
Emerson, Ralph Waldo. 1841. "Self-Reliance." In *Harper American Literature*, edited by J. McQuade et al., 1032–1048. New York: Harper and Row, 1987.
Enfield, Nick. 2009. *The Anatomy of Meaning: Speech, Gesture, and Composite Utterances*. Cambridge: Cambridge University Press.
Evans, Gareth. 1977. "Pronouns, Quantifiers and Relative Clauses (I)." In his *Collected Papers*, edited by John McDowell, 76–152. Oxford: Oxford University Press.
___. 1980. "Pronouns." In his *Collected Papers*, edited by John McDowell, 214–248. Oxford: Oxford University Press.
Everett, D. L. 2008. *Don't Sleep, There Are Snakes: Life and Language in the Amazonian Jungle*. New York: Vintage Books.
___. 2012. *Language: The Cultural Tool*. New York: Random House.
Ezcurdia, Maite, and Robert Stainton. 2012. *The Semantics-Pragmatics Boundary in Philosophy*. Peterborough, ON: Broadview Press.

Ferro-Luzzi, Giovanni. 1986. "Language, Thought, and Tamil Verbal Humor." *Current Anthropology* 27 (3): 265–272.

Fortescue, Michael. 1984. *West Greenlandic*. Dover: Croom Helm.

Francén, Ragnar. 2010. "No Deep Disagreement for New Relativists." *Philosophical Studies* 151 (1): 19–37.

Frege, Gottlob. 1892. "On Sense and Reference." In *Collected Papers on Mathematics, Logic, and Philosophy*, edited by Brian McGuinness, 157–177. Oxford: Blackwell, 1984.

———. 1979. "17 Key Sentences on Logic." In *Posthumous Writings*, edited by Hans Hermes, Friedrich Kambartel, and Friedrich Kaulbach, 174–175. Oxford: Blackwell.

———. 1980. "Letter to Peano on 29 September 1896." *In Philosophical and Mathematical Correspondence*, edited by Gottfried Gabriel et al., 112–118. Oxford: Blackwell.

García-Carpintero, Manuel. 2007. "Recanati on the Semantics-Pragmatics Distinction." *Critica* 38: 35–68.

———. 2012a. "Foundational Semantics I: Descriptive Accounts." *Philosophy Compass* 7 (6): 397–409.

———. 2012b. "Foundational Semantics II: Normative Accounts." *Philosophy Compass* 7 (6): 410–421.

Garcia-Carpintero, Manuel, and Manuel Pérez Otero. 2009. "The Conventional and the Analytic." *Philosophy and Phenomenological Research* 78 (2): 239–274.

Garmendia, Joana. 2010. "Irony Is Critical." *Pragmatics and Cognition* 18 (2): 397–421.

Gauker, Christopher. 2011. *Words and Images*. Oxford: Oxford University Press.

Gazdar, Gerald. 1979. *Pragmatics: Implicature, Presupposition, and Logical Form*. New York: Academic Press.

Geach, Peter. 1967. "Intentional Identity." *The Journal of Philosophy* 64 (20): 627–632.

Geertz, Clifford. 1984. "Anti Anti-relativism." *American Anthropologist* 86 (2): 263–278.

Glanzberg, Michael. 2007. "Context, Content, and Relativism." *Philosophical Studies* 136 (1): 1–29.

Goodman, Nelson. 1977. *The Structure of Appearance*. Cambridge, MA: Harvard University Press.

Greene, Brian. 1978. *Ways of Worldmaking*. Cambridge, MA: Harvard University Press.

———. 2003. *The Elegant Universe*. New York: Vintage Books.

Grice, Paul. 1969. "Utterer's Meaning and Intentions." In *Studies in the Way of Words*, 86–116. Cambridge, MA: Harvard University Press.

———. 1975. "Logic and Conversation." In *Studies in the Way of Words*, 22–40. Cambridge, MA: Harvard University Press.

———. 1989. *Studies in the Way of Words*. Cambridge, MA: Harvard University Press.

Groenendijk, J., and M. Stokhof. 1991. "Dynamic Predicate Logic." *Linguistics and Philosophy* 14 (1): 39–100.

Halpern, M. 2006. *Language and Human Nature*. Oakland, CA: Regent Press.
Hautamäki, Antti. 1983a. "The Logic of Viewpoints." *Studia Logica* 42 (2/3): 187–196.
___. 1983b. "Dialectics and Points of View." *Ajatus* 39: 218–231.
___. 1986. *Points of View and Their Logical Analysis*. Philosophica Fennica, Vol. 41. Helsinki: Acta.
___. 2020. *Viewpoint Relativism*. Cham: Springer.
Heim, Irene. 1983. "On the Projection Problem for Presupposition." In *The Second West Coast Conference on Formal Linguistics (WCCFL)*, edited by M. Barlow, D. P. Flickinger, and N. Wiegand, 114–125. Palo Alto, CA: Stanford University Press.
___. 1992. "Presupposition Projection and the Semantics of Attitude Verbs." *Journal of Semantics* 9 (2): 183–221.
Hill, J., and B. Mannheim. 1992. "Language and World View." *Annual Review of Anthropology* 21: 381–406.
Huang, Y. 2006. *Pragmatics*. Oxford: Oxford University Press.
Hume, David. 1751. *An Enquiry into the Sources of Morals*. Translated and edited by Jonathan Bennett, 2007. http://www.earlymoderntexts.com/assets/pdfs/hume1751.pdf.
Humphreys, Paul W., and James H. Fetzer. 1998. *The New Theory of Reference: Kripke, Marcus, and Its Origin*. Cham: Springer.
Huvenes, Torfinn. 2012. "Varieties of Disagreements and Predicates of Taste." *Australasian Journal of Philosophy* 90 (1): 167–181.
___. 2014. "Disagreement without Error." *Erkenntnis* 79 (1): 143–154.
Iacona, Andrea. 2008. "Faultless or Disagreement." In *Relative Truth*, edited by Manuel García-Carpintero and Max Kölbel, 287–295. Oxford: Oxford University Press.
Irvine, J. T., & Gal, S. 2000. "Language ideology and linguistic differentiation." In *Regimes of Language: Ideologies, Polities, and Identities*, edited by P. V. Kroskrity, 35–84. Santa Fe, NM: School of American Research Press.
Johnson, W. E. 1921. *Logic, Part I*. New York: Dover Publications.
Kamp, Hans. 1972. "Formal Properties of 'now.'" *Theoria* 32 (2) 227–273.
___. 1981. "A Theory of Truth and Semantic Representation." In *Semantics: A Reader*, edited by S. Davis and B. S. Gillon, 234–262. Oxford: Oxford University Press, 2004.
Kaplan, David. 1989. "Demonstratives" and "Afterwords." In *Themes from Kaplan*, edited by Joseph Almog, John Perry, and Howard Wettstein, 481–563 and 565–614. Oxford: Oxford University Press.
Karttunen, Lauri. 1974. "Presupposition and Linguistic Context." *Theoretical Linguistics* 1 (2): 181–194.
Karttunen, Lauri, and Stanley Peters. 1979. "Conventional Implicature." In *Syntax and Semantics 11: Presupposition*, edited by Ch.-K. Oh and D. Dineen, 1–56. New York: Academic Press.
Kay, Paul, and W. Kempton. 1984. "What Is the Sapir-Whorf Hypothesis?" *American Anthropologist* 86 (1): 65–79.

King, Jeffrey. 1987. "Pronouns, Descriptions and the Semantics of Discourse." *Philosophical Studies* 51 (3): 341–363.
___. 1991. "Instantial Terms, Anaphora and Arbitrary Objects." *Philosophical Studies* 61 (2): 239–265.
___. 1993. "Intentional Identity Generalized." *The Journal of Philosophical Logic* 22 (1): 61–93.
___. 2004. "Anaphora." *Stanford Encyclopedia of Philosophy*.
___. 2007. *The Nature and Structure of Content*. Oxford: Oxford University Press.
Kockelman, Paul. 2005. "The Semiotic Stance." *Semiotica* 157 (1): 233–304.
___. 2006. "Representations of the World: Memories, Perceptions, Beliefs, Intentions, and Plans." *Semiotica* 162 (1): 73–125.
___. 2009. "Meaning and Time: Translation and Exegesis of a Mayan Myth." *Anthropological Linguistics* 9 (3–4): 308–387.
___. 2010a. "Enemies, Parasites, and Noise: How to Take Up Residence in a System without Becoming a Term of It." *Journal of Linguistic Anthropology* 20 (2): 406–421.
___. 2010b. "Value Is Life under an Interpretation: Existential Commitments, Instrumental Reasons and Disorienting Metaphors." *Anthropological Theory* 10 (1): 149–162.
___. 2011a. "A Mayan Ontology of Poultry: Selfhood, Affect, Animals, and Ethnography." *Language in Society* 40 (3): 427–454.
___. 2011b. "Biosemiosis, Technocognition, and Sociogenesis: Selection and Significance in a Multiverse of Sieving and Serendipity." *Current Anthropology* 52 (5): 711–739.
___. 2012. "Meaning, Motivation, and Mind: Some Conditions and Consequences for the Flexibility and Intersubjectivity of Cognitive Processes." *New Ideas in Psychology* 30 (1): 65–85.
Kockelman, Paul, and A. Bernstein. 2012. "Semiotic Technologies, Temporal Reckoning, and the Portability of Meaning. Or: Modern Modes of Temporality—Just How Abstract Are They?" *Anthropological Theory* 12 (3): 320–348.
Kölbel, Max. 2004. "Faultless Disagreement." *Proceedings of the Aristotelian Society* 104: 53–73.
___. 2009. "The Evidence for Relativism." *Synthese* 166 (2): 375–395.
Korta, Kepa, and John Perry. 2011. *Critical Pragmatics*. Cambridge: Cambridge University Press.
Kripke, Saul. 1972. *Naming and Necessity*. Cambridge, MA: Harvard University Press.
___. 1977. "Speaker's Reference and Semantic Reference." *Midwest Studies in Philosophy* 2 (2): 255–276.
___. 2005. "Russell's Notion of Scope." *Mind* 114 (456): 1005–1037.
___. 2009. "Presupposition and Anaphora: Remarks on the Formulation of the Projection Problem." *Linguistic Inquiry* 40 (3): 367–386.
Krupnik, I., and L. Müller-Wille. 2010. "Franz Boas and Inuktitut Terminology for Ice and Snow: From the Emergence of the Field to the 'Great Eskimo Vocabulary Hoax.'" In *SIKU: Knowing Our Ice: Documenting Inuit Sea Ice Knowledge and*

Use, edited by I. Krupnik et al., pp. 377–400. Cambridge: Cambridge University Press.

Kulvicki, J. 2008. "The Nature of Noise." *Philosophers' Imprint* 8 (11): 1–16.

Lasersohn, Peter. 2005. "Context Dependence, Disagreement, and Predicates of Personal Taste." *Linguistics and Philosophy* 28 (3): 643–686.

___. 2008. "Quantifications and Perspective in Relativist Semantics." *Philosophical Perspectives* 22: 305–337.

___. 2009. "Relative Truth, Speaker Commitment, and Control of Implicit Arguments." *Synthese* 166 (2): 359–374.

___. 2011. "Context, Relevant Parts and (Lack of) Disagreement over Taste." *Philosophical Studies* 153 (3): 433–439.

___. 2017. *Subjectivity and Perspective in Truth-Theoretic Semantics*. Oxford: Oxford University Press.

LaVine, Matt. 2020. *Race, Gender, and the History of Early Analytic Philosophy*. Lanham, MD: Lexington Books.

Lee, D. D. 1938. "Conceptual Implications of an Indian Language." *Philosophy of Science* 5 (1): 89–102.

Levinson, Stephen, 1983. *Pragmatics*. Cambridge: Cambridge University Press.

___. 1997. "Language and Cognition: The Cognitive Consequences of Spatial Description in Guugu Yimithirr." *Journal of Linguistic Anthropology* 7 (1): 1–35.

___. 2000. *Presumptive Meanings: The Theory of Generalized Conversational Implicature*. Cambridge (MA): MIT Press.

___. 2003. *Space in Language and Cognition*. Cambridge: Cambridge University Press.

Lewis, David. 1975. "Languages and Language." In *Philosophical Papers, Volume 1*, 163–188. Oxford: Oxford University Press, 1983.

___. 1979. "Scorekeeping in a Language Game." *Journal of Philosophical Logic* 8 (2), 339–359.

___. 1980. "Index, Context, and Content." In *Papers in Philosophical Logic*, 21–44. Cambridge: Cambridge University Press.

Liu, Mingya. 2009. "Adverbs of Comment and Disagreement." In *Logic, Language, and Meaning. Proceedings of the Amsterdam Colloquium 2009*, edited by M. Aloni et al., 335–344. Heidelberg: Springer.

López de Sa, Dan. 1999. *Response-Dependencies: Colors and Values*. PhD Dissertation, Universitat de Barcelona.

___. 2008. "Presuppositions of Commonality: An Indexical Relativist Account of Disagreement." In *Relative Truth*, edited by Manuel García-Carpintero and Max Kölbel, 297–310. Oxford: Oxford University Press.

___. 2009. "Relativizing Utterance-Truth?" *Synthese* 170 (1): 1–5.

Lucy, J. A. 1992. *Language Diversity and Thought*. Cambridge: Cambridge University Press.

___. 1996. *Grammatical Categories and Cognition*. Cambridge: Cambridge University Press.

MacFarlane, John. 2003. "Future Contingents and Relative Truth." *The Philosophical Quarterly* 53 (212): 321–336.

___. 2005. "Making Sense of Relative Truth." *Proceedings of the Aristotelian Society* 105: 321–339.
___. 2007. "Relativism and Disagreement." *Philosophical Studies* 132 (1): 17–31.
___. 2009. "Non-Indexical Contextualism." *Synthese* 166 (2): 231–250.
___. 2014. *Assessment Sensitivity*. Oxford: Oxford University Press.
Mandelbaum, D. G. 1958. *Selected Writings of Edward Sapir*. Berkeley: University of California Press.
Marques, Teresa. 2014. "Relative Correctness." *Philosophical Studies* 167 (3): 361–373.
___. 2015. "Doxastic Disagreement." *Erkenntnis* 79 (1): 121–142.
Martí, Luisa. 2006. "Unarticulated Constituents Revisited." *Linguistics and Philosophy* 29 (2): 135–166.
Martin, L. 1986. "'Eskimo Words for Snow': A Case in the Genesis and Decay of an Anthropological Example." *American Anthropologist* 88 (2): 418–423.
Massimi, Michela. 2018. "Four Kinds of Perspectival Truth." *Philosophy and Phenomenological Research* 96 (2): 342–359.
McTaggart, J. E. 1908. "The Unreality of Time." *Mind* 17: 456–473.
Mill, John Stuart. 1843. *A System of Logic*. Honolulu, HI: University Press of the Pacific, 2002.
Montague, Richard. 1970. "Pragmatics and Intensional Logic." *Synthese* 22 (1): 68–94.
Morgan, Jerry. 1969. "On the Treatment of Presupposition in Transformational Grammar." In *Papers from the Fifth Regional Meeting of the Chicago Linguistic Society*, 167–177. Chicago: University of Chicago Press.
Morris, Charles W. 1938. *Foundations of the Theory of Signs*. Chicago: University of Chicago Press.
Mott, Peter. 1973. "Dates, Tenseless Verbs and Token-Reflexivity." *Mind* 82 (325): 73–85.
Neale, Stephen. 1990. *Descriptions*. Cambridge, MA: MIT Press.
___. 2006. "Pronouns and Anaphora." In *The Blackwell Guide to the Philosophy of Language*, edited by M. Devitt and R. Hanley, 335–373. Oxford: Blackwell.
Needham, Paul. 1975. *Temporal Perspective: A Logical Analysis of Temporal Reference in English*. Uppsala: *Philosophical Studies*, vol. 25.
___. 1976. "The Speaker's Point of View." *Synthese* 32 (3/4): 309–327.
Nowak, Ethan. 2020. "Language Loss and Illocutionary Silencing." *Mind* 129 (515): 831–865.
Pagin, Peter. 2007. "Assertion." *Stanford Encyclopedia of Philosophy*.
Pavese, Carlotta. 2017. "On the Meaning of 'Therefore.'" *Analysis* 77 (1): 88–97.
Percus, Oren. 2000. "Constraints on Some Other Variables in Syntax." *Natural Language Semantics* 8 (1): 173–229.
Perry, John. 1979. "The Problem of Essential Indexicals." In *The Problem of the Essential Indexical and Other Essays*, 3–52. Oxford: Oxford University Press.
___. 1986. "Thought without Representations." Proceedings of the Aristotelian Society, Supplement 60, 263–283. In *The Problem of the Essential Indexical and Other Essays*, 205–226. Oxford: Oxford University Press.

Pinker, Steven. 1994. *The Language Instinct: How the Mind Creates Language*. New York: Harper Perennial.
___. 2007. *The Stuff of Thought: Language as a Window into Human Nature*. New York: Penguin Group.
Plumer, Gilbert. 1988. "Kaplan Rigidity, Time, and Modality." *Logique et Analyse* 31 (123/124): 329–335.
Potts, Christopher. 2005. *The Logic of Conventional Implicature*. Oxford: Oxford University Press.
Predelli, Stefano. 1998. "I am not here now." *Analysis* 58 (2): 107–115.
___. 2005. *Contexts*. Oxford: Oxford University Press.
___. 2011. "I am still not here now." *Erkenntnis* 74 (3): 289–303.
Prior, Arthur. 1948. "Determinables, Determinates and Determinants, I and II." *Mind* 58: 1–20 and 178–194.
___. 1957. *Time and Modality*. Oxford: Oxford University Press.
___. 1967. *Past, Present and Future*. Oxford: Oxford University Press.
___. 1968. *Papers on Past and Tense*. Oxford: Oxford University Press.
Pullum, G. K. 1989. "The Great Eskimo Vocabulary Hoax." *Natural Language and Linguistic Theory* 7 (2): 275–281.
Quine, Wilard van Orman. 1960. *Word and Object*. Cambridge, MA: MIT Press.
___. 1969. *Ontological Relativity and Other Essays*. New York: Columbia University Press.
___. 1970. *Methods of Logic*. London: Routledge.
___. 1977. "Facts of the Matter." In *American Philosophy: From Edwards to Quine*, edited by R. W. Shahan and K. R. Merrill, 176–196. Norman: University of Oklahoma Press.
Recanati, François. 2001. "What Is Said." *Synthese* 128 (1): 75–91.
___. 2002. "Unarticulated Constituents." *Linguistics and Philosophy* 25 (3): 299–345.
___. 2004. *Literal Meaning*. Cambridge: Cambridge University Press.
___. 2006. "Predelli and García-Carpintero on *Literal Meaning*." *Crítica: Revista Hispanoamericana de Filosofía* 38 (112): 69–79.
___. 2007. *Perspectival Thoughts*. Oxford: Oxford University Press.
___. 2008. "Moderate Relativism." In *Relative Truth*, edited by Manuel García-Carpintero and Max Kölbel, 41–62. Oxford: Oxford University Press.
___. 2013. *Mental Files*. Oxford: Oxford University Press.
Reding, J-P. 1986. "Greek and Chinese Categories: A Reexamination of the Problem of Linguistic Relativism." *Philosophy East and West* 36 (4): 349–374.
Reichenbach, Hans. 1958. *The Philosophy of Space and Time*. New York: Dover.
Reimer, Marga, and Elizabeth Camp. 2006. "Metaphor." In *Handbook of Philosophy of Language*, edited by Ernest Lepore and Barry Smith, 845–863. Oxford: Oxford University Press.
Richard, Mark. 2004. "Contextualism and Relativism." *Philosophical Studies* 119 (2): 215–242.
Ricoeur, Paul. 1993. *Language and Symbolic Power*. Cambridge, MA: Harvard University Press.

Romero, Sergio. 2012. "They Don't Get Speak Our Language Right": Language Standarization, Power and Migration among Q'eqchi' Maya." *Journal of Linguistic Anthropology* 22 (2): 21–41.

Rosenberg, Jay. 2002. *Thinking about Knowing*. Oxford: Oxford University Press.

Rovelli, Carlo. 2018. *The Order of Time*. New York: Penguin.

___. 2020. *There Are Places in the World Where Rules Are Less Important Than Kindness*. New York: Penguin.

___. 2021. *Helgoland*. New York: Penguin.

Russell, Bertrand. 1905. "On Denoting." *Mind* 14 (56): 479–493.

___. 1911. "Knowledge by Acquaintance and Knowledge by Description." *Proceedings of the Aristotelian Society* 11: 108–128.

___. 1959. *My Philosophical Development*. London: George Allen and Unwin.

Salmon, Nathan. 1991. "The Pragmatic Fallacy." In *Content, Cognition and Communication. Philosophical Papers, Volume 2*, 298–308. Oxford: Oxford University Press.

___. 2004. "The Good, the Bad, and the Ugly." In *Content, Cognition and Communication. Philosophical Papers, Volume 2*, 309–339. Oxford: Oxford University Press.

___. 2005. "Two Conceptions of Semantics." In *Content, Cognition and Communication. Philosophical Papers, Volume 2*, 340–350. Oxford: Oxford University Press.

Sapir, Edward. 1929. "The Status of Linguistics as a Science." *Language* 5 (4): 207–214.

Sauerland, Uli, and Mathias Schenner. 2009. "Content in Embedded Sentences. A Typology by Context Shift." In *Multimodal Signals: Cognitive and Algorithmic Issues*, edited by Anna Esposito, Amir Hussain, and Maria Marinaro, 197–207. Heidelberg: Springer.

Sbisà, Marina. 1984. "On Illocutionary Types." *Journal of Pragmatics* 8 (1): 93–112.

___. 2006. "Communicating Citizenship in Verbal Interaction. Principles of a Speech Act Oriented Discourse Analysis." In *Analysing Citizenship Talk. Social Positioning in Political and Legal Decision-Making Processes*, edited by H. Hausendorf and A. Bora, 151–180. Amsterdam: John Benjamins. https://doi.org/10.1387/theoria.

___. 2014. "The Austinian Conception of Illocution and Its Implications for Value Judgements and Social Ontology." *Ethics & Politics* 16 (2): 619–631.

Schneider, L. 1985. *Ulirnaisigutiit: An Inuktitut-English Dictionary of Northern Quebec, Labrador, and Eastern Artic Dialects (with an Englis-Uniktitut index)*. Quebec City: Les Presses de l'Université Laval.

Sellars, Wilfred. 1956. *Empiricism and the Philosophy of Mind*, edited by Robert Brandom. Cambridge, MA: Harvard University Press, 1997.

___. 1969. "Language as Thought and as Communication." *Philosophy and Phenomenological Research* 29 (4): 506–527.

Shaul, D. L., and N. L. Furbee. 1998. *Language and Culture*. Prospect Heights, IL: Waveland Press.

Sidnell, J., and N. J. Enfield. 2012. "Language Diversity and Social Action: A Third Locus of Linguistic Relativity." *Current Anthropology* 53 (3): 302–333.

Silverstein, Michael. 1976. "Shifters, Linguistic Categories, and Cultural Description." In *Meaning in Anthropology*, edited by K. Basso and H. Selby, 11–55. Albuquerque: University of New Mexico Press.

___. 1979. "Language Structure and Linguistic Ideology." In *The Elements: A Parasession on Linguistic Units and Levels*, edited by P. R. Clyne et al. Chicago: Chicago Linguistics Society.

___. 1981. "The Limits of Awareness." *Work Papers on Sociolinguistics* 84.

___. 1985. "Language and the Culture of Gender." In *Semiotic Mediation*, edited by E. Mertz and R. Parmentier. Orlando, FL: Academic Press.

___. 1991. "Snowing Again." *Lingua Franca* 1 (3): 29.

___. 2000. "Whorfianism and the Linguistic Imagination of Nationality." In *Regimes of Language*, edited by P. Kroskrity. Santa Fe, NM: School of American Research Press.

___. 2003. "The Whens and Wheres—as well as Hows—of Ethnolinguistic Recognition." *Public Culture* 15 (3): 531–557.

___. 2004. "'Cultural' Concepts and the Language-Culture Nexus." *Current Anthropology* 45 (5): 621–652.

___. 2005. "Axes of Evals: Tokens versus Type Interdiscursivity." *Journal of Linguistic Anthropology* 15 (1): 6–22.

___. 2006. "How We Look from Where We Stand." *Journal of Linguistic Anthropology* 16 (2): 269–278.

Slobin, D. I. 1987. "Thinking for Speaking." In *Proceedings of the Thirteenth Annual Meeting of the Berkeley Linguistics Society*, 435–444. Berkeley: UC Berkeley Press.

___. 1996. "From 'Thought and Language' to 'Thinking for Speaking.'" In *Rethinking Linguistic Relativity*, edited by J. J. Gumperz and S. Levinson, 70–96. Cambridge: Cambridge University Press.

___. 2003. "Language and Thought Online." In *Language in Mind: Advances in the Study of Language and Thought*, edited by D. Gentner and S. Goldin-Meadow, 157–192. Cambridge, MA: MIT Press.

Spencer, C. 2007. "Is There a Problem of the Essential Indexical?" In *Situating Semantics. Essays on the Philosophy of John Perry*, edited by Michael O'Rourke and C. Washington, 179–198. Cambridge, MA: MIT Press.

Sperber, Dan, and Deirdre Wilson. 1986. *Relevance*. Oxford: Blackwell.

Stainton, Robert. 2006. "Terminological Reflections of an Enlightened Contextualism." *Philosophy and Phenomenological Research* 73 (2): 460–468.

Stalnaker, Robert. 1970. "Pragmatics." *Synthese* 22 (2): 272–289. https://doi.org/10.1007/BF00413603.

___. 1973. "Presuppositions." *The Journal of Philosophical Logic* 2 (4): 447–457.

___. 1974. "Pragmatic Presupposition." In *Context and Content*, 47–62. Oxford: Oxford University Press.

___. 1978. "Assertion." In *Syntax and Semantics, vol. 9: Pragmatics*, edited by P. Cole, 315–322.

___. 1984. *Inquiry*. Cambridge, MA: MIT Press.

___. 1991. "Reference and Necessity." In *A Companion to the Philosophy of Language*, edited by Bob Hale and Crispin Wright, 534–554. London: Blackwell.
___. 1997. "Reference and Necessity." In A Companion to the Philosophy of Language, edited by Crispin Wright and Bob Hale, 534–54. Oxford: Blackwell.
___. 2002. "Common Ground." *Linguistics and Philosophy* 25 (5–6): 701–721.
___. 2014. *Context*. Oxford: Oxford University Press.
Stanley, Jason. 2000. "Context and Logical Form." *Linguistics and Philosophy* 23 (4): 391–434.
___. 2005. "Review of F. Recanati's *Literal Meaning*." *Notre Dame Philosophical Reviews*. http://ndpr.nd.edu/news/literal-meaning/.
___. 2007. *Language in Context*. Oxford: Oxford University Press.
Stanley, Jason, and Zoltán G. Szabó. 2000. "On Quantifier Domain Restriction." *Mind & Language* 15 (2–3), 219–261. http://dx.doi.org/10.1111/1468-0017.00130
Steckley, J. L. 2008. *White Lies about the Inuit*. Peterborough, ON: Broadview.
Steinberg, S. 2008. *Introduction to Communication*. Cape Town: Juta.
Stephenson, Tamina. 2007. "Judge Dependence, Epistemic Modals, and Predicates of Personal Taste." *Linguistics and Philosophy* 30 (3): 487–525.
___. 2010. "Control in Centred Worlds." *Journal of Semantics* 27 (3): 409–436.
Stern, Josef. 2000. *Metaphor in Context*. Cambridge, MA: The MIT Press.
Stirling, L., and A. Dench. 2012. "Tense, Aspect, Modality, and Evidentiality in Australian Languages." *Australian Journal of Linguistics* 32 (1): 1–6.
Stojanovic, Isidora. 2007. "Talking about Taste: Disagreement, Implicit Arguments, and Relative Truth." *Linguistics and Philosophy* 30 (4): 691–706.
Strawson, Peter. 1950. "On Referring." *Mind* 59 (235): 320–344. https://doi.org/10.1093/mind/LIX.235.320.
___. 1964. "Intention and Convention in Speech Acts." *Philosophical Review* 73 (3): 439–460
Sturm, M. 2009a. *Apun: The Artic Snow*. Fairbanks: University of Alaska Press.
___. 2009b. "Composite List of Iñupiag Snow Words." Unpublished manuscript.
Swoyer, C. 2010. "Relativism." *Stanford Encyclopedia of Philosophy*, edited by Edward Zalta. http://plato.stanford.edu/entries/relativism.
Szabó, Zoltán G. 2005. *Semantics versus Pragmatics*. Oxford: Oxford University Press.
___. 2006. "Sensitivity Training." *Mind & Language* 21 (1): 31–38.
Taylor, Kenneth A. 2001. "Sex, Breakfast, and Descriptus Interruptus." *Synthese* 128 (1): 45–61.
Travis, Charles. 2006. "Insensitive Semantics." *Mind & Language* 21 (1): 39–49.
Von Fintel, Kai, and Anthony S. Gillies. 2008. "CIA Leaks." *The Philosophical Review* 117 (1): 77–98.

Whorf, Benjamin Lee. 1950. "An American Indian Model of the Universe." In *Language, Thought, and Reality: Selected Writings of Benjamin Lee Whorf*, edited by J. B. Carroll, 57–64. Cambridge, MA: MIT Press.

Wierzbicka, A. 1997. *Understanding Cultures through Their Key Words*. Oxford: Oxford University Press.

Winawer, J., N. Witthoft, M. C. Frank, L. Wu, A. R. Wade, and L. Boroditsky. 2007. "Russian Blues Reveal Effects of Language on Color Discrimination." *Proceedings of the National Association of Science* 104 (19): 7780–7785.

Wittgenstein, Ludwig. 1922. *Tractatus Logico-Philosophicus*. London: Kegan Paul.

___. 1953. *Philosophical Investigations*. Oxford: Blackwell.

Wolff, P., and K. Holmes. 2010. "Linguistic Relativity." *WIREs Cognitive Science*. doi:10.1002/wcs.104.

Woodbury, A. C. 1991. "Counting Eskimo Words for Snow: A Citizen's Guide." *Linguistics List*. http://www.princeton.edu/~browning/snow.html.

Woolard, K. 1997. "Between Friends: Gender, Peer Group Structure, and Bilingualism in Urban Catalonia." *Language in Society* 26 (3): 533–560.

Zeman, Dan. 2012. "Unarticulated Constituents, Variadic Function, and Relativism." *Logique et Analyse* 54 (216): 617–632.

Index

accommodation principle, 142
African Americans, 100–101
ambiguity, 9–11, 15, 18, 42
anaphora, 143–52, 153nn3–4
appropriation, 100–101
assertion, 139–40, 142, 147, 150, 152.
    See also speaker intentions
assessment, 107–8, 111, 120, 128
association, 19
attributive: definitions, 10, 18–19
audience interpretations: and meaning,
    2, 9, 28, 34, 42–43, 48–49, 75, 155;
    and speakers, 3, 5–6, 48, 60, 62, 152;
    and theory, 54; and truth value, 108.
    See also uptake
Austin, J. L., 34, 35n4, 49–50, 53, 76,
    78n12, 103, 105nn13–14, 108, 157
auto-centric perspective, 122
Availability Principle, 29, 31, 63–64

Bach, Kent, 35n5, 44, 53, 77n7, 141
Barcan, Ruth, 21n6
Bertalanffy, Ludwig von, 103n3
Bezuidenhout, Anne, 43, 45
bilingualism, 104n9
Black, Max, 85
Boas, Franz, 87–88, 103n2
Boroditsky, Lera, 104n11

Camp, Elizabeth, 5, 39–47, 51n3,
    51n5, 52n6
Cappelen, Herman, 24, 29–33,
    35n5, 39–40, 61
Cardi B., 100
Carnap, Rudolf, 55–56, 61
Carston, Robyn, 24–27, 30–31, 35n1,
    42–43, 77n7
cataphora, 153n1
causal theory of referentiality, 20, 21n6
CDQ (Context Dependent
    Quantifier), 146
Chomsky, Noam, 81–82, 85
Cichocki, Piotr, 87
classical theory. *See* Frege, Gottlob;
    logical theory; Russell, Bertrand;
    semanticism
cognition, 3–4, 25, 27, 81, 83, 86, 104n7
color perception, 92–94, 98–99,
    105nn12–13
the common ground, 19, 47, 59–65,
    70–75, 78n9, 78n12, 108,
    131, 140–42
Common Indexical
    Contextualism, 136n6
communication, 21n7, 53, 74–75, 91
community standard, 130
composition, 14, 23, 55
Comrie, Bernard, 90–91, 104n8

175

connotation, 12, 21n2
Context Dependent Quantifier (CDQ), 146
context set, 131, 142
contextualism: communalist, 130, 137n11; criticism of, 31–32, 43–44; and descriptive definitions, 10, 16; and disagreement, 121, 129–31; and explicature, 27, 29, 31, 44; and meaning, 3, 5, 23, 28, 41–42, 55, 61, 66, 69–70, 112; and metaphor, 39–45; and pragmatics, 37, 127; and presupposition, 68, 72; and psychological realism, 4, 29–31; radical, 30, 35n1; and semanticism, 4–5, 23–24, 35n1, 119; single scoreboard, 130; and speaker's point of view, 110, 128–30; and Speech Act Pluralism, 32–33; and theory, 6, 35n1, 41–45, 54, 66; three tests of, 39–40; and utterance, 5, 24, 27–30, 33, 35n5, 39–42, 51n4, 54–62, 66–71, 75, 78n15, 79n17, 107, 110–14, 118n7, 119–20, 126, 128, 132, 135n1, 136n7, 150, 153n4
contradictory sentences, 112, 115, 122–26, 128–35, 141. *See also* dialectical contradictions; speaker's point of view
conventions, 23, 34, 35n2, 39–50, 52n9, 66–68, 73–76, 100–103, 131, 140. *See also* norms
cooperative communication, 47
covert specification, 65–66, 69–71
culture-language-thought relationship. *See* thought-language-culture relationship
cumulative thesis, 142–43, 148, 151

data. *See* research
Davidson, Donald, 51n4
Davies, Martin, 146–47
definite descriptions, 10, 16–20, 53, 58, 142, 147
denotation, 12–14, 18, 21n2, 53

denotational theory, 10, 18
DeRose, Keith, 130
descriptive semantics, 37–39
determinable, 97–98, 102
determinate, 98
diachronic analysis, 90–91
dialectical contradictions, 133, 137nn13–14. *See also* contradictory sentences
discourse anaphora, 144
Discourse Representation Theory (DRT), 145–46
donkey anaphora, 145
Donnellan, Keith, 10, 18–19, 151–52
DRT (Discourse Representation Theory), 145–46
Dynamic Logic, 147

egocentric systems, 94–97
embedded variables, 61–62, 122
Emerson, Ralph Waldo, 136n12
empirical data. *See* research
empty names, 15–16
enchronic analysis, 90–92, 97–102
Enfield, Nicholas, 90
English language, 88, 92–99, 104n5, 109
entailment, 67–69, 139
epistemic modality, 124–25
epistemology, 7, 20, 54, 66, 133, 137n13
existence, 14
existential expressions, 17
expansion, 77n7
explicature, 26–27, 31, 44
expressions, 54–55
expressive language, 43–44, 51n5
externalism, 62, 64–65

faultless disagreements, 119–35, 135n2. *See also* taste
foundational semantics, 37–38
Frege, Gottlob, 1–2, 4, 9–20, 73, 141–42, 147, 150. *See also* reference; sense
fundamentum divisionis, 97

Index

Furbee, N. L., 88

Gal, S., 104n8
Gazdar, Gerald, 51n1
GCI (generalized conversational implicatures), 26
Geach's discourse, 144–45, 150–51
gender, 104n9
generalized conversational implicatures (GCI), 26
generic pronouns, 132, 134
genetics, 90–91
geocentric systems, 94–97
geography, 89
Goodman, Nelson, 78n13, 115
grammar, 74–75, 82–83, 87, 98, 145
Gricean program (Paul Grice), 1, 23–27, 30–31, 41–44, 47, 49, 53, 66–69, 76, 76n3
Guugu Yimithirr language, 95–97

Hagahai language, 90–91
Haruai language, 90–91
Hautamäki, Antti, 137nn13–14
Heim, Irene, 143, 145–46
hierarchies, 99, 105n12
honorifics, 104n9

identity, 49, 75
illocutionary act, 47–50, 52n10, 101, 105n14
implicature, 26–30, 42–44, 50, 66–70, 76, 141
incomprehension, 121
indefinite description, 151–52
indexical sentences, 15, 55–56, 65
indirect speech acts, 140–41
Individualized Indexical Contextualism (IIC), 136n6
individuation, 61, 72–73, 78n13
inference, 11, 14, 26, 28, 74
instantial term, 146
intentionality, 74
interactive perspective, 6–7

Interactive Theory: explanation of the, 54, 69–75, 86, 108, 120, 155–58; introduction to the, 2–7, 20. *See also* audience interpretations; norms; speaker intentions; tensed sentences; unarticulated constituents
internalism, 62
Inuit language, 87–90, 103n2, 104n6
Invariantist Truth-Conditionalism (ITC), 124–26
irony, 46
Irvine, J. T., 104n8
ITC (Invariantist Truth-Conditionalism), 124–26
iteration, 110

Johnson, W. E., 97–98
judge parameter, 120, 126–27, 134

Kamp, Hans, 109–11, 145–46
Kaplan, David, 38, 51n3, 112–13, 118n4, 118n6, 126, 128–30, 135n1, 136n6
Karttunen, Lauri, 147
Kay, Paul, 92–94, 98
Kempton, W., 92–94, 98
Kilarski, Marcin, 87
King, Jeffrey, 144, 146, 151
Kobon language, 90–91
Korta, Kepa, 77n6
Kripke, Saul, 10, 19–20, 140, 143, 147–51, 153nn3–4

Langendoen, D. T., 143
language-culture-thought relationship. *See* thought-language-culture relationship
language loss, 48–50, 52n10. *See also* natural languages
Lasersohn, Peter, 126–28, 135n3
Leibniz, Gottfried Wilhelm, 10–11
Lepore, Ernest, 24, 29–33, 35n5, 39–40, 61
Levinson, Stephen, 95

Lewis, David, 38, 46, 60, 72, 112, 118n6, 126, 140
lexemes, 87–88, 103n4
lexicon, 82–83, 88–90, 93–94
lexico-semantics, 147–49
linguistic determinism, 96, 102–3
linguistic parsimony, 61, 73
linguistic relativism, 61, 67, 73, 75, 84–86, 89, 107, 119–22, 127–28, 136n9
linguistic relativity, 81–89, 96–97, 102. *See also* SRT (strong linguistic relativity thesis); WRT (weak linguistic relativity thesis)
literalism, 4, 23, 28, 41–45, 119, 122, 157
locutionary acts, 47, 50, 52n10, 105n14
logical space of reasons, 74
logical theory, 1–2, 10–11, 14–16, 20, 97
Logicism, 21n1
Lowland Q'eqchi,' 91
Lucy, J. A., 102

MacFarlane, John, 114–15, 126
Martí, Luisa, 61–62, 64–70, 78n16, 79n17, 79n21
Massimi, Michela, 117, 118n9
mathematics, 10–11, 112, 118nn1–2, 147–48
Maxwell, James Clerk, 92
Maya language, 91
meaning. *See* ambiguity; reference; referentiality; sense
meaning of thoughts, 13
mental files, 65, 79n19
metalanguage, 109
metaphor, 39–47, 51nn3–5, 52n6
metaphysical modality, 124–25
metaphysics, 63, 65–66, 68, 79n21, 124–25
metasemantics, 2, 9, 38–39, 152, 155. *See also* semanticism
Mill, John Stuart, 11–14, 54, 76n2
minimalism, 4–5, 24–34, 35n1, 39

mismatch, 121
mnemonic device, 86
modality, 7, 20, 124–25
Montagovian semantics, 109
Morgan, Jerry, 139
Morris, Charles, 51n1
Mott, Peter, 118n5

the name strategy, 94–95
natural languages, 3–4, 10, 37, 74–75, 81–83, 109, 155. *See also* language loss
Neale, Stephen, 146–47
Needham, Paul, 110–11, 118n7
NITC (Non-Invariantist Truth-Conditionalism), 124–26
nonexistence, 14
Non-Invariantist Truth-Conditionalism (NITC), 124–26
normalized interpretations, 26–27, 74
normalized interrelation, 26
norms: and context, 43, 46, 54, 60; and proposition, 12–13, 33–34; and speech communities, 3, 5–6, 9, 41, 46–54, 60–63, 71–75, 116–17, 121, 155, 157; and truth, 108. *See also* conventions
Nowak, Ethan, 48–50
the N-word, 100–101

objective metaphysical content, 124–25
observation sentences, 5, 57, 59–60, 62
occasion meaning (what is meant), 25, 28–29, 37, 42–45, 68
occasion sentence, 55, 57, 75–76, 76n3, 110–11, 115, 118n7
ontology, 2, 14, 21n4, 82, 98–99, 108, 116, 132
operators, 109–10, 127, 140, 143, 149
optionality, 61–62, 65, 67–69, 79n17, 79n21
ordinary language philosophy, 33–34
organizing space, 94–97, 104n11
original baptism, 20

particularized conversational
   implicatures (PCI), 26
Pavese, Carlotta, 68
PCI (particularized conversational
   implicatures), 26
Peano, Giuseppe, 11, 13
performatives, 100–101
perlocutionary act, 49–50, 52n10,
   101, 105n14
Perry, John, 56, 61, 63, 76n4, 77nn5–6,
   78n15, 79n21
perspectivism, 81, 86, 96–97, 108,
   116–17, 121–26
Peters, Stanley, 147
philosophy, 94, 102
phonetics, 104n8
Pierce, Charles Sanders, 55
Pinker, Steven, 81, 85–86, 96
Pirahã language, 95
Plumer, Gilbert, 118n7
pluralistic perspectivism, 81, 108, 157
PO (The Psychological Objection),
   24, 29–32, 39
poetry, 42–43, 46
the Pragmatic Fallacy, 36n6
pragmatic presuppositions,
   139–40, 142–43
pragmatics, 4–7, 26–34, 37, 40, 51n1,
   53–54, 58–67, 70–72, 77nn7–8, 131
Predelli, Stefano, 113, 118n7
presentism, 109
presupposition, 7, 57–65, 68–75, 77n8,
   78n9, 79n18, 131, 139–43, 147–52,
   153nn4. *See also* projection
presupposition of commonality, 131
pretense, 46, 52n6
Prior, Arthur, 98, 109–11,
   118nn1–2, 118n5
PRO, 127, 136n5
projection, 7, 57–58, 71–72, 140,
   142–43, 147–48, 151–52. *See also*
   presupposition
pronominalization
   transformations, 145, 148
pronouns, 132, 134, 144–48

proper names, 15–17, 19, 53, 91–92
properties, 132
proposition: and concepts, 14, 57–59;
   and content, 33, 126; and context,
   119, 152; and conversation, 29–30,
   33; definition of, 1, 9; functions,
   15–17; and meaning, 67; and
   metaphor, 39; and pluralism, 4, 6,
   155–57; and pragmatism, 72; and
   presupposition, 73–74; and reference,
   66; and semantics, 27, 30, 143;
   singular, 16–17; and speaker's point
   of view, 108, 139; and theory, 1–3,
   12, 15–16, 19, 40, 56; variables, 109
propositionalism, 35n5
The Psychological Objection (PO),
   24, 32, 39
psychologism, 54, 61–62, 75
psychology: and context, 29, 31–34, 70,
   73; and language evolution, 4; and
   minimalism, 24–34; and verbs, 55,
   57, 62. *See also* speaker intentions
Puerto Ricans, 101
puzzle of belief reports, 72

Q'eqchi,' 91
quantificational expressions, 17
Quantifier Domain Restriction, 78n16
Quine, Wilard van Orman, 55, 57,
   59–60, 76n3

racism, 100–101
radical relativism, 127
rationality, 5, 76
realism, 14, 29–32
Recanati, François, 27–32, 35n1, 43–45,
   56–57, 62–66, 73, 77n7, 79nn17–21,
   130–31, 137n11
recognition, 28
reductivism, 2–3, 10, 20, 156
reference: and descriptive definitions,
   10, 20; expressions, 143–45;
   and natural languages, 2, 11, 15;
   and propositions, 66, 141; and
   sense, 12–14, 17, 53; and speech

communities, 10, 18. *See also* Frege, Gottlob
referential definitions, 10, 16, 18–19
referentiality, 11–12, 17, 20
referential presupposition, 141–42
reflexivization transformations, 145
Reichenbach, Hans, 110
relativity. *See* linguistic relativity; SCRT (sociocultural relativity thesis); SRT (strong linguistic relativity thesis); WRT (weak linguistic relativity thesis)
relevance principle, 43
Relevance Theory, 30, 35n1
research, 6, 81–83, 86, 90–103, 156
rigid designator, 10, 20
Rosenberg, Jay, 118n9
rules, 10, 14, 18, 20, 53, 74–75
Russell, Bertrand, 1–2, 4, 9–10, 14–20, 21n4, 53, 142, 147, 149, 153n2
Russian language, 99

salience, 62–68, 70, 79n18
Salmon, Nathan, 32
Sapir, Edward, 83–85. *See also* SWH (Sapir-Whorf Hypothesis)
Sapir-Whorf Hypothesis (SWH), 83–89, 97, 102, 103n3
sarcasm, 43–46
saturation, 77n7
Sbisà, Marina, 50, 52n9
SCRT (sociocultural relativity thesis), 81–82, 84–86, 89–92, 97, 99
Sellars, Wilfrid, 74, 79n22
semantic domain, 90–92
the Semantic Fallacy, 33–34, 36n6
semanticism: criticism of, 4, 10, 18–20; and disagreements, 120–21, 125–32; introduction to, 1–3. *See also* contextualism; contradictory sentences; descriptive semantics; foundational semantics; lexico-semantics; metasemantics; minimalism; pragmatics; presupposition; psychology; sentence meaning (what is said); SPAP (Speech Act Pluralism)
semantic perspectivism, 5
semantic presuppositions, 139–40
sense, 12–14, 17. *See also* Frege, Gottlob
sentence meaning (what is said), 25–32, 37, 40, 42–44, 46, 68, 76n3, 155–56
Shaul, D. L., 88
Silverstein, Michael, 87–88
sincerity, 31, 33–34, 41
Slobin, Dan, 90
slurring words, 48, 51n5, 99–102, 105n14
Soames, Scott, 153n4
social conventions, 99–101
sociocultural relativity thesis (SCRT). *See* SCRT (sociocultural relativity thesis)
space. *See* organizing space
SPAP (Speech Act Pluralism), 32–34, 35n5, 39, 48
speaker-indexical position, 129–32
speaker intentions: and the audience, 3, 5–6, 28, 45–46, 49, 60, 62, 152, 155; and convention, 100–101, 132, 157; and meaning, 1–4, 9, 24, 39, 46–47, 50, 66–67, 73, 75, 151–52; and reference, 150; and theory, 54–55, 63–64. *See also* assertion; psychology
speaker's point of view, 6–7, 39–50, 108–16, 120–24, 129–35, 137n15. *See also* contradictory sentences; taste
SRT (strong linguistic relativity thesis), 84–86, 90, 92, 97, 103. *See also* linguistic relativity; WRT (weak linguistic relativity thesis)
Stalnaker, Robert, 38, 57–60, 77n8, 140, 142
standards of performance adequacy, 117, 118n9
Stephenson, Tamina, 127–28, 132, 136n5

stereotypes, 91, 99–100
Stern, Michael, 51n3
Strawson, Peter, 10, 18–20, 23, 49, 53, 76n1, 108, 142
strong disagreement, 121
Strong Linguistic Relativity Thesis (SRT). *See* SRT (strong linguistic relativity thesis)
subjectivity, 82, 93, 107, 113, 116, 120, 122–25, 134–35, 136n9, 156
subject-predicate, 16–17
SWH (Sapir-Whorf Hypothesis), 83–89, 97, 102, 103n3
the S-word, 100–101
syntax, 51n1, 65, 156

Tarahumara language, 92–94, 98, 104n10
taste, 122–26, 128–35, 135n3. *See also* faultless disagreements; speaker's point of view
taxonomy, 98
TCP (truth-conditional pragmatics), 60–62, 65, 78n16
TCS (truth-conditional semantics), 61–62, 78n16
temporal coordinates, 7, 108
temporal perspectives, 116–17
temporal sentences, 6–7, 107
tensed sentences, 108–17, 118nn1–2
thinking for speaking, 90
thought-language-culture relationship, 81–103, 104n10
time, 104n11, 107, 109–11, 113–17. *See also* world-time-judge triple
truth-conditional pragmatics (TCP), 60–61, 65, 78n16
truth-conditional semantics (TCS), 61–62, 78n16
truth conditions: and character, 112–13; and communication, 29, 31, 33–34, 61; and content, 112–13; and context, 5–6, 33, 56, 59, 61, 67, 120, 131, 135n1; and denotations, 12–13; and entailment, 68; and faultless disagreements, 123–24; and indexical sentences, 55–56; and local determination, 70–71, 75; logical, 7; and meaning, 2, 119; objective, 126; and propositions, 1, 33, 57; and semanticism, 23, 37, 58, 120, 126; and speakers, 67, 111; subjective, 126; and theory, 54, 66; and verbs, 72
truth value: and content, 113, 126; and context, 107, 110–17, 126–28, 130–32, 135, 155; and language, 54–55; and literalism, 122; and meaning, 1–2, 38–39, 112–17, 142; and perspective, 7, 122–23; and pragmatism, 29, 31, 37, 61; and presupposition, 58; and reference, 12, 14–15; and speech communities, 108; and theory, 4, 6, 18–20, 37; and time, 107–8; and truth-utterance, 65, 107, 111–15, 119–20, 126, 135n1; variability, 111, 115–17, 118n7, 128
two-dimensional semantics, 112–13, 126, 128–29
Tzeltal language, 95

unarticulated constituents, 55–57, 60–61, 63–65, 70–72, 74–75, 76n4, 77nn5–6, 136n7
undetermined sentences, 15
uptake, 48–50, 52n9, 105n14, 108. *See also* audience interpretations

variables, 61–62, 65–70, 109–11, 146
verbal morphology, 91
vocabulary, 82, 86–90, 98

weak disagreement, 121
weak linguistic relativity thesis (WRT). *See* WRT (weak linguistic relativity thesis)
what is meant. *See* occasion meaning (what is meant)
what is said. *See* sentence meaning (what is said)

Whorf, Benjamin Lee, 83–85, 87, 92, 103. *See also* SWH (Sapir-Whorf Hypothesis)
Wierzbicka, Anna, 104n6
Wittgenstein, Ludwig, 74
Woodbury, A. C., 87
world-time-judge triple, 113–15, 126–27

WRT (weak linguistic relativity thesis), 81, 84–86, 89–90, 97, 99. *See also* linguistic relativity; SRT (strong linguistic relativity thesis)

Zeman, Dan, 57

About the Author

Juan J. Colomina-Almiñana is assistant professor in the Department of World Languages, Literatures, and Cultures and the Interdepartmental Program in Linguistics at Louisiana State University. He is also an affiliate of LSU's Department of Philosophy. Dr. Colomina-Almiñana is interested in pragmatics and the philosophy of language, in which he has published several articles in journals such as *Philosophia*, *Lingua*, *Foundations of Science*, *Language and Dialogue*, *Pragmatics and Society*, and *The Journal of Mind and Behavior*. His book *Formal Approach to the Metaphysics of Perspectives* (Springer) appeared in 2018. Dr. Colomina-Almiñana is currently working on two book projects: one about the semantics of racial epithets and an intellectual biography of Alice Ambrose.